iPad® Action Gaming for Teens

Michael Duggan

Cengage Learning PTR

CENGAGE
Learning®

Professional • Technical • Reference

Australia • Brazil • Japan • Korea • Mexico • Singapore • Spain • United Kingdom • United States

CENGAGE
Learning·

Professional • Technical • Reference

iPad® Action Gaming for Teens
Michael Duggan

**Publisher and General Manager,
Cengage Learning PTR:** Stacy L. Hiquet

Associate Director of Marketing:
Sarah Panella

Manager of Editorial Services:
Heather Talbot

Senior Marketing Manager:
Mark Hughes

Senior Acquisitions Editor: Emi Smith

Project Editor: Jenny Davidson

Technical Editor: Clayton Crooks

Teen Reviewer: Shelby Hiquet

Interior Layout Tech: MPS Limited

Cover Designer: Mike Tanamachi

Indexer: Sharon Shock

Proofreader: Michael Beady

For product information and technology assistance, contact us at
Cengage Learning Customer & Sales Support, 1-800-354-9706

For permission to use material from this text or product,
submit all requests online at **cengage.com/permissions**

Further permissions questions can be emailed to
permissionrequest@cengage.com

Library of Congress Control Number: 2013944589

ISBN-13: 978-1-285-44009-5

ISBN-10: 1-285-44009-9

Cengage Learning PTR

20 Channel Center Street

Boston, MA 02210

USA

Cengage Learning is a leading provider of customized learning solutions with office locations around the globe, including Singapore, the United Kingdom, Australia, Mexico, Brazil, and Japan. Locate your local office at: **international.cengage.com/region**

Cengage Learning products are represented in Canada by Nelson Education, Ltd.

For your lifelong learning solutions, visit **cengageptr.com**

Visit our corporate website at **cengage.com**

Printed in the United States of America
1 2 3 4 5 6 7 15 14 13

To my students, who were delighted to learn more about Unreal Development Kit, and to my wife, who puts up with my obsessions.

ACKNOWLEDGMENTS

I want to thank the team at Epic Games for their continued efforts to support indie game designers and their Unreal Development Kit software that has made this book possible. I want to thank the editorial and layout teams at Cengage Learning PTR for all their assistance making this book a reality, because without them you would not be reading this. Lastly, I want to thank my family for their continued support as I spent long hours piecing these pages together and grumbling when frustrated that something wasn't working correctly. For their patience and kindness to me, I applaud them.

ABOUT THE AUTHOR

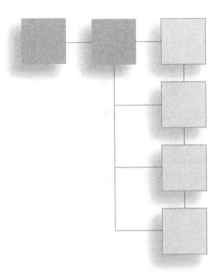

Michael Duggan is an Oklahoma-born author and illustrator with a background in game and web design. His education includes a bachelor of science degree in Game Art and Design from the Art Institute of Pittsburgh. Michael currently lives in the Ozark Mountains with his wife and step-kids. He is an applications developer and digital media instructor at North Arkansas College by day and a tattoo artist by night.

Contents

x   Contents

INTRODUCTION

Today's video game designers are akin to rock stars. They have their photos on the cover of magazines. They are interviewed by television networks. They foster a collection of adoring fans. What is truly remarkable is that they do all this without having to step on stage or scream into a microphone. What they do is spend long hours putting together a video game and getting it played by the public.

Have you ever wanted to design a video game yourself? Are you a hardcore or casual gamer? Have you ever considered creating an iPad game yourself but had no idea how or where to start? No matter where you look, the task seems to be a difficult one, full of math, physics, and late nights staying up staring at a computer screen, not knowing how to implement the features you dream about.

You, too, can become a game designer, and you do not have to get a fancy job at Epic Games to do so! The instructions within this book reveal one route to making your own video games and getting people to play them. You can become a modern-day rock star by embracing the role of a maker of video games, if that is truly what you want to do.

During the 1970s and 1980s, video game playing was often seen as a hobby and substitute for physical sports or outdoor activities. Video games have changed a lot since then. Today, video gaming is viewed as a serious industry comparable to the movie or music industries. News outlets cover video game console releases in the same manner as they would the release of a highly anticipated motion picture.

A video game is any electronic game with human interaction and a user interface that generates visual feedback on a video device. The type of electronic system you use to play a video game is known as its platform. Examples of different platforms include personal computers, laptop computers, mobile devices, and video game consoles such as the Xbox 360 and Nintendo Wii.

The platform we will focus on in this book includes mobile devices, especially the iPad. Mobile devices are highly personal devices that are carried and used in a completely different context than other devices. Thus, they are ever-present (in other words, always with the user) and are usable just about anywhere. Though mobile devices are often thought of as an inferior gaming platform compared to console or PC games, notably because of having a smaller screen size and lesser processing power, they are quickly becoming one of the most popular game media in the world.

The video-game industry is a rapidly developing phenomenon. Technological innovation results in continual improvement in the devices people use to play video games. As the market develops, players become more sophisticated, and the types of games they play change. As well as what goes on in the mainstream media, thanks to the Internet, there is plenty of activity on the fringe of game development, such as web browser–based games, user-developed modifications (mods), and independent game design.

With so many possibilities, this is an exciting time to become involved in making video games. It can also seem like a frightening time, because where do you start and what skills do you need to become a video game developer?

Video game development and authorship, much like any form of entertainment, is frequently a cross-disciplinary field. Video game developers primarily include programmers and graphic designers. Over the years this has expanded to include almost every skill set you might see in the creation of a film or television show, including sound engineers, musicians, and other technicians, as well as skills specific to video games, such as the game designer and character modeler. All of these roles are managed by directors and producers.

Video games are comprised of the following:

1. **2D/3D design:** Making pretty pictures on the computer.
2. **Animation:** Making those pictures move.
3. **Computer logic:** Making those pictures interact with each other and react to player's input.

While the first two contribute to the appearance of the game, the game is nothing without the gameplay. That leads you to computer logic, which is the bread and butter of any video game. From designing a heads-up display that ticks off the player avatar's health to dialog boxes that pop up in game to the character movement controls, none of this would be possible without the logic. As you will see, the game authoring software you will use following the steps in this book makes the logic part a cinch.

In the early days of the industry, it was more common for a single person to manage all of the roles needed to create a video game. As platforms became more complex and powerful in the type of material they could present, larger development teams were needed to generate all the art, programming, and other substance required of a video game.

However, this is not to say the age of the "one-man shop" is gone, as you still see this happen in the casual and handheld gaming markets, where smaller games remain prevalent. Independent game developers still have clout, and game-authoring technology that makes the process simpler for users keeps the independent market alive.

With the growth in the size of development teams in the game industry, costs have increased. Development studios need to be able to pay their staff a competitive wage in order to maintain the best talent, while publishers are constantly seeking to keep costs down in order to make a profit. The growth of team size combined with the pressure to get completed projects into the market to begin recouping production costs has led to an increasing occurrence of missed deadlines, rushed games, and the release of unfinished projects.

Therefore, there is more practical simplicity in keeping a project smaller. For one, you can build an iPad game yourself in a reasonable amount of time with a limited amount of resources, especially if you select a game creation tool that will afford you the greatest flexibility for the least cost.

This book will show you one such game creation tool, the Unreal Development Kit (UDK), and how you can use this 100% free tool to make your very own iPad games.

UDK is a freely available-for-download version of Epic Games' popular Unreal game development engine. First created in 1998 to power the original *Unreal* game, the C++ based game engine has received positive criticism and awards, one right after the other, and has not only formed the backbone of Epic Games' titles, such as the popular *Gears of War* series, but has also been successfully licensed to third-party developers. Later titles ranged among the following:

- *American McGee's Alice*
- *American McGee's Alice: Madness Returns*
- *American McGee's Grimm*

- *Batman: Arkham Asylum*
- *Batman: Arkham City*
- *BioShock*
- *BioShock 2*
- *BioShock Infinite*
- *Borderlands*
- *Borderlands 2*
- *Bulletstorm*
- *Devil May Cry*
- *Game of Thrones*
- *Hunted: The Demon's Forge*
- *Infinity Blade*
- *Infinity Blade 2*
- *Lollipop Chainsaw*
- *Mass Effect*
- *Mass Effect 2*
- *Mass Effect 3*
- *Silent Hill: Downpour*
- *Singularity*
- *Thief*
- *X-Men: Destiny*
- *X-Men Origins: Wolverine*
- *Zumba Fitness*

Currently, the Unreal engine itself is in its fourth edition and is considered to be one of the top game engines in the world. UDK has evolved as the Unreal engine has evolved, and thus it is a powerhouse quite capable of delivering some amazing experiences.

The offering of their game creation tools as a concept came along very early, as Epic Games often shared its tools, such as the UnrealEd editor tool (which allowed players to build their own in-game levels), with its gamers, spawning a healthy thriving modification (modding) community. Originally, it was tools like these that were made available to anyone who bought the game. In 2009, however, Epic made their tools available to everyone, whether they owned an *Unreal* game or not. This proved to be a successful transition and expanded the Unreal developer base considerably.

In 2010, Epic added iOS functionality, ensuring that UDK could provide games for the ever-growing mobile customer base that the iPhone, iPad, and iPod Touch devices by Apple introduced. The first demonstrated ability of this was in a live tech demo called *Epic Citadel*, a free download on the iTunes store that played like an interactive walkthrough of a fantasy medieval town. This attracted a lot of attention and record downloads as at that time it was truly groundbreaking to see high-resolution, real-time graphic rendering on a mobile device.

This book shows you how you can use UDK to build iOS games, and more specifically, how to build action games for the iPad device. However, be aware that you will not start making blockbuster game titles as seen on contemporary consoles or the PC for iPads using UDK. Do not expect to make anything like you see in *Gears of War*. For instance, most console games usually have 40, 100, or more developers working around-the-clock to make them, and they are using expensive hardware to do so. Most of those developers have college experience in programming, 3D art, and/or graphic design.

What You'll Find in This Book

No single book could ever hope to provide utterly comprehensive coverage of such a vast and dynamic subject as game development. Rather like a guidebook, this book provides you, a novice designer, a good grounding in gaming principles and suggestions of how to achieve your aspirations.

You will use Epic's free game development tool, UDK, to mix your own video games through practical exercises that require some of the skills and techniques necessary to become a video-game designer. With UDK, any game you build you can convert to and publish for all kinds of different gaming platforms, including Mac, PC, mobile devices, and online.

The lessons in this book will show you how to adapt to the UDK interface and move around in that interface to bring life to your ideas. The content of this book is intended to start you off on the long but exciting journey to becoming a professional in the gaming industry. May you find your time with it, and your experiences with UDK, rewarding.

WHO THIS BOOK IS FOR

Want to try your hand at making your own video game? It might seem impossible at first, but it can actually be done more easily than you might think. If you want to make a video game, this book will teach you how from start to finish.

You do not have to be a math whiz, a computer genius, or a talented artist to make a video game with UDK. It helps, but by all means, you could be an amateur when it comes to those fields and you will still be capable of following along with the instructions located within these pages. You will still be able to make iPad action games using UDK, regardless of your previous experience or skill level.

If you already have prior experience making video games, or just dealing with art editors or programming languages, you will find this text's instructions familiar and perhaps more relaxed than if you did not have previous knowledge. Nevertheless, I guarantee you will learn something you did not know before, and the things you build in UDK will be no less satisfying. In fact, you may take what you know and push the parameters of UDK even further, developing your own unique creations to show off your abilities to the world.

So, if you're a beginner or intermediate computer user, you will find something deeply rewarding with *iPad Action Gaming for Teens*.

You will need a Windows PC or Macintosh computer to run UDK. The instructions contained within this book refer to general commands for use on a Windows PC. Moderate changes to these commands allow you to use a Mac. For example, when you see the use of the ALT key, simply switch it for the Option key, and when you see the CTRL key mentioned, think of it as the CMD key. However, to publish your game to the App Store, there are two requirements: first, that you have an Apple Developer license, which costs (at the time of this writing) $99 per year; and second, a Mac to publish your game. To play test your game remotely on a mobile device using UDK Remote, you will also need an iPad. If you feel comfortable with these requirements, you are set to publish and distribute your iPad games once you have made them. Otherwise, you can still learn how to make iPad games with UDK.

HOW THIS BOOK IS ORGANIZED

This book is divided into neat and easy-to-follow chapters that contain the instructions you need to become familiar with UDK and how to build iPad action games with it.

- **Chapter 1—What Is Game Development?**: This chapter will introduce you to the game industry and what it takes to make a video game, from the initial concept to a pen-and-paper design plan to an actualized game in stores. This chapter will also familiarize you with some of the basic game industry terminology and more popular game genres, including action games (which this book focuses on).

- **Chapter 2—How Video Games Come to Be**: Before delving into the step-by-step instructions to making video games, it is better to know a little about the game industry and how game studios push a project from green light to gold master, and what actually goes into making a top-shelf video game title. This chapter will illustrate what each step takes.

- **Chapter 3—Making iPad Games**: Of the many platforms to choose from, this book looks primarily at making video games that can be played on the iPad. This chapter will provide the preliminary information about the iPad and how it is suited as a gaming platform.

- **Chapter 4—Introduction to UDK**: Before taking your first steps building an actual iPad game, it is best to learn the UDK interface and how it is flexible enough that you can construct mobile games with it. This chapter teaches you the basics of UDK and what it can be useful for.

- **Chapter 5—Level Construction in UDK**: Want to know how to make game worlds and story environments to fit your project needs? This chapter will show you how to construct the basic level architecture for games using UDK.

- **Chapter 6—Building Static Meshes**: Once you have the basics down for making a game world, I will show you how to put objects in it. This requires designing 3D models and textures in third-party software packages and then importing those assets into UDK. If you have ever wanted a peek at what it takes to develop 3D models, this chapter is the place to start!

- **Chapter 7—Quick-Start Design Example**: Now for something totally different. After you have finished learning the UDK interface and experimenting with building levels and objects for a game, it is time for you to learn how to script characters and events in Unreal Kismet. This chapter uses the Jazz Jackrabbit tutorial as a basis for making an iPad action game.

- **Chapter 8—Enhanced UDK Development**: With everything you have already learned, it is time to try your hand at developing a slightly more complex iPad action game with UDK.

- **Chapter 9—Taking Your Game to Market**: Lastly, you will learn some of the basics of publishing your game. With multiple networks for you to target, you can hit a broader market for your games and garner even more players. You will also learn a few trade secrets about Web advertisement, including how to promote yourself in social networks and via Web design.

- **Appendix A—Resources**: This appendix includes bulleted lists of all the Web-based resources demonstrated within this book, for easy reference.

- **Appendix B—Glossary**: Forgot what a specific term means? You can refer back to the glossary to look up the definition of a specific behavior, function, or other important vocabulary word.

CHAPTER 1

WHAT IS GAME DEVELOPMENT?

Have you ever wanted to make video games? Chances are, if you play video games more than occasionally, the thought of making games has at some point crossed your mind.

Making video games is a truly cross-disciplinary task. Not only do you need to be able to create great stories, you also have to illustrate interesting settings and aesthetically pleasing characters. In addition, having a knack for working with computer programs and understanding how those programs work helps.

Merriam-Webster defines a video game as any game "played by electronically manipulating images produced by a computer program on a television screen or display." Most Americans under the age of 40 have played video games since childhood and are more than passingly familiar with them. Some are even what you might call "core" gamers, who play video games between 12 and 30 hours per week. Video games have found a strong niche within the media market, right beside music and movies.

Using basic software applications, this book will show you how you can design your very own video games and export them for play on the iPad. Why the iPad? Because many games are going mobile, and the Apple iPad (shown in Figure 1.1) has cornered the current market on tablets running mobile games.

Figure 1.1
The Apple iPhone and iPad in relation to one another.
Source: Big Bucket Software® Corporation.

Before plunging in, you need to find out what a game developer does and doesn't do, and the history of game technology.

I WANT TO BE A GAME DEVELOPER

Game developers use cutting-edge computer technology to create video games. Why do they do it? Besides the sheer pleasure of making games, they do it because video games make money. Right now, sales of video games have topped sales of CDs and DVDs, making more money than the movie or music industry combined. This consumer-driven expansion has ushered in a need for skilled developers to join the growing video game field.

You can make games simply as a hobby, all by yourself. But let's discuss game development as a whole for a bit. A single published triple-A game title requires a team of 20 to 300 or more individual developers and is very expensive to make. The triple-A (AAA) game title description refers to an individual title's success or anticipated success. In other words, you define triple-A titles by the cost and the return on investment. Most triple-A title games cost between $10 and $12 million to make and can become smash hits, selling well over a million copies. Unfortunately, iPad games have not quite hit the status of a triple-A title yet, partly due to their lower cost initiative. *Infinity Blade* (shown in Figure 1.2) comes close.

Figure 1.2
Infinity Blade for the iPad.
Source: Epic Games.

A game development (game dev) team for big titles is often funded by a game publisher, such as Microsoft, Nintendo, Electronic Arts, or Activision, for exclusive publishing rights. Once the game is made, it must hit the store shelves and make as much money in the first month as possible, or it could wind up in the bargain bins or returned to the manufacturer as unsold product.

As I mentioned above, iPad games do not come close to triple-A titles. In fact, thousands of games exist for download on iTunes that have production costs that you can afford to make, even with very little experience.

Components of a Development Team

Perhaps you are making video games as more of a hobby, and therefore you will fill the shoes of all the game developer roles. However, to get the "big picture," it is vital to look at how the big-time game developers work.

Team leaders hire game developers based on personality—because everyone on the team must work well together—and on demonstrable skills. Developers fall into several classes based on their skillsets.

- **Programmers.** Programmers must typically know many different scripting languages because no single language standard exists in software development. Some languages include C++, C#, Java, Perl, Lua, and Ruby, among many others. If you are good at logic, math, and algebra, programming is probably for you.

- **Artists.** Artists create the game's visual assets, including its environments, characters, props, weapons, vehicles, monsters, and more. The look of a game can make or break its commercial viability. Game art includes two-dimensional (2D) and three-dimensional (3D) art, both of which are important in video game design. If you are good at drawing, or can visualize imaginary objects and people really well, you may have what it takes to be a game artist.

- **Writers.** Not only are writers responsible for constructing the storyline behind the game, they also script the dialogue and events that take place in the game. It takes proper use of grammar and written expression to be a game writer. Typically, writers are outsourced on game projects, so most of their income comes from freelance jobs. If you find yourself making up stories and coming up with unique characters and events, you could be a game writer.

- **Audio specialists.** Audio specialists set up sound effects, compose music mixes, and make games sound sweet. Have you ever played a video game on mute? It is not the same experience, is it? Sound is a vital component of the total gaming experience. If you enjoy music and have a distinct ear for the way things sound, you might make a good audio specialist.

- **Testers.** There is this persistent myth that testers get paid big money to play games all day, but that is not true. Game dev teams outsource to testers to get a fresh pair of eyes on their games. Testers sit in offices, testing just one level or one part of the overall game, day in and day out, and they have to fill out loads of paperwork. Testers let the team know what works and what doesn't, and then they test the same area to see if the issue has been fixed.

- **Leaders.** Leaders make sure everyone is doing what they should be doing and that deadlines are met. Leaders include directors, team leads, producers, and managers. Leaders often have to communicate with everyone, from artists to programmers, so understanding the culture and vocabulary of each department can add to their effectiveness. If you find yourself coming up with ideas and talking your friends into making those ideas reality, you may make a great leader.

Of course, many teams have noted cross-pollination between these disciplines. A writer may become an artist, and a programmer may become a leader, often switching between game projects.

"My primary responsibility at Rockstar San Diego is to build buildings that will populate the environment of the game I'm working on. To do my job, I've got to keep up with various levels of technology, all the way from simply making cool stuff in Maya (based on a detailed photo reference) to applying various shaders to these objects so that they look good within the context of the finished game."

—Tom Carroll, environment artist at Rockstar San Diego

Indie Game Developers

Although much of the game industry's big-budget efforts come from large team efforts, toiling on the production line is not the only model for game development out there. Lovingly crafted creations from independent (indie) game developers have proven that creativity flourishes when the development process is put back into the hands of a solo designer.

As an indie developer, you can make any game you want. Because you are not taking anyone else's money to make your game, you can try radical things no one else has tried before. Working alone to build a game with art, music, and compelling play may seem daunting to a first-timer, but it has never been easier for developers to create original titles without committing themselves to programming from scratch or shelling out an exhaustive budget.

Best of all, there is no reason to wait to start working on a game. You can start right now and do it all by yourself. Working alone on a game not only gives you complete control, but it infuses your work with a personality that big team development rarely has.

The music industry has existed for a lot longer than the game industry, and as anyone who knows music can tell you, the top-of-the-chart pop music lists are fine for most listeners, but if you want to hear some edgy tunes, indie music is where it is.

Indie musicians are artists who are not afraid to take risks. They settle for smaller gigs and less pay to play the music they want to and experiment with their art. Indie musicians are often seen as rebels who thumb their noses at the big industry giants.

Games work precisely the same way. When a corporate giant such as Electronic Arts pours thousands of dollars into creating a big-market game, they expect huge payoffs to compensate for their costs. They are understandably unwilling to take risks, even if the payoff might come in better innovation or storytelling.

This undeniable fact is why you see so many game sequels and imitation knockoffs instead of original or groundbreaking games on store shelves. If you want to see real innovation in the game industry, you have to peer at the margins, at the indie game developers. You can find out more by watching the documentary film *Indie Game* (see Figure 1.3).

Figure 1.3
Still from the movie *Indie Game*.
Source: Blinkworks® Corporation.

Indie games are often shorter, less expensively made games developed by fewer than 20 people, and are free or sell for a low price over the Internet. Indie games usually rise out of amateur and hobbyist game designers.

The indie game movement grew out of the modification (mod) community, where players of popular games such as *Quake* and *Unreal* modified the components to build their own game experiences and swap them online.

Giving away your game doesn't sound very smart, admittedly, and when you see prices at $10 a purchase, it makes you wonder if indie developers ever make their money back. However, if an indie developer can sell a minimum of 4,000 copies in one year, at $10 per unit, this tally comes to $40,000, which is not bad at all for a person's part-time hobby. Even in the Apple App Store market, where most apps fall between 99 cents and $10, you can quickly make several extra thousand on even the most casual game.

There are communities online as well as conferences and workshops for indie game developers sprouting up nationwide. Other indie developers often help their brethren up rather than seek to push them down. As an indie developer, you, too, can network with others like yourself.

Game Developer Pay and Location

As a hobbyist, pay is not important, but if you go on and want to make a career out of being a game developer, it will be. Pay is commensurate with location. Most game companies headquarter in large metropolitan areas like Austin and San Diego. Companies pay better in those areas.

A game artist in New York may make close to $68,000 a year, whereas a freelance game artist living in Wisconsin may only make $27,000. However, the person living in New York will have higher living expenses, as the cost of living is higher there than for the person living in Wisconsin.

So your expected salary earning must balance with your personal comfort level and where you want to live.

Demonstrable Game Developer Skillsets

Skillsets are important within a game design team. In fact, even if you graduate from a game school, the majority of employers will not judge you on the classes you took or did not take in school but on your present skillset. The best demonstration of your skillset is a powerful portfolio.

Therefore, if you want to get a job in the industry as a 3D animator, you have to show prospective employers what 3D software you know, and you will have to show them a portfolio of original 3D artwork you have personally created.

An employer may also want to see a demo reel of animations you have made yourself. Demo reels can be videos you post online or burn to DVD.

Breaking Into the Industry

There are a couple ways to get started as a professional game developer, if that is your desire: going to a school that offers a degree in game technology, or getting your foot in the door at a game company.

Going to a Game School

Electronic games are spanning the earth, and this global expansion has ushered in a need for skilled programmers and talented game artists. Most tech schools have started offering degree programs in game design to help fill this need, creating a brand-new foundation in game education.

If you decide game design will be your career goal, look for a technical college that teaches game software development or game art. Perhaps there is one near you. Here are a few:

- **3D Training Institute**—http://www.3dtraining.com
- **Academy of Art University**—http://www.academyart.edu/game-design-school/
- **DeVry University**—http://www.devry.edu
- **DigiPen Institute of Technology**—https://www.digipen.edu
- **Digital Media Arts College**—http://www.dmac.edu
- **Emagination Game Design**—http://www.computercamps.com
- **Ex'pression College for Digital Arts**—http://www.expression.edu
- **Full Sail University**—http://www.fullsail.edu
- **iD Tech Camps**—http://www.internaldrive.com
- **International Academy of Design and Technology**—http://www.iadt.edu
- **ITT Technical Institute**—http://www.itt-tech.edu/teach/list/degd.cfm
- **Pacific Audio Visual Institute**—http://www.pacificav.com
- **Seneca College's Animation Arts Centre**—http://www.senecac.on.ca/school/animationartscentre.html
- **The Academy of Game Entertainment Technology**—http://academy.smc.edu
- **The Art Institutes**—http://www.artinstitutes.edu
- **The Florida Interactive Entertainment Academy**—http://www.fiea.ucf.edu
- **The Guildhall at SMU**—http://guildhall.smu.edu
- **University of Advancing Technology**—http://www.uat.edu
- **Vancouver Institute for Media Arts**—http://www.vanarts.com
- **Westwood College of Technology**—http://www.westwood.edu/programs/

To become more proficient at the technology used in game development and to build your resume for future job applications, you can go to a school that offers a game design program, but honestly, you do not have to get a formal education to become a computer-age rock star.

Getting a Job in the Industry

If you have your education and want to get a job at a game development company, like Bungie Software, chances are you will have to start with an entry-level position.

The most common entry-level position at game development companies is as a game tester. Game testers perform focus testing and beta testing and take part in quality assurance for games being developed. They write many reports to document bugs or glitches. This can be downright tedious and nerve-wracking sometimes. Yet if you show a good head for design and stick with it, you can see promotion to another job title in the company in your future.

Occasionally, if you have a connection or a really good job placement counselor at your college, you can bypass servitude as a game tester and start out with a good game job title. It really helps, too, to have an amazing body of work or portfolio to show employers.

Again, to get a job making games, you have to show employers you can make games. The best way to do this is to start right now, with what you learn in this book, by making as many cool games as you can to put into your portfolio.

For more information on game developer jobs and projected salaries, visit www.gamecareerguide.com today. The makers of *Game Developer* magazine can help you prepare for a future career in game development.

Common Game Developer Myths Dispelled

As cool as a professional career in game development can be, it's also a lot of work. What follows are just a few myths of being a professional game developer and the underlying truths.

"I will be paid to play games all day long." You are making games, not playing them. It is true you will probably play-test your game maps as you build them, to check for errors, but you will not be gaming; you will be playing through the same map repeatedly, checking for every minor glitch that might escape passing notice.

"I won't have to work all that much."   This is definitely not true! As you will see throughout this book, working on a game development project is rewarding, but it is also difficult, and at times, tedious.

Besides coming up with art and audio assets, brainstorming game ideas, programming bits of code to make your games work, and laying out your levels, you will also have to document and promote your games.

Most developer's workdays do not stop at eight hours. Often, they may find themselves working twelve or more hours a day, and this takes them away from their families, friends, and doing what they love (which may include playing video games!).

"I'll make more money than my parents ever dreamed."   Most developers start out on the bottom rung, working as a game tester. Testers may only make minimum wage, and their days are full of testing game maps repeatedly for errors and filling out long documented reports of their findings. Testing is dull, and interaction with the rest of the team is limited.

After a couple years, a tester may work his way into joining the rest of the team, especially if he has appropriate skillsets the team requires. Then, pay is about equal to what you might make as a nurse at a hospital. Eventually, though, with enough influence, you could work your way up to becoming a project lead or art director, where the money really is.

"I don't want to do art or programming. I want to be the idea person."   Everyone who enters the game industry has tons of ideas for new games rolling around in their head, and of those people now working in the industry, most come up with original ideas practically every week.

What game dev teams really need are hard-working artists and programmers, especially the latter. Programming is such a virulent field right now, and if you have a head for logic and numbers, you might think of becoming a programmer. Programmers also get paid more than artists do.

Game Components

Just as books, movies, and music are categorized by genre, so, too, are video games. In addition, games are categorized by their perspective, or point of view. I have a list of four items of priority to keep in mind when building games in order to make them great. We'll discuss all of these topics in the following sections.

Game Genres

Just as the fiction book category has its genres, like westerns, science-fiction, and horror, video games have their genres, too. Video game genres may mirror fiction book genres, but game genres are also divisible by their gameplay, or the underlying way the games are played.

What follows are some traditional video game genres.

Action Games

Action games include all the different games where a player's reflexes and hand-eye coordination make a difference in whether she wins or loses. The most popular action games consist of:

- **First-Person Shooters (FPS):** Seen through the eyes of the main character, these games focus on fast-paced movement through detailed game levels, and of course, shooting and blowing up everything in sight. Because of the intimacy of "being the character," these games have the deepest player immersion. However, because of the frantic pacing of these games, the player rarely has time to stand still and take in all the scenery, no matter how much detail the level designers have imparted in the game environments. See Figure 1.4.

Figure 1.4
Cold War, a typical first-person shooter.
Source: Mindware Studios® Corporation.

- **Third-Person Shooters:** The player sees the action through a camera, which hovers above the ground in the air and aims down at the main character or over the character's shoulder. These games still focus on shooting and blowing stuff up, but the character is always visible onscreen and may have additional controls for actions like jumping, climbing, and performing martial arts.

- **Platform Games:** The player's character is visible onscreen, sometimes from a side angle. The action no longer focuses on shooting and blowing up enemies; instead, the main action focuses on the character running and jumping from one platform to the next in a fast-paced animated world. The first platform games were side-scrollers, where two-dimensional characters started on the left of the screen and jumped and ran their way to the right of the screen (think *Super Mario Bros.*, *Sonic the Hedgehog*, and *Earthworm Jim*). Games like *Mario 64* (shown in Figure 1.5), *Ratchet and Clank*, *Jak and Daxter*, and *Crash Bandicoot* revolutionized platform jumpers by bringing them into fully realized 360-degree 3D game worlds.

Figure 1.5
Classic platformer *Mario 64*.
Source: Nintendo® Co., Ltd.

- **Racing Games:** Racing games feature fast vehicles along twisting tracks and difficult terrain in an all-out race to the finish line. The goal is usually to come in first and as far ahead of the rest as possible.

- **Sports Games:** Featuring rules and scenarios just like the real-world counterparts, sports games focus on popular sports such as golf, soccer, basketball, football, volleyball, and baseball, although any pastime can be a prospective electronic game.

- **Fighting Games:** Fighting games set the player against a single combatant in an enclosed arena. Games such as *Street Fighter*, *Mortal Kombat*, and *DOA* have set the standards for this genre.

- **Stealth Games:** For those players who do not like rushing headlong into battle, there are games that reward the players for sneaking in and out of places without being seen, striking enemies silently. Sometimes the player is taking on the role of a master thief (*Thief: Deadly Shadows*), while at other times the player is a slick assassin (*Hitman: Absolution*).

Adventure Games

Adventure games traditionally combine puzzle-solving with storytelling. What pulls the game together is an extended, often twisting narrative, calling for the player to visit different locations and encounter many different characters. Often the player's path is blocked and she must gather and manipulate certain items to solve a puzzle and unblock the path.

One of the first interactive fiction games played on a computer (and one of the best games ever released for the Commodore 64), *Zork* was the forerunner of modern adventure games. The name *Zork* is hacker jargon for an unfinished program, but by the time Infocom was set to release their game with the name *Dungeon* in 1979, the nickname *Zork* had already stuck. For many, the name *Zork* conjures up dim images of a computer game prehistory, before graphics became the norm. *Zork* set several precedents for the genre.

Adventure games primarily center on story, exploration, and mental challenges. Many have players solve mysteries through gathering specific clues, as in *Sherlock Holmes: The Awakened* (shown in Figure 1.6).

Figure 1.6
Sherlock Holmes: The Awakened.
Source: Frogwares® Corporation.

There are at least four different types of adventure games. There are completely text-based adventure games, graphic adventure games, and visual novels (which are a popular Japanese variant featuring mostly static anime-style graphics and resemble mixed-media novels).

Another type of adventure game you might have seen and even played before is the hunt-the-pixel or "hidden image" adventure game. This manner of adventure games, a trendy genre for amateur game developers to undertake, consists of a series of graphic puzzles that has the player going on a virtual scavenger hunt.

Examples of adventure games include *Colossal Cave, Secret of Monkey Island, Myst, Siberia, Still Life, Legend of the Broken Sword, Gabriel Knight, Grim Fandango*, and *Maniac Mansion*.

If you would like to make an adventure game, you can download one of the following game-authoring tools:

- **WinterMute Engine (WME)**—http://dead-code.org/home
- **Adventure Game Studio (AGS)**—http://www.adventuregamestudio.co.uk/
- **Lassie Adventure Studio**—http://lassiegames.com/lassie/about/

Role-Playing Games

Role-playing games (RPGs) got their start in pencil and paper in the 1970s with Gary Gygax's *Dungeons and Dragons*, a variation of British war-gaming (which used miniature soldiers and world maps). Players of *Dungeons and Dragons* sit around a table and, using paper character logs and rolling many-sided dice, imagine they are wizards, warriors, and rogues exploring vast treacherous dungeons in a fantasy world.

Today's more complex computer role-playing games, like *Neverwinter Nights* (see Figure 1.7), *Asheron's Call*, *World of WarCraft*, and *Elder Scrolls V: Skyrim*, help players create their own characters from scratch, and the goal of each game is often making their characters stronger and finding better weapons while facing a rising level of adversity. The adversity comes in many startling guises, from trolls to giant spiders to fire-breathing dragons.

Figure 1.7
Neverwinter Nights.
Source: BioWare® Corporation.

One of the major resources you can acquire in almost every RPG is *experience*. Players earn experience for completing missions and beating monsters, and they spend experience to raise their character's skills or gain new powers. Another popular part of RPGs is communicating with non-player characters, or NPCs, through multiple-choice conversations. Depending on what players decide to say to NPCs, they might make friends, or they might find the NPCs rushing them with swords drawn!

There is a great application you can use to make fantasy RPGs called RPG Maker, and if you want to learn more about it, look for my book *RPG Maker for Teens*, from Course Technology PTR, 2011 (featured in Figure 1.8). In that book, I show you how to make a fantasy game RPG using Enterbrain's RPG Maker software.

Figure 1.8
RPG Maker for Teens by Michael Duggan.
Source: Cengage Learning®.

Strategy Games

Strategy games envelop a great deal of mental challenge–based games, including real-time strategy (RTS) games, turn-based strategy (TBS) games, and construction-management simulations (CMS).

In each, the core play has the player building an empire, fortress, realm, world, or other construct, managing the resources therein, and preparing against inevitable problems like decay, hardship, economic depravity, revolution, or foreign invaders. Strategy games emphasize skillful thinking and planning in order to achieve victory.

In most strategy games, the player is given a godlike view of the game world and indirectly controls game units under her command. Thus, strategy games are a closer comparison to classic British war games than RPGs, even though RPGs were the first electronic games to originate from war games.

Keynote strategy games that have helped define the genre include *Age of Empires*, *Civilization*, *StarCraft*, *Command&Conquer*, and *Shattered Galaxy*. CMS game examples include *The Sims*, *Spore*, *Ghost Master* (see Figure 1.9), and *Roller-Coaster Tycoon*.

Figure 1.9
Ghost Master.
Source: Sick Puppies® Corporation.

Casual Gaming

When video games entered homes during the console movement, the rules for video games became more complex and only the most hardcore gamers dominated the consumer market. However, this is not the only type of video game audience out there, and developers, especially mobile game developers, have recognized that.

A casual game is a video game targeted at or used by an audience of casual gamers. What are casual gamers? Casual gamers are those who do not have the time, patience, or obsessive passion to learn difficult, complex video games but still want to be entertained. Casual gamers include the young and old, but most (74%) are female. Casual gamers tend to seek out games with comfortable gameplay and a pick-up-and-play entertainment that people from almost any age group or skill level can enjoy.

Casual games can include any type of genre, but you can distinguish them by a simple set of rules and particular lack of time commitment required. Casual games often have one or more of the following features:

- Extremely modest gameplay, played entirely with a single-button mouse click or cell phone keypad.
- Gameplay accomplished in short episodes, such as during work breaks or, especially in the case of mobile games, on public transportation.
- Either the capacity to quickly attain a finishing stage or continuous play with infrequent or no need to save your spot in the game.
- Usually free or try-before-you-buy downloads.

Microsoft's *Solitaire*, which comes free with Microsoft Windows, is widely considered the very first casual game, with more than 400 million people having played it since its inception.

When Nintendo released their Gameboy, the free built-in *Tetris* game, a casual game if there ever was one, was partially credited with the success of that handheld console.

With the invention of the Flash animation software, there came a sudden boom of web-based casual games, one of the most prominent titles being *Bejeweled*, seen in Figure 1.10. Even former president Bill Clinton admitted to being addicted to playing *Bejeweled*. Flash game sites have cropped up left and right over the Internet, and Facebook third-party application developers got into the action with casual games like *Farmville* and *Mobsters*.

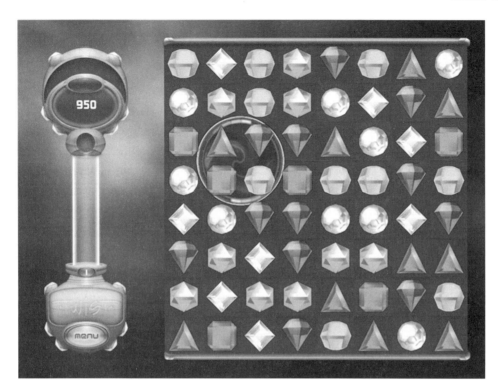

Figure 1.10
Bejeweled.
Source: PopCap Games® Corporation.

The arrival of Apple's iPod in the casual gaming market made games that are more powerful widely available on a mobile platform. PopCap Games created *Peggle*, which was an instant success on Apple's music player. Its success proved the need for more high-quality casual games on mobile devices.

Today, casual games played on the web and on mobile devices have exploded, with a wider and much more approachable audience than any other known game type. Casual games are also remarkably well placed for indie game developers to get their foot in the door.

Other Game Genres Worth Mentioning

Besides the genres already described, there are some others.

- **Traditional Games:** Chess, Poker, Texas Hold 'em, Solitaire, Mahjong, trivia games, and others share a clustered category under traditional games. These are all games once played physically and now given a virtual makeover to become video games. In some cases, the video game versions become more popular than the originals.

- **Artificial Life Games:** The player of an A-life game cares for a creature or virtual pet. In *Nintendogs*, for instance, players feed, play, and care for virtual canines. A game that first started out as an A-life game and grew to encompass multiple games in an online community is *Neopets*.

- **Puzzle Games:** These games never have much of a story. Instead, they focus on single-player mental challenges. Popular examples include *Bejeweled* and *Tetris*. One very addictive game that has truly redefined the puzzle game genre, and is in fact a redesign of the traditional "tower defense" style of play, is *Plants vs. Zombies*, where the player controls a yard full of cartoon plants defending against an oncoming zombie horde.

- **Serious Games:** Serious games are a serious business; many of them are educational games, which help schools teach subjects in the guise of having fun, or they can be training games, helping companies to instruct their employees in specific tasks. This is developing into a much larger genre as years go by, and some professionals have started referring to it as "edutainment."

"One of the more interesting trends today is the plethora of 'mixed-genre' games. It seems that one way to mitigate risk, while still trying to innovate, is to take several popular genres … and mix them to create a new style of game. *Deus Ex* is a great example of this hybrid."

—Tracy Fullerton, Assistant Professor, Electronic Arts Interactive Entertainment Program at USC School of Cinema-Television

Camera Modality

There is another component to consider when designing a video game, besides genre. It is the playing perspective, also known as the point-of-view (POV), just as in the development of fiction stories.

In film, cinematographers have to arrange the composition of all their camera shots to tell the story, but games use fixed or active cameras, which you can think of as floating eyes, to witness the action in video games. The position of these cameras, whether fixed or not, defines the POV of the game. The following are the most popular playing perspectives seen in video games today.

First-Person View

Just as fiction has a first-person perspective—the "I," "me," and "our" voice, told from the perspective of the narrator—so too do games. The approved choice of 3D shooters because of the ease of aiming, first-person perspective enhances sensory immersion by putting the player directly into the shoes of the character played. In other words, the player sees through the eyes of her character, and usually the only part of the character the player can see is the hand holding the gun out in front of her.

The player will start to think of herself as the avatar character, so cut-scenes that suddenly show the character or asides with a particularly incongruous voiceover supposedly belonging to the character, will take away the player's suspension of disbelief and (worst-case scenario) cause frustration.

Third-Person View

Just as in fiction writing, where the third-person (omniscient) style is typified by the "he," "she," "they," and "it" voice, games, too, have a third-person perspective.

The video game third-person perspective is much more cinematic and immediate in that the gamer can see her character on the screen and therefore can watch every move she makes. This leads to a greater identification with the player character but less player immersion overall.

The worst restriction to this viewpoint is that the character is *always* onscreen and the view is often from behind, so the character must look exceptional or gamers are going to complain.

Both Mario from *Mario 64* and Lara Croft from the *Tomb Raider* series were used in this perspective and rose to "movie star" fame because they literally became game icons and representatives of their gameplay.

Film cinematography features an over-the-shoulder (OTS) camera view, which has recently seen its way into video games as a variation of the third-person perspective. Surprisingly well-done examples of this are Capcom's *Resident Evil 4* and *5* (see Figure 1.11). These games help the players aim their weapons at enemies without having to resort to first-person visuals.

Figure 1.11
Resident Evil 4 for the iPad demonstrates the over-the-shoulder (OTS) perspective.
Source: Capcom® Corporation.

Top-Down (Aerial) View

The top-down or aerial view is a view looking straight down at the playing field. You see this perspective in games like *Solitaire*, the early *Ultima*, or *Zelda: Link to the Past* (see Figure 1.12). It limits the horizon for the player, so she has a harder time seeing what obstacles might be coming up, but it adds finer detail to what is on the surrounding map. *Grand Theft Auto*, before its 3D days, began as a vintage 8-bit top-down game.

Figure 1.12
Zelda: Link to the Past.
Source: Nintendo® Co., Ltd.

Isometric View

Isometric view is the tilted "three-quarter" view hovering off to one side of certain RPGs such as *Diablo*, *Baldur's Gate*, *Bard's Tale*, and *Planescape: Torment*. Developers use this perspective to give a fair impersonation of 3D even when the characters and environments are 2D, as in the popular iPad game *Bastion* (see Figure 1.13). Isometric games for this reason are popular in RTS and RPG but are rarely seen in action shooters because of the limitations to aim and visibility. Developers argue this to be the premiere perspective for strategy games, because players have a good overview of terrain and resources and can therefore manage their pawns better. Isometric games offer player movement in eight directions: north, northwest, west, southwest, south, southeast, east, and northeast.

Figure 1.13
Bastion has an isometric view.
Source: Supergiant Games® Corporation.

Side View

The side view reflects the traditional view of Sega and Nintendo's side-scrolling platformers as popularized in *Sonic the Hedgehog*, *Super Mario Bros.*, and *Earthworm Jim*. Although largely unused in newer games, thought of as too "retro," this view *can* be mimicked quite well even when working in 3D if you set up satellite cameras from the side and provide a fenced-in path terrain.

Adventure Scenes

Adventure games are well known for having their characters explore static backdrops, each scene acting like a diorama. Sometimes there is not a player character at all, just a diorama to explore. This type of perspective is fixed and unmovable. Whenever the player moves to an exact location onscreen, say a door leading to a hallway, another scene is drawn, say the interior of that hallway.

The player navigates and clicks through each adventure scene, sometimes having to backtrack many times or click throughout a scene to find elements to interact with, and if the designer is not careful, this can quickly degenerate into "hunt-the-pixel" frustrations.

Closed-Circuit Cameras

First pioneered by the game *Alone in the Dark*, the closed-circuit camera (CCTV) perspective style became the basis for the *Resident Evil* cameras. In fact, many developers simply call this playing perspective "RE cameras" for that reason. The style was copied by *Silent Hill* and countless other survival horror games in succession, because developers believed it made for heightened suspense.

In the closed-circuit camera view, fixed cameras pan to follow the player characters as they wander through their virtual environments. When a player character gets too far away from one camera, another camera will "switch on" and pick up the action, so that the player character is always on display.

Unfortunately, this perspective style has faced a lot of opposition. Players have complained that this style can be downright frustrating when trying to aim and shoot enemies coming around corners, or when determining if you are coming up on a potential hazard. This complaint is one of the reasons that *Resident Evil*, starting with RE4, switched to using over-the-shoulder, third-person perspective.

Four Fs of Great Video Games

There are four Fs of great game design. They are listed in order of priority and should be reflected on whenever you have to make any design decision. They help ensure every game you build is fantastic.

The four Fs are Fun, Fairness, Feedback, and Feasibility.

Fun

> "I still think that people who make their own games forget that it's supposed to be fun. I still play enough games where I'm really into it, and there's something just amazingly frustrating. Never give your player a reason to put your game down."
>
> —Todd Howard, Bethesda Softworks

Games are supposed to be fun by their very definition. Fun is a word often synonymous with play. Even the smallest child will begin inventing his or her own personal game when bored, an innate instinct meant to stave off boredom.

You know what fun is intrinsically, but fun is actually very abstract and subjective. You cannot dissect fun and have it laid out before you in its constituent parts. It loses its nature when you do so. Yet there are some tricks you can do to make sure your game will be fun.

A game is any fun activity conducted in a pretend reality that has a core component of play. Because it is play (not work), that is a huge distinction to keep in mind when making a game. However, even play has rules.

Rules of Play Play is any grouping of recreational human activities, centered on having fun. The pretend reality of most games is based on the players' mental capacity to create a conceptual state self-contained within its own set of rules, where the pretender can create, discard, or transform the components at will. The complexity and character of people's games evolve with their age and mental acuity. A game that outreaches a participant's age or understanding will swiftly tire the participant and leave her feeling bored.

The pretend reality created by a game's rule set is referred to as Huizinga's Magic Circle, first established by Johan Huizinga in 1971. Huizinga's Magic Circle is a concept stating that artificial effects appear to have importance and are bound by a set of made-up rules while inside their circle of use.

For example, the American game of football is about players tossing a pigskin ball back and forth to each other, but inside Huizinga's Magic Circle, the players abide by clearly outlined rules to reach a victory for one team or the other. Consequently, the concepts of winning and losing are not essential to all games, but they do make a game more exciting, competitive, and positioned within a clear frame of reference.

Electronic games are special types of games in which the Huizinga's Magic Circle is tied to an electronic device, whether that device is a computer screen and keyboard, TV screen and console, or handheld machine. Video games have graphics, audio, and interaction, but beyond those things, the elements of a video game differ widely based on game genre and platform.

Video games are different from traditional board or card games: in video games, developers hide most of the rules. The game still has its rules, but those rules are not always written down for the player to consult before jumping into play. Instead, video games allow players to learn the rules of the game as they play. Harder games, or games with entirely new/unheard-of rules, will sometimes offer players training levels to learn the rules early in the game. These are levels where players learn the rules through moderated experimentation. Given this route for learning rules, gamers with practice playing a specific game are better informed and therefore can optimize their choices.

Hiding the rules offers video games one huge advantage over traditional games: because the computer sets the boundary of the Huizinga's Magic Circle, the player no longer has to think of the game as a game! This level of immersion is lacking in most traditional games.

Player Interaction   When a player picks up the controller, takes over the keyboard and mouse, or puts her thumbs on the touchscreen, she wants to be able to explore make-believe worlds, encounter responsive creatures, and interact with her game environment. Games are not passive entertainment forms, such as watching movies. Games are active; they expect you to react!

Games are not like traditional stories. Stories are typically a series of facts that occur in a sequential order. In a game, however, the audience cannot understand the story from a typical sequential order but, rather, are free to make choices and come at the options from every angle.

This freedom of interactivity leads to immersion, which sells games. Indeed, a game with a lot of immersion in it is a game that players will want to play repeatedly to explore new opportunities and avenues for expression.

Players do not want to be told a story; they want to discover the story themselves. Listening to long-winded expositions, being forced to watch long animated sequences, and even talking with characters should always be secondary to exploration, combat, manipulation, and puzzle solving. In other words, story is supplementary to interactivity.

Putting the controls in the player's hands can sound scary for any designer at first. You are abdicating some control to allow the player to interact with, and possibly lose, at the game you have provided. However, without elevating your player to the status of co-author of your game, you will never make a fun game because fun games are all about interactivity.

If you fail to empower your player with interactive control, your game will fail.

Giving Players Fun Choices to Make

Part of interactive control is giving the player fun choices to make. Two main ideas must be present in your game for it to work:

- Difficult, not easy, decisions that have to be made by the gamer.
- Tangible consequences for making these decisions.

There is a partnership between you, the game designer, and your future gamer. You essentially pass off partial control of your game and its contingent story to the person who plays your game. Doing this can be exciting.

When creating decisions for the player to make, keep these simple rules in mind:

- **Make each choice reasonable:** Don't ask your player to go in a door marked "Great Stuff Inside," and then place a brick wall on the other side of it. Likewise, don't ask your player to choose between getting a magnificent sword and a pile of junk, because she'll pick the sword every time. The choices a player are given should be reasonable ones.

- **Make each choice real:** Don't invent arbitrary decisions, such as asking your player if she would rather go through Door A or Door B when both doors lead to the same room. To the player, this is as bad as cheating. The best choices of all to present your gamer with are difficult ones, especially when there is a perceptible tension surrounding the outcome of the decision.

- **Keep your player informed:** You must give the player enough knowledge to make a proper decision when faced with it. If you leave out the fact that if she keeps the Sword of Eons, she will have to slaughter her only surviving sibling, you are sure to see a player throw a tantrum.

Gameplay Balance   Gameplay is defined by developer Dino Dini as "interaction that entertains" and by developer Sid Meier as "a series of interesting choices." Gameplay comes first, because it is the primary source of entertainment in all video games. Art and story are almost "window dressing" in many cases. When designing the core mechanics, gameplay must be the foremost element you consider.

Gameplay differs from game to game, based on the player actions, options, and challenges. The challenges are central to the game, often varying by the game genre, and the options are the interactive abilities open to the player in order to overcome challenges. The player actions are steps players take to achieve their goals throughout the game.

One of the thorniest facets of successful game creation is making sure the game has balanced gameplay. If just one element in play gives the player (or for that matter, the enemy) too much power, the whole game is a wreck.

Players try to find the laziest and most efficient way to beat any game, because they understand games have an underlying competitive challenge. So be on the lookout for minor imbalances in the core mechanics and repair those imbalances so your player cannot cheat.

When you think you have found all the discrepancies, have some friends play through it with fresh eyes and see what they discover. They might find a loophole or problem you missed. Do not feel bad if they find one, because even the large commercial game developers miss glitches until after game releases.

What About Narrative?   Numerous games have narrative elements that give context to the events that take place in a game, making the activity of playing the game less abstract and enhancing the game's entertainment value. But narrative elements are not always clear or present. Some games, in fact, have no narrative at all.

Besides providing context for play, PR teams use narrative for marketing the game, as the game story can help sell the game to players. You might have heard catchy slogans like "Play as a brutal warrior in a fantasyland," or "Save the Mushroom Kingdom from the evil Bowser," or "Discover the magic of Emerald City." These slogans do not tell you about the game's core mechanics or share with you the gameplay, but they do impart the storytelling aspect of the games and make you want to play them.

It is largely up to you whether your game will have story in it or not. A game can still be fun and addictive even without a story.

Always Remember to Make Your Game Fun   Give your players a fun, fresh, and original experience, one encouraging replayability and word-of-mouth advertisement, and you have done your first duty as game designer. If your game is the slightest bit offbeat, offers cathartic release, or is irreverent and funny, it will get played.

Games can seem like hard work and can sometimes be frustrating to play, but players are willing to put in as much work as required if they get back enough high-quality fun. Fun is what games are all about. If you find your game is not providing the player with enough fun moments, you have to stop, rewind, and erase what you are doing right now and start building your game on the premise that every part of it must be fun.

Fairness

A player's time must be respected. A great game should offer the quickest, easiest ways to have fun and accomplish all the challenges, unless there is some entertaining reason to prevent it. Frustration can be a healthy motivator in games, challenging gamers to achieve greater heights for themselves, but frustration can also lead to the player giving up before beating the game. So tamp down frustration by playing fair with your player and you will receive greater rewards in the end.

Do not force gamers to repeat complicated moves in the game or learn their lesson by seeing their character die repeatedly. Endless repetition can be maddening, so never let your player fall into a rut. Never set the player up so that she has to perform a knotty set of maneuvers to get her avatar to the top of a hundred-foot platform, only at the last minute making her fall back down to the bottom where she has to start all over again. Likewise, do not kill the player's character suddenly for no reason. Avoid meaningless repetition or wrist slapping such as this.

Avoid frustration by making the game easier for the player. Do not remove challenges from the game completely, but relieve the build-up of tension that could potentially lose the player's attention. For instance, it is common practice now to have extremely brief death or game-over sequences and allow the player to jump right back into play without missing a beat. Although this reduces the realism of game scenarios, it is intrinsic in making the game seem fair.

A game would not be a game if it did not offer the player some goal to reach or challenge to overcome. Your game can be challenging while still being fair. The types of challenges games offer vary widely, from the accumulation of resources to intellectual challenges to self-preservation. Many challenges are staples of the game genres they belong in; others fit with the gameplay and are thus included.

The most common game challenges include the following:

- **Gates:** Gates, also called lock mechanisms, fence the player in, preventing access to some area or reward in the game world until that moment when the player beats the challenge and unlocks the next area or recovers the reward. The simplest and most prosaic gate is a locked door. The player is so familiar with this kind of gate she knows to immediately start looking for a key to unlock it (or a passcode, like in Figure 1.14).

Figure 1.14
A security panel requires a passcode before the gamer can continue in *Silent Hill: Downpour*.
Source: Konami® Corporation.

■ **Mazes:** Below-average gamers can get lost in standard game levels, so making the level more difficult by adding lots of twists, turns, and dead-ends might quickly make for a gamer headache. On the other hand, used wisely, a maze can become a wonderfully entertaining way to break the monotony of locked doors.

■ **Monsters:** Battles with monsters typify the combat mechanic in many games, including fighting games, shooters, and role-playing games. As classic as the gateway guardians of mythic lore, monsters are another form of obstacle to overcome, and always with some reward. The toughest of all are the "boss monsters" that pose the largest threat in a level.

■ **Traps:** Traps are a hodgepodge of suspense, scenery, and intrigue. Good traps can have whole stories behind them. Give some thought to each trap you place. Traps, like monsters, have become a staple of popular games ever since the days of pen-and-paper games like *Dungeons and Dragons*. One of the earliest games to focus solely on traps was Atari's *Pitfall* in 1982. In it, the player character Pitfall Harry had to leap or swing over tar pits, quicksand, water holes, rolling logs, crocodiles, and more.

- **Quests:** Quests are special sets of challenges that take place in both stories and games, thus linking narrative and gameplay. When playing quest games, like the *King's Quest* game series, the player must overcome specific challenges in order to reach her goal. When the player successfully surmounts the challenges of the quest and achieves the goal, another part of the game story is unlocked.

"Quests in games can actually provide an interesting type of bridge between game rules and game fiction in that the games can contain predefined sequences of events that the player then has to actualize or effect."

—Jesper Juul, *Half-Real: Video Games Between Real Rules and Fictional Worlds*

- **Puzzles:** Aside from actual puzzle games like *Bejeweled* and *Tetris*, developers can use puzzles to further the story or as mini-games within a game. Some puzzles are cryptographic or clue-driven in nature, where the player must supply a crucial bit of info, such as a password, key code, or similar, to pass by a guard, a locked door, or open a wall safe. Clues can be left lying around in convenient journals, computer e-mails, tape recordings, or discovered by talking to people.

Feedback

Video games are all about pushing a player's buttons. A game world is little better than a Skinner Box, a special lab apparatus developed by psychoanalyst B.F. Skinner to show you can train a rat to hit a button to get food. Feedback is just one of the primary components of the human-computer interface. Providing the player with adequate feedback will help the player know what to expect out of the game and frames the choices she will make from then on.

In other words, if the player does something dumb, show her it was wrong to try that particular action by punishing her. On the other hand, if the player does something right, give her a reward.

There are two critical rules to remember with regard to punishments and rewards. First, you should make your punishments and rewards fit the actions and environment, and you should always be consistent with your use of them. Second, you should make your punishments and rewards happen immediately so the gamer sees the cause-and-effect relationship.

Gamers are eager to know that they are doing something right or wrong so they can adjust their play style and master the game. They listen for the bells and whistles to instruct them in how to play better. You can use this knowledge to your advantage by creating a better game.

Also, the game world must react reasonably to the player. The environment must be somewhat reactive. Having reactive environments means that the game world responds to the player in logical and meaningful ways that help immerse the player in that game world.

This can mean that if the player sees a weak spot in a wall, a strong enough force should be able to knock a hole through it. This empowers the player to explore the game's environment and to treat it as if it were its own self-contained world. When in doubt about whether to make the game background more interactive, always opt for the affirmative answer, even though it usually means more work for you.

Feasibility

Encourage player immersion whenever and wherever you can in your game. To this end, avoid inconsistencies. Keep your games simple. Anything goes as long as it is fun, fair, provides adequate feedback, and makes sense.

Not all games have to appear to make a whole lot of sense. For instance, take *Super Mario Bros*. You play an overweight plumber who runs around stomping on killer mushrooms and kamikaze turtles while navigating giant pipes and flaming pits in a vast world full of titanic toadstools and floating platforms in the clouds. Finally, you face off with a huge redheaded turtle to save a princess named Peach. The game does not make sense, but it is fun and feasible; the core mechanics, in other words, remain consistent, and the player understands the workings of the game world.

As president of Cerny Games and video game consultant Mark Cerny puts it, "Keep the rules of the game simple. Ideally, first-time players should understand and enjoy the game without instructions." Keep your game rules simple and feasible.

CHAPTER 2

HOW VIDEO GAMES COME TO BE

Perhaps you remember the classic video games, such as those played on Atari or Nintendo console systems, and you wonder how games came from such primitive 8-bit beginnings to the glorious 256 RGB color range today.

In this chapter, I describe the process by which professional game companies make video games and the origin stories of those game companies. If you are creating games totally on your own, then some of the following topics may not apply.

THE GAME DEVELOPMENT PROCESS

Game companies do not create video games willy-nilly. Every game made has a process behind its development. When you play a game, you do not see the sweat and hard work it took to polish that game into the final piece of electronic make-believe you play.

Although there are many steps involved, the procedure can be broken down into three stages: pre-production, production, and post-production.

Pre-Production

The pre-production stage is where the concept is created and finalized, the game company seeks funds, and a team is put together to produce the game.

Inspiration can come from anywhere. Typically, an individual (often the head game designer) thinks up the game, but the game concept can also be discovered through random brainstorming by the whole group of developers. Once the idea originates, the team work together to iron out all its wrinkles by asking multiple questions about the game until they have a framework they can use. It is then that the team knows how many team members they will need, if they need to recruit more help in making the game, and what kind of software they need.

If more funds are required to purchase software, purchase hardware, hire team members, or commit to other investments in the build, then the team must devise a way to pay for it all. Sometimes they will do this by borrowing money or finding investors. Of course, the smaller, simpler projects like the ones for iPads are not very cost-intensive.

Production

The team is now ready to begin game development in earnest. The asset artists design 3D models, 2D artwork, textures, and environments on their computers. The programmers code the player controls and character behaviors, as well as the physics engine. The writers create dialogue and scripted events. The cinematic artists take storyboards and create short animatic cut-scenes that appear throughout the game (cut-scenes are those pauses in games where the player's controls are taken away, and she must pay attention for narrative purposes, such as the cut-scene from *Infamous* in Figure 2.1).

Figure 2.1
Cut-scene from the game *Infamous*.
Source: Sucker Punch® Productions.

The production process often starts dreamy and becomes more stressful the closer you get to deadlines. Team members may work obscene hours during the "crunch" time.

Finally, the team creates a gold master, which they send to the manufacturer for publication. The gold master is the final unalterable version of the game as it will appear when it's published.

Post-Production

After the game is finished, there is still more to be done. Testing, quality assurance, and bug fixing commences, followed up by a public relations scheme that will market the game to its target audience.

Game Testing and Quality Assurance

Testing involves the team members taking the time to play the game repeatedly, carefully following checklists to make sure every possible glitch is caught and fixed. After the team tests their game, they pull in people not related to the team to test the game with fresh eyes. A beta version of the game may even be released online, requesting players to tell the team if they discover a bug, or offering prizes if a player discovers a glitch. Even after the game is released and sitting on store shelves, more bug fixes may be required in the form of patch software.

Team leaders are responsible, primarily guided by the project manager or head game designer, for making doubly sure the game's overall look and playability remain consistent with the original concept.

Game Launch and Marketing

Before the game hits store shelves, it has to start selling well, so the public relations (PR) department makes sure people know about the game before its release and that the target audience wants to buy it. Most companies release their games to coincide with the Christmas rush, although games may come out year-round, and new games hit retail stores every week.

Game magazines will feature previews of early prototypes of the game or interviews with its developers. Web forums are also a great place to hit the target audience. Any way the PR people can whet the appetite of the public and make folks curious about an upcoming game is a good way to advertise it before its release.

Supplemental Materials

Should the game prove wildly successful, the developer may have to begin work on expansion packs, downloadable content, or sequels. If not, the game dev team may get a moment to take a few breaths before starting their next game project.

ORIGINS OF VIDEO GAMES

Games have existed as long as humankind has walked the face of the planet. A game is any variety of entertainment people use as a means of amusing themselves when they aren't busy hunting, gathering, preparing, cooking, or taking care of business.

This is still true today, in this digital age, with video games. Video games have become so integrated into our daily lives that they frequently become a distraction to computer users at work and school. They are a distraction because they can be addictive, but also because of the increasing rise of the social game market. Social games offer a component of play in which users share their victories with friends online, through co-op play or demonstrations of achievements.

But where did video games come from? And who made them? Studying the invention and evolution of video games will help you make better, more novel games today.

The First Video Game

In 1961, Digital Equipment Corporation (DEC), a leading American company in the computer industry, donated their latest computer to the private research university Massachusetts Institute of Technology (MIT). Computers in the 1960s would typically fill up whole rooms and appear as large banks of metal and flashing lit buttons. This computer DEC gave to MIT was comparatively modest in size, only as big as a large automobile. They called it the Programmed Data Processor-1 (PDP-1).

Like many universities, MIT had several campus organizations, one of which was the Tech Model Railroad Club (TMRC). TMRC appealed to students who liked to build things and see how they worked. They decided to reprogram the PDP-1 for fun.

One of the students, Steve Russell, was a typical science-fiction-loving nerd who joined TMRC at that time. He put nearly six months and 200 hours into completing an interactive game in which two players controlled rocket ship images on the PDP-1 screen. Using toggle switches built into PDP-1, players controlled the speed and direction of their rocket ships and fired torpedoes at one another. Russell called this game *Spacewar!*

In 1971 Nolan Bushnell and Ted Dabney took Steve Russell's *Spacewar!* game and developed a coin-operated arcade version of it they called *Computer Space* (shown in Figure 2.2), which used a black-and-white television for its video display.

Figure 2.2
Computer Space.
Source: Nutting Associates®.

Atari

Just one short year later, Nolan Bushnell and Ted Dabney founded a company called Atari, which would revolutionize video games. The word "Atari" comes from the Japanese strategy game *Go* and is a term similar to the phrase "Checkmate!" used in Chess. The Atari company was primarily responsible for the formation of the video arcade and modern video game industry.

You don't see as many video arcades as you used to, but back in the day these were places where upright coin-operated game machines stood in rows and, with their bright lights and loud noises, drew the attention of the young and interested everywhere. I used to frequent the Aladdin's Castle video game arcade in the local shopping mall. Instead of taking real money, the Aladdin's Castle coin-op arcades took special minted tokens with the Aladdin's Castle symbols on them (see Figure 2.3). I remember spending many Aladdin's Castle tokens on Don Bluth's game *Dragon's Lair*.

Figure 2.3
Aladdin's Castle game token (front and back).
Source: Namco Cybertainment® Co.

In 1972 (the same year Atari was founded), Atari launched its keynote game *Pong*. *Pong* featured a black-and-white television from Walgreens and a coin mechanism from a laundromat with a milk carton inside to catch coins as gamers deposited them in the slot. *Pong* was placed in a Sunnyvale, California, tavern called Andy Capp's to test its viability. When Atari workers showed up the next morning to fix the machine, which had died around 10 o'clock the night before, they discovered a line of people waiting to play the game. On examination, they found what had caused the Pong machine to quit working—the coin collector was overflowing with quarters, and when frustrated gamers kept shoving quarters in anyway, the machine shorted out. The Atari folks realized they had a hit on their hands, and after that, video games really took off!

Another leap in video game history came when Bushnell had the idea in 1975 to make a home console machine. It was a novel idea at the time, to take the excitement of the arcade and make it available on a person's home television. By early 1976, the Atari 2600 home console system (shown in Figure 2.4) became one of the hottest commercial items in history, followed by several successors and competitors. The home console machine was a huge marketing success.

Figure 2.4
The Atari 2600 home console.
Source: Atari® Inc.

Nolan Bushnell left Atari to start a chain of video arcade pizza parlors in 1977. He called his theme restaurant chain Chuck E. Cheese's Pizza Time Theatre, and it was the first family eating establishment to combine food, animated entertainment, and an indoor video game arcade.

The North American video game crash of 1983 (known as The Atari Debacle by some critics) brought an end to what some consider the second generation of video game consoles in North America. There were several viable reasons for the crash: too many different game consoles, too many different game companies, and a constant price war to catch as many gamers as possible. The market was flooded with hundreds of cheap, low-quality games that resulted in loss of consumer confidence.

One of these high-profile titles that didn't do well in the market was the 1982 game *E.T. the Extra-Terrestrial*, a movie tie-in with the Spielberg franchise. The game *E.T. the Extra-Terrestrial* has been called "one of the worst video games ever" and is even the subject of a music video—"When I Wake Up" by Wintergreen. Thousands of the game cartridges were returned unsold to the manufacturers, who eventually dumped them in landfills in the desert.

Nominally due to The Atari Debacle, Atari was dissolved in 1985. Yet, thankfully, video games were not dead forever. The market saw a resurrection in the late 1980s, thanks in huge part to Nintendo.

Nintendo

According to Nintendo's Touch! Generations website, the name "Nintendo" translated from Japanese to English means "leave luck to heaven."

Nintendo (a multinational corporation based in Kyoto, Japan) was founded in 1889 by Fusajiro Yamauchi to make handmade trading cards for the game Hanafuda, but in 1956, Hiroshi Yamauchi (grandson of Fusajiro Yamauchi) visited the U.S. to talk with the United States Playing Card Company, the dominant playing card manufacturer in America, and found their esteemed company headquartered in a rinky-dink office. This was a turning point for Nintendo, because Yamauchi realized the limitations of the playing card business and knew Nintendo had to do something different if it was going to survive.

By 1963 Nintendo had tried several other entrepreneurial ventures, including a taxi cab company, an instant rice manufacturer, a television network, and a love hotel. None of these panned out. Then in 1974, Nintendo secured the rights to distribute the Magnavox Odyssey home video game console in Japan. By 1977, Nintendo had begun producing its own home video game consoles. It wasn't until 1978, one year later, that Nintendo made their first video game.

In 1985, Nintendo released the Nintendo Entertainment System (NES) in North America, making video game consoles "cool" again. The NES featured a more accurate controller than the Atari joystick, higher-quality hardware, and games like *Super Mario Bros.* and *The Legend of Zelda*. In 1988, Nintendo made $1.5 billion, fifteen times the industry revenue three years before.

In 1977, Nintendo lucked out hiring Shigeru Miyamoto, a 24-year-old student product developer. Among Miyamoto's first tasks was to design the casing for several color TV game consoles. However, Miyamoto had some imaginative ideas of his own. In 1981, Nintendo released Miyamoto's first creation, *Donkey Kong*, somewhat inspired by *Beauty and the Beast*. *Donkey Kong* (seen in Figure 2.5) changed the history of Nintendo forever. The game got its name when Miyamoto said he wanted a "stubborn ape," and chose "donkey" as a demonstration of stubbornness and "kong" from the biggest ape in fiction, King Kong.

Figure 2.5
Donkey Kong.
Source: Nintendo® Co., Ltd.

In the game, a mad ape kidnaps a young woman, and her carpenter boyfriend (originally called Jump Man, but who later became a certain well-known plumber named Mario) must rescue her from the ape's clutches by navigating a shell of an unfinished building while avoiding barrels hurled at him by the enraged ape. *Donkey Kong* was the first video game I ever played. I spent several rolls of quarters on the arcade machine in the back of a local laundromat, getting up to the highest level I could.

Miyamoto's legend didn't stop with *Donkey Kong*. He went on to develop some of the most influential games in history, including *Super Mario Bros.* and *The Legend of Zelda*. In the early 1990s, a survey revealed Mario as more recognizable to American children than Mickey Mouse, placing Miyamoto in the same creative visionary category as Walt Disney.

In 1980, Nintendo launched Game & Watch, a handheld video game series developed by Yokoi. In 1989, Yokoi came out with an even greater follow-up: the GameBoy. This spawned a new age in video games, where a handheld console device could be taken with you anywhere, in a bag or pocket. When the GameBoy Advance came out a decade later, it continued the growing handheld gaming fever.

Nintendo outdid its GameBoy system in 2010 with its release of the 3DS. The Nintendo 3DS was a complete revamping of its previous DS handheld system. The 3DS was the first auto-stereoscopic handheld Nintendo engineered, and it included 2GB NAND flash memory for storage and 3D-capable 24-bit color. The 3DS currently competes against all other handhelds on the market, even with the cloud of controversy around rumors of possible health-risks among children concerning vision problems due to persistent play.

Nintendo conceived the Wii console in 2001 at the same time the GameCube console launched. According to an interview with Nintendo's game designer Shigeru Miyamoto, the concept for the Wii involved focusing on a new form of human interaction: "The consensus was that power isn't everything for a console. Too many powerful consoles can't coexist. It's like having only ferocious dinosaurs. They might fight and hasten their own extinction."

The Wii continues to dominate console wars in North America, maintaining Nintendo's legacy. A little-known fact is that more U.S. households own a Nintendo Wii (38%) than they do a cat (33%). The Wii is best known for its unique game controller, often referred to as a "magic wand" because it fits in the palm of your hand, and you can wave it around like a magician's wand. A handheld version of the Wii, Wii U, was released fourth quarter of 2012.

A game controller is an input device used for human interaction and is typically connected to a console or personal computer. A game controller can be a keyboard, mouse, gamepad, joystick, paddle, or any other device designed for gaming that receives input. Special-purpose devices also exist, such as steering wheels for driving games, light guns for shooting games, and fishing rods for fishing games.

Rhythm games like *Guitar Hero* and *Rock Band* utilize controllers shaped like musical instruments; dance games like *Dance Dance Revolution* and *Pump It Up* use dance mats with sensors built into them to detect foot motion; and other games use microphones and voice-recognition software.

Nintendo today has a U.S. market value of over $85 billion, and it lists as the fifth largest software company in the world, with over 3,400 employees. Five out of ten video game consoles sold are Nintendo products, and based on global unit sales in million units (as of December 2011), Nintendo's *Wii Sports* game dominates as the best-selling console game ever. Behind it, in terms of number of sales, the top Nintendo franchises include the *Mario* series, *Pokémon* series, and the *Zelda* series, in that order—and have outsold even *Halo* and *Mortal Kombat*.

Nintendo has earned a reputation as a "family company," because of its strict content criteria and its efforts to release family-friendly titles. The Nintendo gold seal of approval originally went on every cartridge released to impart the message of their strict quality concerns.

Sega

When gamers think of Sega, they immediately picture a spike-headed blue character called Sonic. Sega was Nintendo's competitor during the second game dynasty. A small Hawaiian company called Standard Games began operations in 1940, and in 1951, Raymond Lemaire and Richard Stewart moved the company from Hawaii to Tokyo, Japan, in order to develop and distribute coin-operated amusements like jukeboxes and slot machines. At that time, they renamed the company Service Games and dispersed their machines to American military bases throughout Japan.

An American Air Force officer named David Rosen started making coin-op games in 1957 and began competition with Service Games. Around 1965, Rosen merged with Service Games and changed the name of the company. Using the first two letters of Service Games, the company became known as Sega. Rosen continued to helm Sega until 1984.

Sega prospered heavily from the video game arcade boom of the late 1970s, with revenues climbing over $100 million by 1979. In 1982, Sega's revenues reached $214 million, but in the following year, following the North American video game crash, Sega's revenues dropped to $136 million. Sega then pioneered the use of laser discs and built their first video game console machine (the SG-1000) around the concept.

Sonic the Hedgehog became a virtual mascot for Sega in 1991 in an effort to compete with Nintendo's Mario character. (See Figure 2.6.) With his hip attitude and style, Sonic was marketed to seem "cooler" than the plumber. This effort worked in Sega's favor, pushing the Sega Genesis machine over the top in the console wars for a short time.

Figure 2.6
Sega's *Sonic the Hedgehog.*
Source: Sega® Corporation.

Sega enjoyed several console market hits, including their Dreamcast machine, but they officially announced they were quitting the console market race in 2001. Although out of hardware manufacturing, Sega continues in software development and video arcade distribution.

Sony

Sony Computer Entertainment (SCE) is a video game company subsidiary of Sony Consumer Products & Services Group. The company was first established in late 1993 prior to its launching of the original PlayStation video game console.

Sony originally developed the PlayStation (codenamed PSX during development; now known as PS1) to be a CD-ROM drive add-on for Nintendo's Super Nintendo Entertainment System (SNES) as a response to the Sega CD. Negotiations between Sony and Nintendo fell through, so Sony decided to release its add-on as a stand-alone game system under their own brand name. Nothing prepared them for how well received it would be. In fact, it propelled them into being part of the game console triad.

The PlayStation 2 (PS2), released in 2000, was the first video game console to have DVD playback functionality included straight out-of-the-box, making it a dual-purpose entertainment device. Even though the proprietary hardware and multifaceted development technologies received criticism at first, the system still received widespread support from third-party developers and went on to sell over 150 million units internationally. Sony released its successor, PlayStation 3 (PS3), later in 2006.

The PlayStation Network (PSN) competed with Windows Live and did very well, because PSN did not have the monthly subscription fees Windows Live did. The PSN allowed multiplayer functionality for several popular PS3 titles.

The PlayStation Portable (PSP) was SCE's first foray into the handheld gaming market, which Nintendo had dominated ever since its invention of the GameBoy. Released in 2004, the PSP has since seen significant redesigns, including smaller size, more internal memory, higher-quality LCD screen, and slimmer fit. The latest design, the PSP Go, came out in 2009 and supports Bluetooth. It is 45 percent lighter and 56 percent smaller than the first PSP.

Sony Ericsson has also taken the smartphone market with its Xperia phone, which combines the popular Android and HD screen technologies and puts them together in one mobile device. The name "Xperia" is derived from the word "experience" and is used in the Xperia branding.

Besides hardware, Sony has had a strong and persistent software angle as well from the very start. Sony Computer Entertainment Worldwide Studios (SCE WWS) is a subsidiary of SCE and is a group of video game developers fully owned and operated by Sony. This includes developers such as Naughty Dog Studio, which garnered title recognition for *Crash Bandicoot*, *Jak and Daxter*, and *Uncharted* series.

Microsoft

In 1998, engineers from Microsoft's DirectX team, including Seamus Blackley, Ted Hase, and Otto Berkes, disassembled some old Dell laptops to construct a prototype Windows-based video game console. The team hoped their console would compete with the Sony PlayStation 2, which had lured many players away from Windows games. Early on, they named their prototype the DirectX box, but later shortened it to "Xbox" because of the name's popularity with the test demographic.

In 2000, Microsoft founder and CEO Bill Gates unveiled the Xbox (see Figure 2.7) at the Game Developers Conference to rave reviews. Games like *Halo: Combat Evolved* helped secure Xbox's place in households worldwide.

Figure 2.7
The Xbox.
Source: Microsoft® Corporation.

The Xbox was the first video game console to feature a built-in hard disk drive, used primarily for storing game saves. This eliminated the need for separate memory cards. Xbox users could also rip music from audio CDs to this hard drive, and users could often apply these songs as custom soundtracks in some Xbox titles.

In November 2002, Microsoft launched its Xbox Live online gaming service, allowing subscribers to play online Xbox games with other subscribers around the world and download new improved game content directly to the system's hard drive. Approximately 250,000 subscribers signed up within the first two months, and by May 2009 that number had swelled to 20 million subscribers.

By August 2005, NVIDIA ceased making Xbox's GPU, and Xbox became a dinosaur. At the same time, Microsoft launched the new and improved Xbox 360, which featured superior storage, audio, and video capabilities.

Microsoft announced as part of its Live Anywhere initiative that it would bring the Windows Live online gaming and entertainment network to a wide host of platforms and devices, including the Xbox, Xbox 360, Windows PC, Windows Phone 7, Zune, and more. As part of the Windows Live experience, Microsoft encourages independent developers to make games for these media to be integrated into the Live network. This has drawn an audience of amateur game developers to learn Microsoft XNA Studio and related technologies. Microsoft's Windows Live accounts often require paid subscriptions, as opposed to Sony's PlayStation Network.

The forthcoming Xbox One got a bit of a kicking when it was first announced, landing itself in hot water with some unpopular features, including a mandated 24-hour online check-in and restrictions on the used games market. However, in light of the reaction from disgruntled gamers, these features have been scrapped, pulling the Xbox One out of its initial downward spiral. The Xbox One console will go on sale in November 2013.

Macintosh

Before the first Macintosh was released by Apple, marketing execs voiced their concerns that including games on the operating system would only exacerbate the notion the Mac was toy-like. Plus, the small amount of RAM would not be big enough to house and run a game.

Eventually, however, developer Andy Hertzfeld created a desk accessory called *Puzzle* that used only 600 bytes of memory and shipped with the Mac in 1984. *Puzzle* remained a constant part of the Mac OS until 1994, at which time *Jigsaw*, a puzzle game that came with Mac OS 7.5, replaced it.

In the 1990s, Apple computers didn't attract the same amount of video game development as Windows computers did, due largely in part to the high popularity of Windows and, especially useful for 3D gaming, Microsoft's DirectX technology. DirectX featured a lot of program code that made 3D game making easier, and developers loved it. However, it was pretty much Windows-dependent.

In recent years, however, the introduction of Mac OS X and support for Intel processors has eased the porting of many games, including 3D games that use OpenGL. Virtualization technology and Boot Camp (a product that allows Intel-based Macintosh machines to boot directly into Windows) have also permitted the use of Windows games on the Mac.

Steam's Mac Games

The Valve Corporation shocked many users in 2010, when they hinted at a Mac version of Steam, their popular online gaming distribution and multiplayer communications platform. Steam had already gained a huge following of PC gamers. Rather than typical Mac emulations, Steam highlighted fully downloadable native content for Macs.

The first game released simultaneously for Mac and Windows by Valve was *Portal 2*.

Apple Mobile Gaming

An even more successful movement by Apple was mobile gaming. A mobile game is a video game played on a cell phone, smartphone, PDA, handheld computer, or portable media player. This is not to be confused with handheld video games such as the GameBoy, Nintendo DS, or PlayStation Portable (PSP).

The iPhone   Apple's iPhone, a smartphone first unveiled in 2007, combines a video camera, a camera phone, a media player, and a web browser with phone technology that accepts both SMS text messages and voice mail and uses Wi-Fi and 3G/4G for Internet connection.

Development of the iPhone first began in 2005 when Steve Jobs decided Apple engineers ought to investigate touchscreen technology. Touchscreen means that there are no physical buttons, but the entire surface of the viewscreen can be programmed to react to touch. It proved to be a huge success, mostly due to its native integration with Apple iTunes, one of the top stores for MP3 media, and for mobile gaming.

The iPod and iPod Touch   The iPod Touch was a significant improvement on the original iPod design. Essentially, the Touch is a portable media player, personal digital assistant (PDA), handheld game console, and Wi-Fi mobile platform. The iPod

Touch runs iOS, the Macintosh operating system custom-designed for mobile technology. The iPod Touch was the first to add the multi-touch graphical user interface to the iPod line and was also the first iPod to have wireless access to the iTunes store, making downloading new apps a cinch.

The iPad   The iPad is one of a line of tablet computers designed, developed, and marketed by Apple. Apple designed it primarily as a platform for audio-visual media, which includes electronic-format books (ebooks), periodicals, movies, music, games, and web content. Its size and weight put the iPad in a category between Mac laptops and contemporary smartphones.

Speculative names for the device before its final release included "iTablet" and "iSlate." Apparently, the final name "iPad" was a nod to the science fiction show *Star Trek*, which featured a fictional device called a PADD that had an analogous look to the iPad. The PADD prop from *Star Trek* even operated very similarly to the iPad (see Figure 2.8).

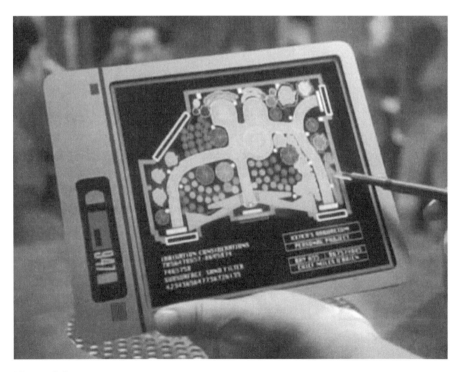

Figure 2.8
The PADD from *Star Trek* helped inspire the iPad tablet.
Source: Paramount® Domestic Television.

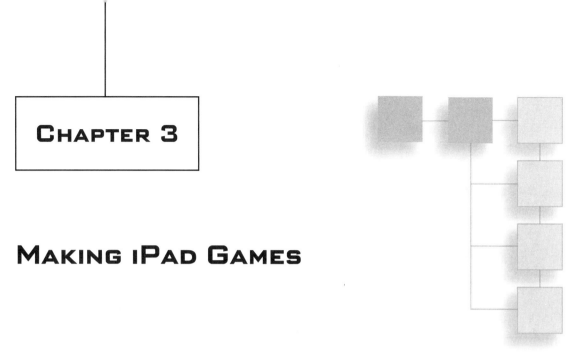

CHAPTER 3

MAKING iPAD GAMES

Now let's focus on the iPad. With what you will learn, you could develop games for the PC, Macintosh, Xbox, PlayStation, Web, or other platform, but for the sake of tapping a vital growing niche market (mobile gaming), you will gather all the pertinent information you need for making three-dimensional (3D) action games on the most popular tablet invented yet, the iPad.

Before we examine the software side of the matter, you should know a little more about the iPad's specs and what it can and cannot do.

THE IPAD

Do you have, or have you ever used, an iPad? If the answer's negative to both, you might have some difficulty understanding the audience and creating video games played on an iPad. However, it's not impossible.

Even if you consider yourself a proud iPad owner and user, you might find information here you never knew before. Furthering your understanding of the technology can help you determine the best course of action when developing applications to be used on it. If you want to make great mobile games, you may also want to look at other pertinent technology such as the iPhone and Android. There are subtle nuances between the tablets and smart phones, especially when it comes to screen resolution and processing power.

History of the iPad

In 1993, Apple created the Newton MessagePad, Apple's first stab at a tablet, which you can see in Figure 3.1. Critics considered it just an oversized personal digital assistant (PDA) instead of a true mobile computing device. Since the product never reached the acceptance hoped for, Apple discontinued the Newton in 1998.

Figure 3.1
The Newton MessagePad.
Source: Apple Inc.

The iPad, which you can see in Figure 3.2, launched in 2010 and sold 3 million units in the first 80 days. The fervor has only increased. The iPad is the number one tablet on the market today, holding over 65% of the market.

Figure 3.2
The iPad.
Source: Apple Inc.

Typical Uses of the iPad

There has been rapid growth of American iPad users since its initial release. In 2010, there were 11.5 million iPad users. Today, there are over 53.2 million users. 66% of those are male and 34% are female. The average age of the iPad user is between 25 and 36 years old.

Although general consumers are the most common users of the iPad, several growing user groups have begun making the iPad a common sight in their prospective fields.

- **Business:** Several companies have adopted iPads in their offices by distributing or making iPads available to their staff. A Frost & Sullivan survey shows iPad usage in the workplace is linked to the increase of employee productivity, a greener and more paperless work environment, and increased revenues. The iPad is compact, making it easy to use to jot down office notes, and its presentation apps can make in-office presentations, especially connected to screen projectors, eye-catching and quicker to start.

- **Education:** Many classrooms have adopted the iPad and even praised it in many circles as a much-needed tool for homeschoolers. Shortly after the iPad's release, reports came out that noted over three-quarters of the top book apps were for school-age children. Many secondary educational institutions have also started using iPads, even going so far as to make them available in student bookstores as a requisite learning utility.

- **Music:** In 2010, the rock band Gorillaz released an album called *The Fall*, which singer/songwriter Damon Albarn created almost exclusively using just his iPad while on tour with the band. With its iTunes playback software and samplers, music creation is a snap on the iPad, and many sound mixers and DJs have started considering the iPad a major tool in their arsenal.

- **Flight:** In 2011, Alaska Airlines become the first airline to replace pilots' printed flight manuals with iPads in the hope of having fewer back and muscle complaints. The movement has spread with the U.S. Federal Aviation Administration approving the iPad for pilot use to cut down paper consumption. This is related to the push for iPad usage in offices (noted above).

The iPad is truly a "go anywhere" computer tablet, which makes it great for on-the-go casual gaming. Users can play games on the iPad wherever they want, as long as they don't disrupt the people around them, of course.

App Development for the iPad

There are 650,000 total apps currently in the Apple App Store at the time of this writing, and 225,000 of those are iPad apps.

When rumors first circulated back in 2009 that Apple was considering making another tablet, most people wanted to know what operating system (OS) it would run, because the OS would be a keynote in whether the tablet would have true sustaining power. Apple played it smart. Rather than stick their current Macintosh OS X on their new tablet, the company built an OS capably fixated on touchscreen navigation to create all-in-one mobile operations. The iPad is powered by a tablet-enhanced version of iOS. With millions of satisfied iPhone and iPod Touch users already familiar with the iOS interface, the iPad has an immediate and intuitive feel. It looks easy to use because it is, and people have raved about the cross-demographic simplicity.

Because the iPad runs the same iOS as the iPod Touch and iPhone, it not only can run its own iPad apps, it can also run a vast majority of iPhone apps. When running iPhone apps, the iPad user is given the choice to view it normal iPhone size (the small 480×320 pixel dimensions of the iPhone), centered in a black screen, or to tap the "2x" icon in the lower right to see the app full iPad size (the 1024×768 pixel dimensions). You can see a visual comparison of the two devices in Figure 3.3.

Figure 3.3
The specs for both the iPhone and iPad.
Source: Piotr Kowalczyk and Apple Inc.

The iPad is an ideal target platform for game developers wanting to tap the popular iOS market. Syncode's Matthew Lesh said, "Apple has provided developers with some powerful and unique tools to create stylish applications for the iPad. The challenge now is to create them." This book will show you how to create them.

Several game titles are making use of the iPad's lightweight on-the-go size and touchscreen functionality to give players unique experiences. You can see examples of these in the following illustrations from various rising iPad games: *Dungeon Hunter 2 HD* (Figure 3.4), *Infinity Blade II* (Figure 3.5), *N.O.V.A. Near Orbit Vanguard Alliance HD* (Figure 3.6), and *Fieldrunners HD* (Figure 3.7).

Figure 3.4
Dungeon Hunter 2 HD.
Source: Gameloft®.

Figure 3.5
Infinity Blade II.
Source: Chair Entertainment® Group.

Figure 3.6
N.O.V.A. Near Orbit Vanguard Alliance HD.
Source: Gameloft®.

Figure 3.7
Fieldrunners HD.
Source: Subatomic Studios®.

Besides titles made just for the iPad, you can find all kinds of games from other platforms now being ported over to the iPad, including popular games like *Bastion* (Figure 3.8) and *Dead Space* (Figure 3.9).

Figure 3.8
Bastion.
Source: Supergiant Games®.

Figure 3.9
Dead Space.

Source: Visceral Games® (formerly EA Redwood Shores).

The iPad only runs programs sanctioned by Apple and distributed via Apple's App Store (shown in Figure 3.10), with the exception of programs that run inside the Safari web browser.

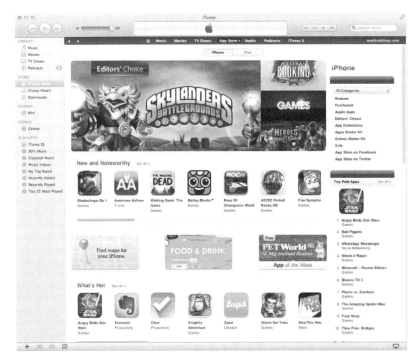

Figure 3.10
Screen grab of the App Store.

Source: Apple Inc.

iPad ships with Safari, Mail, Photos, Video, YouTube, iPod, iTunes, App Store, iBooks, maps, Notes, Calendar, Contacts, and Spotlight Search. Several of these apps have improved since their use on iPhone and Mac. Apple ported its iWork suite, Mac's answer to the Microsoft Office Suite, from the Mac to the iPad and sells pared down versions of Pages, Numbers, and Keynote apps in the App Store.

Apple's Strict Proprietary Control on Apps

Critics have voiced concerns that Apple's centralized app approval process and control of the platform could downgrade software innovation. In fact, Apple retains the facility to remotely disable and/or delete apps, media, or data from any iPad at any time. Apple employs Digital Rights Management with the intent to control certain software and prevent its use outside the iPad. For instance, pornographic material is intentionally prohibited on iPads.

The iPad's development model also requires anyone who wishes to create an app for an iPad to sign a non-disclosure agreement (NDA) and pay for a registered developer subscription, which doesn't come cheap. Currently, it costs close to $100 to become an Apple developer, even if all you want to do is fiddle around with making iOS apps. This has discouraged some software developers from entering the Apple market.

Digital rights advocates have criticized Apple for its restrictions. Apple has full control of what can be loaded and what can stay on an iPad, regardless of the iPad owner's wishes. Critics consider this a breach of the freedom of speech provided for by the Bill of Rights.

As GigaOM analyst Paul Sweeting said on National Public Radio, "Apple is offering you a gated community where there's a guard at the gate, and there's probably maid service, too." This concept of the iPad as a safe haven from viruses and malware is the positive thing about the restrictions, but it makes developing for the platform harder. As Paul went on to say, "With the iPad, you have the anti-Internet in your hands. It offers [major media companies] the opportunity to essentially re-create the old business model, wherein they are pushing content to you on *their* terms rather than you going out and finding content, or a search engine discovering content for you."

Questions About Jailbreaking the iPad

Like similar iOS devices, the iPad can be jailbroken, a hack that allows applications and programs not authorized by Apple to run on an iOS device. Once the iPad is jailbroken, whether through a "userland" jailbreak or other method, the user is able to download apps not presented in the Apple App Store as well as illegally pirated apps. The jailbreak app stores, of which there are several (Cydia, Icy, and RockYourPhone, among others), have apps that do pretty much anything you want on the iPad.

Apple claims that jailbreaking voids factory warranty on the device in the United States, even though, officially, jailbreaking is legal. I am not condoning jailbreaking, but if you are unafraid of voiding your warranty, you can Google a how-to on jail-breaking. Cydia's JailbreakMe is shown in Figure 3.11.

Figure 3.11
Screen grab of JailbreakMe.
Source: comex.

There is no reason to compel you to jailbreak your iPad for the purpose of iPad game design. In fact, I do not approve or condone the practice. The following, however, covers the most general questions you might have about jailbreaking your iPad.

"Does jailbreaking affect my App Store apps?"   No, it doesn't. You can use your current apps from the App Store, buy new apps, and sync them to your computer just as you would normally.

"If I jailbreak my iPad can I download App Store apps for free?"   Yes, you can. Jail-breaking allows you to circumvent the App Store and install apps for free. But this is really not a nice thing to do. It is considered similar to pirating software, and there-fore is not suggested.

"Will jailbreaking break my iPad?"   Probably not, but downloading and installing apps can seriously mess up your iPad if you're not careful. You might even find yourself needing a factory restore, and though there haven't been any reports so far, there's the outside chance you might break your iPad altogether.

Also, you should keep future upgrades in mind, because Apple will patch the holes that make jailbreaking possible, and then you might be stuck.

"Does jailbreaking void the warranty on my iPad?"   Yes, it does! When you jailbreak your iPad, you are essentially taking it off the grid. Apple Store Geniuses will regard your jailbroken device with complete and utter indifference. Of course, if you reset your iPad to its original factory settings, things should go back to normal, and it's possible no one will ever be wise to your jailbreaking.

"Can I ever get my old iPad back?"   Yes. Restoring your iPad to factory settings in iTunes will remove all traces of jailbreaking activity and lets you resume your previous iPad experience.

"Why should I jailbreak my iPad?"   One of the most obvious reasons would be to access content Apple wouldn't normally allow, especially apps that don't pass Apple scrutiny.

Another reason is multitasking; currently, the iPad does not let you switch tasks, but Backgrounder, an iPhone jailbreak favorite, works great on the iPad and bestows upon you the capacity to browse the Web while listening to your favorite music. You can also customize your icons and deck your iPad out with custom themes.

Again, there is no actual reason to jailbreak an iPad to design games for the iPad.

"How easy is jailbreaking?"   It's very easy, in most cases. The Spirit jailbreak, for instance, is practically a one-click process. Any jailbreak system you use will have its own set of instructions. What's really important is to remember to not play around with your iPad or iTunes while jailbreaking and definitely do *not* unplug the device while the jailbreaking is taking place.

"How beneficial is jailbreaking in the long run?"   Jailbreaking, believe it or not, has often been a trendsetter for official Apple revisions to its iOS. When a jailbreak app becomes exceedingly popular, you will likely see Apple release an official app very similar to it not too long after. Before you could do Wi-Fi tethering on iOS devices, MyWi provided a jailbreak way to add Wi-Fi tethering without having to go through a carrier. Apple later made Wi-Fi tethering official with iOS 4.3.

So jailbreak apps, in many ways, are like a testing ground for future iOS updates.

Developing iPad Games

When it comes to game development, most developers use a pipeline of software technologies. They use paint-editing programs to make 2D art, modeling and animation programs to make 3D graphics, sound-editing programs to make audio, and then put it all together with a game engine. Big-name companies build their game engines from the ground up, but some game engines (especially Unreal) are becoming popular turn-to solutions even for corporate giants.

Most game engines have restrictions about what platforms they can port their games to, based on how the engine was programmed. There are several applications that port games to Apple iOS devices, particularly the iPad. What follows are some game authoring software packages you might consider for making iPad games.

GameSalad

Info on GameSalad (see Figure 3.12):

Figure 3.12
GameSalad.
Source: GameSalad® Inc.

- ■ **Website:** http://gamesalad.com/products/creator
- ■ **Price:** Free. $299 for pro version (price subject to change)
- ■ **Platforms:** Macintosh, iOS device, or Web
- ■ **Target Audience:** Single player
- ■ **Learning Curve:** Easy or beginner

GameSalad Creator, which features a dynamic drag-and-drop game editor, comes with a variety of templates that you could use to start making 2D Macintosh or iOS games.

GameSalad's biggest selling point is that the game creation tool doesn't require any programming knowledge to use, although a basic understanding of computer game logic and digital media is preferable. As they say on their website, "GameSalad aims to open the doors of game design to anyone who wants to create." With the editor's visual interface and versatile programming, their mission statement shows.

The best detail about GameSalad? It's free!

Besides Mac and iOS platforms, GameSalad can also publish titles directly to HTML5, so developers can embed their titles for play on any compatible web browser, Safari or otherwise.

"I'm not here to say that Flash is done, but we do envision that the web game industry will move towards the open standard of HTML5," GameSalad Chief Product Officer Michael Agustin reported to Gamasutra. "We're placing a bet: GameSalad wants to be ahead of the curve with HTML5 … It's widely expected to become the next standard language for the Web, and is poised to quickly disrupt Flash."

Since most major web browsers now support HTML5, GameSalad offers a much larger potential audience than Flash or Unity does currently. The company is also promoting emerging web-based games through the GameSalad Arcade section of their website.

If you are looking to make a 2D game for an audience of one, you might give Game-Salad a try. It's easy to download and begin working with, requiring very little experience.

cocos2d for iPhone

Info on cocos2d for iPhone (see Figure 3.13):

Figure 3.13
cocos2d for iPhone.
Source: Michael Heald.

- **Website:** http://www.cocos2d-iphone.org
- **Price:** Free (open source)
- **Platforms:** Macintosh or iOS device
- **Target Audience:** Single or multiplayer
- **Learning Curve:** Intermediate

More than 2,500 App Store games reportedly use cocos2d for iPhone. cocos2d for iPhone is a free, fast, and lightweight framework for building 2D games and other applications. The name itself is misleading, as cocos2d for iPhone can be used to build iPhone, iPad, and iPod Touch games. It is entirely open source, so it is heavily community fed and driven. The language cocos2d for iPhone uses is Objective-C and is a sight better than using direct OpenGL. Its core is flexible, allowing integration with third-party code libraries, and it uses optimized data structures.

There is a third-party extension created and maintained by The Brenwill Workshop (http://brenwill.com/cocos3d/) for manipulating cocos2d into making 3D games.

Here are some features of cocos2d for iPhone:

- Scene management and transitions
- Basic menus and buttons
- Integrated behavior scripting
- Particle system
- Special effects such as lens, ripple, waves, liquid, and twirl
- Integrated physics engines
- Touch and accelerometer support for iOS
- Portrait and landscape modes for iOS

iTorque 2D
Info on iTorque 2D (see Figure 3.14):

Figure 3.14
iTorque 2D's iPhone emulator.
Source: GarageGames® Inc. and Apple Inc.

- **Website:** http://www.garagegames.com
- **Price:** Free to try; $99 to buy (price subject to change)
- **Platforms:** Windows PC, Macintosh, or iOS device
- **Target Audience:** Single player
- **Learning Curve:** Easy or beginner

GarageGames, the makers of Torque, knew their popular 2D and 3D game engines needed a wider audience of game platforms to be sustainable. So they began targeting platforms besides the PC and Mac computers. Following the release of Microsoft's XNA Studio, and the potential to develop Windows and Xbox 360 games, Garage-Games launched their hugely successful TorqueX, a game maker for Windows and Xbox 360 platforms.

Most recently, GarageGames set their sights on Apple's iOS mobile devices and have released the iTorque 2D game engine. iTorque 2D can be used to craft simple or complex games for the iPod Touch, iPhone, or iPad devices. iTorque 2D is simple to use and is just one level above drag-and-drop creation. iTorque 2D provides the following features:

- A visual 2D editor at iPhone, iPad, or iPod touchscreen resolutions
- Powerful and simple scripting language (TorqueScript) for rapid prototyping
- Multi-touch and accelerometer input support
- Tutorials and documentation to guide users of all experience levels
- QuickTime movie playback and music playback support

You build your iOS game on PC or Mac and then port it to the iPhone, iPad, or iPod Touch. A Mac is required to perform optimization, device deployment, and Objective-C coding, but if you're a diehard Windows user, you can still program your game on a PC with C++ before moving to the Mac.

Multimedia Fusion 2
Info on Multimedia Fusion 2:

- **Website:** http://www.clickteam.com
- **Price:** Free to try; $119 to buy (price subject to change)
- **Platforms:** Windows PC, iOS, or Android
- **Target Audience:** Single player
- **Learning Curve:** Easy or beginner

Clickteam, a software company founded in 1993 and headquartered in Paris, France, is best known for their easy-to-use game-making toolkits, including The Games Factory and Multimedia Fusion.

Multimedia Fusion is a flexible, powerful, and full-featured authoring tool with no programming skills or knowledge required, and it's a tool used by many multimedia professionals, game creators, and more. You can create a frame containing any 2D graphics you desire and then insert objects called extensions into that frame by drag-and-drop. Set behaviors for those objects in an intuitive, grid-style Event Editor, and you're practically done!

Clickteam offers an iOS runtime option for Multimedia Fusion 2 and Multimedia Fusion 2 Developer, so that you can export 2D games to be played on the iPhone or iPad.

Unity iOS

Info on Unity iOS (see Figure 3.15):

Figure 3.15
Unity iOS.
Source: Unity Technologies® and Apple Inc.

- ■ **URL:** http://unity3d.com
- ■ **Price:** Unity is free; iOS Pro license is $1,500 (price subject to change)
- ■ **Platforms:** Web, Windows PC, Mac, or iOS device (others available)
- ■ **Target Audience:** Single or multiplayer
- ■ **Learning Curve:** Beginner or intermediate

Unity is a popular high-end 3D graphics game engine that caters to most platforms. Through separate purchasable licenses, a single developer can publish to PC or Mac, the Web to be played over a web browser (the Unity Web Player plug-in is required), Android, Nintendo Wii, Xbox 360, Sony PlayStation 3, and iOS devices. Thus, with a single tool and workspace, you can target multiple platforms at once.

Plus, you have complete control over the way your project delivers to these platforms. The built-in Unity Editor emulates your selected platforms so you can see what your game will look like before you publish it.

Unity lets you specify graphic resolution and texture compression, so you can use one Photoshop file and have it blend seamlessly on every device. On top of cross-platform distribution possibilities, Unity has a next-generation look and is optimized for speed and quality when rendering complex environments and controlling ambient lighting and effects. It also has preprogrammed physics that make those environments close to reality. In fact, Unity contains the powerful NVIDIA PhysX Engine, which is top-line in the gaming industry.

UDK Mobile

Info on UDK Mobile (see Figure 3.16):

Figure 3.16
UDK Mobile.
Source: Epic Games.

- **URL:** http://www.unrealengine.com/en/
- **Price:** UDK is free for non-commercial use
- **Platforms:** Web, Windows PC, Mac, or iOS device (others available)
- **Target Audience:** Single or multiplayer
- **Learning Curve:** Beginner or intermediate

Unreal Development Kit (UDK) is the free version of Unreal Engine 3 and provides you access to the award-winning 3D game engine and professional creation toolset used in blockbuster video game development. Unreal has been used to create such popular games as:

■ *Alice: Madness Returns*

■ *Batman: Arkham Asylum and Batman: Arkham City*

■ *BioShock and BioShock 2*

■ *Borderlands and Borderlands 2*

■ *Bulletstorm*

■ *Dungeon Defenders*

■ *Fable: The Journey*

■ *Gears of War 3*

■ *Lollipop Chainsaw*

■ *Mass Effect, Mass Effect 2, and Mass Effect 3*

UDK is the perfect toolset for anyone and everyone, including you, as it has been proven with countless releases and dozens of awards. Plus, it has the flexibility and track record of Unreal Engine 3 to fall back on.

UDK has everything in one total free package. It comes with Unreal Kismet, the visual scripting component of Unreal that allows you to string together actions, inputs, and events in order to dictate how the game world reacts to the player, all without you having to enter a single line of code. UDK also comes with Unreal Marquee, which helps you build dynamic animations without having to leave the editor environment. The Unreal Content Browser makes managing assets like meshes, materials, audio, and animations so easy it's, well, unreal.

You can easily deploy your app from the UDK Mobile Editor to your iOS device with a single click. The packaging assistant (built-in) helps you easily configure your app for deployment.

UDK has a fully implemented OpenGL ES 2.0 Renderer on Windows PC that allows you to preview your content as if it was running on an iOS device, using your mouse to interact with the touchscreen controls, something no other game dev toolset currently offers! This allows you to test iOS gameplay without copying it to your device or passing Apple's App Store approval first.

Of course, if you want device interaction for test-play, Unreal offers a free download of UDK Remote from the App Store. UDK Remote allows you to interact with your iOS device in real time and see the input on the device affect your application currently running on your Windows PC. This greatly reduces iteration time while building your mobile game.

For the purposes of this book, you will be using UDK Mobile to make iPad games, although UDK can also be used to make titles for other target platforms. With everything you will learn, you can make any game you want, not just mobile games.

DOWNLOADING AND INSTALLING UDK

Now that you have the necessary backend tools ready, it's time to install UDK. You can download it by going to: http://www.unrealengine.com/en/udk/downloads/.

For the lessons herein, I have used the November 2012 UDK Beta (1.8 GB .exe). If this is not the latest release, you may find it under the Previous Versions subheading or in their archives. (See Figure 3.17.)

Figure 3.17
A screen grab of the online UDK downloads.
Source: Epic Games.

Recommended requirements for content development if you are using a Windows PC are as follows:

- Windows 7 64-bit operating system (OS)
- 2.0+ GHz multi-core processor
- 8 GB system random access memory (RAM)
- NVIDIA 8000 series or higher graphics card
- Plenty of hard drive disc (HDD) space

I have seen UDK run fine on some laptops and struggle to run on some desktops, so double-check your system specs before installing and running it on your machine. If you have had zero problems running high-end graphic games like *Borderlands 2* on your machine, then you should have no problem at all running UDK.

During installation, you will be asked if you want to install the demo project, which you should do. The setup will also ask if you want to install the optional Perforce server or client app. These are useful if you are collaborating with a large team and want to protect your work in backup format. They are not required for general use, however.

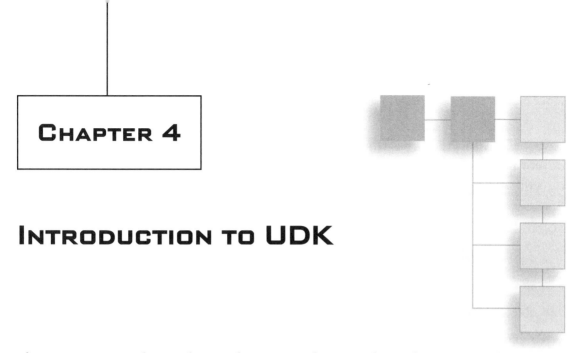

CHAPTER 4

INTRODUCTION TO UDK

If you are interested in making video games, the Unreal Development Kit (UDK) can help you. It can resolve many of the issues you would normally face in a game development atmosphere, such as lighting, object placement, physical interactivity in a virtual world, and so on. In this chapter, you will examine the software and take your first steps in understanding how it works.

The Unreal Development Kit comes with multiple built-in modules that you use for game development. Content that is developed outside of UDK, such as graphics made in a photo editor or 3D models made in 3ds Max, Maya, or another 3D modeling program, can be brought into UDK through the Content Browser module. The programmer scripts the gameplay and provides interactivity between the gamer and the game itself using the Kismet module. And the Matinee module is used to add motion graphics to the game, such as you might see in a cut-scene cinematic.

THE UDK EDITOR

UDK Editor is a fully featured level editor. By "level," I mean a singular game world or scenario environment, the definition of which is somewhat flexible. Most developers stitch games together from multiple levels.

This is perhaps most obvious in classic 2D platformers, where the player runs his sprite character from left to right across an entire level, and once the player reaches the end of that level, his character continues on to the next level.

In more modern games, such as Bethesda Softworks' game *Elder Scrolls V: Skyrim*, levels are less noticeable and are virtually stitched together at the seams. Therefore, for instance, the gamer travels from a mountain peak in one level to a shrouded valley in the next without very much lag or noticeable difference to give away the fact that they are two separate levels.

You do not have to use another program to make game levels, because all of that can be done within the UDK Editor. In addition, unlike some other game engines, you do not have to use command line scripts or third-party programs to import content directly into your levels, because UDK Editor can do everything for you, without having to leave the Editor. This is more efficient and time-conservative.

Here are some examples of things you might add in UDK Editor as a level designer:

- 3D models, meshes, and particle effects
- Static ambient sound effects
- Reactive environment effects and enemy characters via Kismet
- Cinematic effects via Matinee

You installed UDK in the last chapter. Now, it is time to open the UDK Editor, if you have not done so already. When first opening UDK Editor, your first sight should include two preliminary windows overlapping the Editor itself (see Figure 4.1). The first of these windows is the welcome message, which has links to UDK documentation and videos to get you started. These links provide alternative methods for learning and becoming familiar with the UDK Editor and its versatile tools. The second window is the Content Browser.

Figure 4.1
Opening UDK Editor.
Source: Epic Games.

Content Browser

Importing your game content (models, graphics, sounds, and more) is done via the Content Browser, which is included in the UDK Editor. Content creation usually takes place outside UDK Editor. For instance, some content creators will make 3D models (aka meshes) in a separate 3D program, such as 3ds Max or Maya, both of which are high-end Autodesk programs. In UDK, you refer to most 3D objects as meshes.

Other content creators make 2D graphics, which are useful for texturing, bitmaps, and sprites, in photo editors like Adobe Photoshop or Corel Draw. In UDK, you refer to most 2D graphics as textures. Then you have the sound engineers, busy composing music, background noise, and sound effects, in their sound editor of choice.

All this content is what developers consider part of "the pipeline" of material, and that pipeline funnels into UDK Editor through one source: the Content Browser. The Content Browser is shown in Figure 4.2.

Figure 4.2
The Content Browser.
Source: Epic Games.

You can import a wide array of file formats directly into the UDK Editor via the Content Browser. This provides almost a universal importing ability unprecedented compared to other game engines. Your options improve when using the Content Browser, because you are not stuck conforming to one file extension type.

The Content Browser demonstrates all the content you have imported that is ready to use in your game. You can zoom in to look at the thumbnails close up. You can also select or deselect filters (in the top frame) to see only specific file types. For instance, if you choose Skeletal Meshes and Static Meshes, you will see only the 3D models that have been imported.

Another great thing is you can view and play back your files directly in the Content Browser without having to leave the UDK Editor to do so. This helps you see how your content will appear or sound in the game before placing it in the level. You can actually change a couple of things about a file as well. Say, for instance, you have imported a couple of textures, and you need to change their saturation or vibrancy. You can do that within the Content Browser, by double-clicking on a thumbnail image, which saves you from having to import, make edits outside UDK, reimport, and so on. You can simply tweak the files within the Content Browser and move on to the next task effortlessly.

Figure 4.3 shows you how easy it is to edit a texture's saturation or how vibrant and expressive each color appears.

Figure 4.3
Editing a texture's properties.
Source: Epic Games.

You can play back sounds by simply double-clicking them. You can also play back animation sets of a single 3D character in the UDK Editor, so you can see exactly what your animations will look like within the level before dropping the character into that level.

This saves you a lot of iteration time, of having to build, test, and build again, and so on. If something does not look or sound just right, you do not have to leave the UDK Editor to make the appropriate changes. You can make your changes and forge on.

Material Editor

Shaders are parametric templates that can cover 3D objects within a game to make the objects appear shiny, bumpy, rough, slick, and so on. Essentially, shaders make 3D objects appear more realistic.

In UDK, you might hear shaders referred to as materials. This is because a shader is supposed to mimic a real-life material, to create the composition of a real-life object in virtual 3D. Normally, programmers or technical artists would be the ones to create materials, but with UDK, you can make your own materials within the Material Editor, a WYSIWYG (what-you-see-is-what-you-get) module within the UDK Editor.

As you can see from Figure 4.4, the Material Editor, which appears when you double-click on a thumbnail image of a material within the Content Browser, is a visual representation of what goes into making a material. To the left is a preview, and central to the Material Editor is a node tree, with each node applying a step in the making of that material.

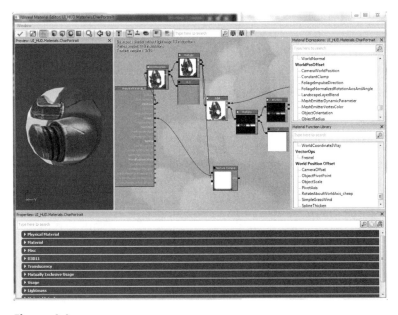

Figure 4.4
The Material Editor.
Source: Epic Games.

You can also see a preview of what each node does by right-clicking on the node and selecting Preview Node on Mesh. This visual interface helps make complicated techniques simple. Effectively, you use this technique to debug the shader, so if something is not looking right, you can narrow down what is causing the problem.

You are not restricted on number of nodes or complexity of your material. For instance, the shader in Figure 4.4 is comprised of several nodes, but you can literally use hundreds of nodes to create increasingly complex shaders.

Another advantage to using the Material Editor within UDK is the ability to make instances to create multiple variations. An instance is a single item that you can duplicate repeatedly for use in multiple situations. If you edit the original, all instances of that original will automatically update. A practical example of this would be if you have two types of enemies, both goblins. One goblin team comes from a nasty swamp full of moss and vegetation, while the other comes from the rugged peaks and lava flows of the mountains. You use the same material to cover both types of goblins, but you use instances. Therefore, you tweak the swamp goblins' hue material property to appear green, and the mountain goblins' hue to appear grayish-brown. This requires less stress on the rendering engine while hitting your target.

You can also group instances to make it easier to organize them. If you have several instances used to tweak color, you might organize them so a level designer working behind you can tell, "Oh, this is the instanced parameter group that helps me change color." You do this most often by selecting a descriptive name for the instances.

Lighting

Think of lights based on tangible objects that provide light sources. You can add lights into your game world to provide both illumination and shadow, including point lights, area lights, directional lights, spotlights, and sky lights.

- **Point light:** You can use a point light, which is a light object placed somewhere in space that emits light in all sorts of directions around it, like a lamp bulb.

- **Area light:** You can model a plane or square and tell the Editor this plane or square emits a glow or light on its own.

- **Directional light:** You can use this type of light, which shines in one single direction like a ray following an arrow. This is useful for sunrays falling through tree canopy.

- **Spotlight:** Similar to a directional light, a spotlight shoots its rays in one direction, but it has a cone with the wide part facing down.

■ **Sky light:** This type of light brightens lighting everywhere within your level, much like an ambient glow. This is useful for adding brilliance or subtly changing the overall color of the level.

Not only do lights add illumination, they also add shadow. You cannot add shadow independent of lights. Wherever you place a light, it will cast shadows (see Figure 4.5). UDK supports both static and dynamic shadows.

Figure 4.5
This brick wall has a light source behind it that casts a shadow down front.
Source: Epic Games.

Most of the time, when you refer to static shadows, you are referring to static lights. When you "cook" the level, the engine does light mass calculation, performing all the radiosity and global illumination, and bakes that down into a light map. Static (aka "baked") shadowing is fast when rendering the game.

Simultaneously, UDK supports dynamic shadows. This refers to mobile objects within the game or scripted events that spawn moving light, and that moving light casts shadows that also travel. For instance, say you give the player's character a torch to carry through a relatively dim dungeon. The torch will flicker and change with the character's motions, and the light given off by the torch will cast moving shadows. These shadows will also affect the static shadows "baked" into the dungeon.

Dynamic shadows can cause lag or even screen freezes when rendering games, as it drags on computer memory during rendering. This lag is something to bear in mind, as both the desktop and iPad platforms have only a limited amount of video memory. Especially when making iPad games, you would not want to use dynamic shadows. In iPad development, the more baked shadows, the better.

Light functions are mathematical formulas of how lights should render and how they should function. You use light functions to perform more complex lighting effects such as textured or flickering lights. A practical example of this would be a flashlight that dims as the battery gets low and reflects dust particles in the cone of light.

Kismet

You use Kismet to add gameplay logic in UDK. Kismet is a visual scripting language that you utilize to create simple or complex in-game logic. Like the Material Editor, Kismet is a WYSIWYG (what-you-see-is-what-you-get) module system.

To see an example, you can go to File > Open and browse to Maps/Examples to find ExampleMap.udk and open it. Once there, click the green K icon button in the shelf menu at the top of your UDK Editor (see Figure 4.6). If you hover over the icon buttons in this shelf, the tooltips will appear to let you know what to call each button. The green K icon is "Open UnrealKismet."

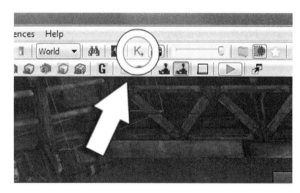

Figure 4.6
The Kismet button.
Source: Epic Games.

Clicking and holding the right mouse button turns your cursor into a grabber hand tool, which you can use to drag the node tree view to see more of the scripting involved here, as shown in Figure 4.7.

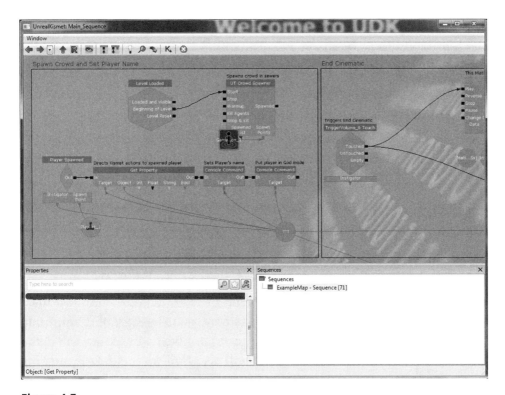

Figure 4.7
Kismet.
Source: Epic Games.

The topmost script's intention, as you can read via the title, is to spawn crowds and set the player character name. You can see there are triggers, like the Level Loaded trigger, which helps to spawn the crowd. You can add comments and perform all sorts of events based on this trigger. Other Kismet script areas in ExampleMap.udk control elevators, explosions, level transitions, end-game cinematic playback, and more.

The game *Gears of War* was originally prototyped in this fashion in Kismet. The great thing about Kismet is you do not have to be a programmer to link these nodes up and figure out how to make complex events happen. You can be a level designer or content creator and go into Kismet and roadmap how you want your game to work. Your roadmap may involve how the player interacts with the game world, how the world reacts to the player, transporting actors across the world, spawning new actors, turning Matinee events on/off, and various other activities. This allows for quick prototyping and fast iteration in game design. This does not replace programmers, because the programmers can still review how the designers used Kismet to write custom game logic as needed.

Epic built Kismet on top of Unrealscript, the underlying scripting language UDK uses. This makes programming much easier, because the programmer can edit the Unrealscript and the game designer can use Kismet to set up in-game triggers to operate the programming logic. Unrealscript provides a safe environment for game programming, because it is both flexible and forgiving.

Landscape

iPad game development does not offer the capability to use terrains in their games. In fact, it is restricted in mobile emulation for that very reason. Why? Because terrains are video memory hogs when it comes to real-time rendering, and as I said before, mobile platforms cannot sustain memory hogs.

Therefore, you will probably not do a whole lot of terrain generation. Nevertheless, I will briefly cover the topic should you ever develop games on another platform.

Landscape is UDK's advanced terrain toolset. You can use Landscape to mimic a massive world. One of its premier features is that it has continuous geographic mip-map level-of-detail (LOD). What this means is that the program itself will reduce the detail of terrain objects farther away from the viewer. It will also buff up the details, making the terrain objects appear more realistic, the closer you get to them. The algorithm is automatic. This makes rendering smoother and requires less memory.

Landscape also uses a high-resolution LOD-independent lighting, which is remarkable when you think about it. To reduce the detail of terrain objects farther away from the player, Landscape removes more and more of the visible planes of those objects. So where, up close, an object might be made up of 350 polygons, off in the distance it might only have 25. Typically, the light reflecting off the lesser polygons will be more obvious and cause strange shadows to pass the terrain, but with LOD-independent lighting, Landscape makes the lighting blend perfectly between the high- and low-detailed objects for better realism.

UDK uses NVIDIA's PhysX for all its collision detection, and so Landscape uses PhysX. Therefore, when vehicles roll over the terrain, PhysX uses its special collision detection algorithms to handle the way the tires bounce and move over the layout of the terrain for you, so you do not have to spend hours programming every detail yourself.

Cascade Editor

You use the Cascade Editor, built into the UDK Editor as another module, to create particle effects for your game. Particle effects are clumps of small particles used to simulate such things as fire, smoke, dust, magic fairy dust, and so on. Cascade Editor lets you craft sprite-based emitters, mesh-based emitters, and beams, which could represent lightning bolts, for example.

You can modify particle effects via Unrealscript. This allows you to define how particles should react to other in-game objects. One case includes the particles coming out of a hand cannon a player character is using. Perhaps when the player is using one type of ammunition, you want empty brass shells to spit out of the hand cannon. If the player is using another type of ammunition, you want broken thorns to pop out the side of the hand cannon. You can do both with a single particle effect and control the parameters via Unrealscript. This makes it nice for you as the developer, because you do not have to create numerous particle effects. You make one and you are done.

Particle effects can also detect for collisions, and based on what you tell the particle effects to do on collision, you can destroy them, transport them, or do something else with them. You can combine PhysX with particle effects for interesting effects.

For instance, this might be useful for smoke particles. As the smoke rises up from a fire in the center of a room and hits the ceiling, you might want the particles to roll across the ceiling to find an opening like a skylight, or you might want the particles to billow and build up, filling the room until it is thick with smoke. Another case might involve a dripping pipe in a basement. You might want the drips to stop when they hit the floor but then form a puddle, and as the puddle builds and spreads, the drips might cause a more noticeable splash back. Yet another case might involve snowfall. You set a particle emitter to emit snowflakes, which sprinkle all about the world, but as the snowflakes fall on rigid objects, they pile up, producing several inches of snow.

To see a direct example, if you are still within the ExampleMap.udk, open the Content Browser and use the filters to look for only Particle Systems. Double-clicking a thumbnail image will open the Cascade Editor. In Figure 4.8, I have opened P_Deployables_ EMP_Mine_VehicleDisabled within the Cascade Editor. You have an emitter that spawns these lightning-like meshes all over the place.

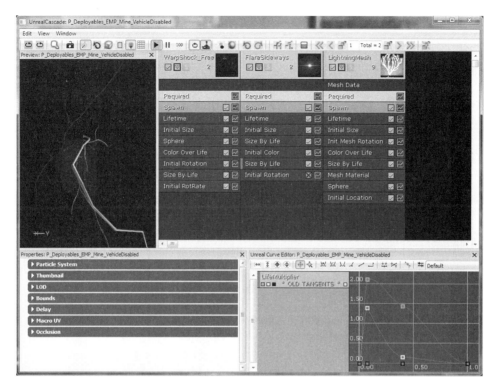

Figure 4.8
Cascade Editor.
Source: Epic Games.

The Cascade Editor is a WYSIWYG module, much like the others, so you will see what you get as you tweak the parameters of a particle system. To the right of the preview window you'll see the functions, which control the size, color, rotation, and more of the meshes emitted. You can right-click to bring up a context menu (seen in Figure 4.9) to add new functions to adjust how the system should be behaving. As you adjust things, the Cascade Editor will refresh what you see on the left.

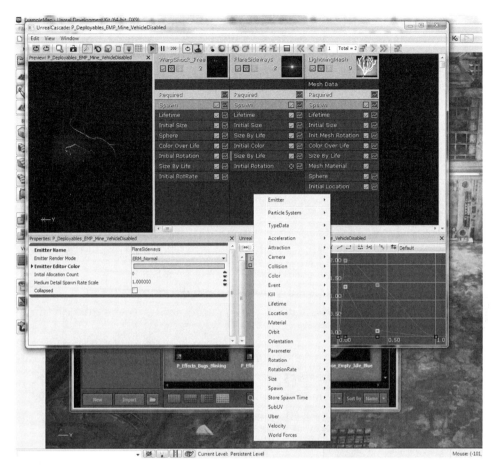

Figure 4.9
Adding new emitter functions.
Source: Epic Games.

Do you see the red X icon beside Initial Rotation? That icon means the parameter is currently disabled. You can enable/disable a parameter by clicking the icon next to it.

PhysX

PhysX is the physics engine integrated into UDK. Also integrated into UDK is APEX, built on top of PhysX. This type of physics control provides you with simulations of cloth, constraints (joints or pulley systems between various objects), rigid body collisions, soft body collisions (think ragdoll physics), vehicle movements, and more. You do not have to program or implement any of this yourself. PhysX does this for you.

If you have never had to program physics before, you might not know that it is very time-consuming. For instance, creating a rigid stone sphere or boulder that rolls when the player character presses on it could take weeks to get just right. This type of collision detection and physical reaction is built in to PhysX for you and simply requires being dropped into your game, saving you time and work.

Need to push the physics simulation even further, or have a custom requirement just not met by the predesigned PhysX? You can use Unrealscript to modify PhysX, designing your own personal simulations. For example, you might want to program a trigger event that creates or destroys constraints, or make a solid object turn into a soft wavy object, like cloth.

Sound Cue Editor

Although sound is an aspect of animation and games often overlooked by viewers, it is still very significant. Without sound, the visuals seen on screen just would not be as complete. Try playing *Call of Duty* or your favorite video game with the sound on mute and see how well the game plays then. Sound is actually one of the most immersive parts of video games, yet developers often push game audio to the end or forget it entirely.

Sound is useful for simulating real-world elements difficult to depict in 3D. One example is wind. If your player character steps out of a cavern onto a mountain peak, having the sound of wind blowing hard at that place in the level helps the player believe it really is windy there, even when 3D has no real wind. He will actually assume there is some invisible force blowing his character around.

That is how strong the sense of immersion is when it comes to sound. Adding some visual cues as well can help, but essentially the sound effects convince the players they are in that space you have designed. Layering the sound effects is common, too. Think about a farmyard scene. To make it realistic, you may want to add the sounds of chickens squawking, cows mooing, horses whinnying, wood creaking, wind blowing through tall grass, a metal wind vane squeaking, kids giggling, birds chirping, tree boughs swaying, and much more. That may seem like too many noises, but with the right pacing and balance, you will have a perfect balance and not a raucous cacophony.

You can also use the aural environment to make a gamer think your level is bigger than it really is. When the player is exploring the middle school in the game *Silent Hill*, strange sneaker squeaks, wood scratching, chair scraping, and other school sounds playing just off camera, as if coming from distant classrooms, builds suspense while making the player believe there is more of a world to explore.

You can import raw sound waves into the Content Browser. UDK has sound cues, which are edited in the Sound Cue Editor, a visual node-based sound system that controls when and how sound is played back. In the Content Browser, use the filters to limit the file types shown to Sound Cues. I have chosen the sound cue called A_Weapon_BioRifle_FireImpactExplode_Cue. Double-clicking it will not open the editor. Instead, double-clicking will simply play the sound once. This sound cue resembles a person smashing a rotten watermelon with a hammer. To open it within the Sound Cue Editor, right-click and select Edit Using Sound Cue Editor.

Here, in the Sound Cue Editor (see Figure 4.10), you can adjust an Attenuation node, so if the player character is far away, the engine plays the sound back at a lower volume. You can fine-tune parameters to determine if the sound has a linear falloff or algorithmic falloff. The Modulator node lets you raise or drop the pitch. Furthermore, the Random node lets you play different sound cues at random times, so if the player character is shooting and hits a rock wall, you might want to play various ricochet pings instead of hit sounds. You do not have to program a script to play random variation into your sound cues, because you can do it with the Random node.

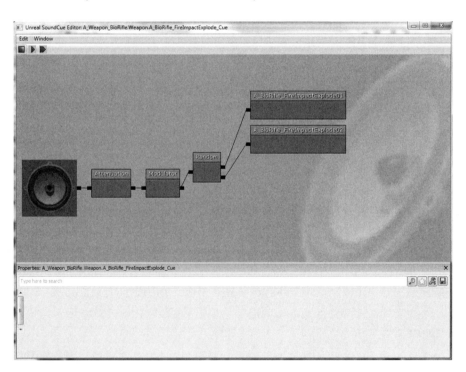

Figure 4.10
Sound Cue Editor.
Source: Epic Games.

You can attenuate, loop, delay playback, modulate the noise, and so forth with sound cue nodes. As you tweak the parameters of each node, you can play back your sound effect by clicking the play button at the top of the editor. You can also right-click in the node tree window to add further functions. Several options are available.

For example, if you want a cannon effect, you might want to use the Distance Cross-Fade option. It sounds like a metal shell scraping as it is being launched from the cannon if the player character is nearby. If the player character is way off in the distance, it will sound like a soft thud.

Sound cues can be grouped into sound classes, which can be independently controlled. For instance, you might group all your weapon sound cues into a sound class, all your music into a sound class, and so on. The reason you would do this is something like the flash-bang grenade flash in a military shooter game. If the player witnesses a flash-bang, you expect all the sounds to dim, almost to mute temporarily, while a sharp-pitched whistle plays for a few seconds. You do this by editing sound classes.

Multiplayer Gaming

Epic Games built client-server replication right into UDK, which makes making multiplayer games a cinch. This replication synchronizes game simulation between clients and servers. This is set up in Unrealscript, so programmers can customize it. UDK has Steam and GameCenter integrated right in, making a multiplayer game prepared in UDK easy to add to those game distribution centers.

TCPLink can also be used in Unrealscript to connect to any TCP server, or you can actually make UDK into a true TCP server. TCP (Transmission Control Protocol) provides reliable, ordered, error-checked delivery of data streamed between programs running on computers connected to a local area network, intranet, or the public Internet. It is not necessary to understand TCP servers or server setup to make iPad games, unless you want to make multiplayer online games.

Games Made with UDK

So what kind of games can you make in UDK? Many people tend to pigeonhole UDK and say that you can only use UDK to build first- or third-person shooter games. This is certainly how UDK is set up by default, but it could not be further from the truth. Some of the different games that users have made with UDK include:

- Side scrolling platformers (Figure 4.11)
- Hack-and-slash action RPGs (Figure 4.12)
- Puzzle games (Figure 4.13)
- Mech games (Figure 4.14)
- Space combat games (Figure 4.15)
- Wild West shooter games (Figure 4.16)

Figure 4.11
Bounty Arms.
Source: Open Reset®.

Figure 4.12
Chivalry: Medieval Warfare.
Source: Torn Banner Studios®.

Figure 4.13
Q.U.B.E.
Source: Toxic Games®.

Figure 4.14
Hawken.
Source: Adhesive Games®.

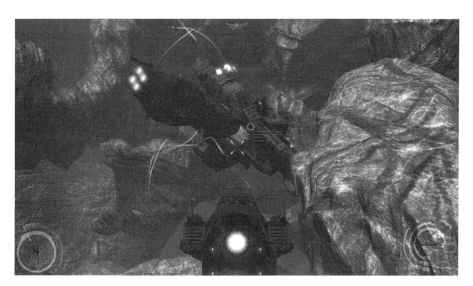

Figure 4.15
AFF: Planetstorm.
Source: treeform®.

Figure 4.16
Warm Gun.
Source: Emotional Robots® Inc.

Resources Available to UDK Users

Epic Games has a forums section on their website: http://forums.epicgames.com/. Here you will find a sub-forum dedicated to UDK. There are several game developer veterans on the forums that do their best to help users. Many of these veterans work within a studio or have been in the industry a while. They use the forums to answer questions and help beginners.

You can also use Unreal Developer's Network (UDN), which is dedicated to documentation on UDK: http://udn.epicgames.com/. Epic constantly updates UDN with new tutorials and reference materials each month. You might notice UDK itself is updated to a new version practically once a month. This requires consistent updates to documentation. There is always something innovative, some new way to do things. UDN's priority is to keep users apprised of these changes.

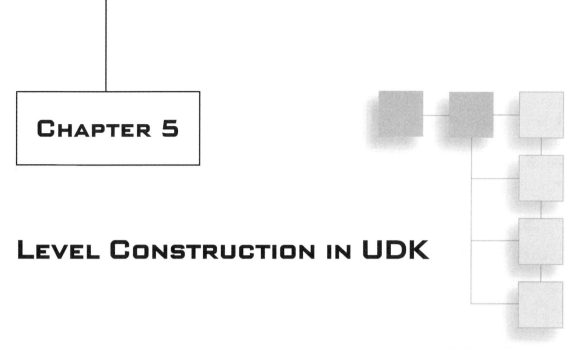

CHAPTER 5

LEVEL CONSTRUCTION IN UDK

If you used to enjoy playing with LEGOs or construction kits as a kid, or if you lost yourself in imaginary worlds of castles and kingdoms, you will find designing game worlds to be an exciting pastime that can make you money.

You are probably eager to begin working in Unreal Development Kit (UDK) to build your iPad game. The UDK Editor, which you learned about in the last chapter, is the main development tool for UDK. It is used to create levels, including using the Content Browser, to import, organize, and set up the content for your game.

Before you begin making iPad games or learning the mobile emulator UDK ships with, you need to know about UDK Editor and, more specifically, how you use it to construct your levels. This chapter will walk you through the interface.

Go ahead and start up the UDK Editor, if you have not done so already, and be prepared to make a virtual world happen.

WHAT IS LEVEL DESIGN?

Inside each game world there are several scenes, or chapters, we call levels. Each level has its own distinctive region with its own set of objectives that the player must reach before she can travel to the next level. Kind of like a haunted house amusement park, levels are like each of the spooky rooms visitors go into to get scared.

Level design is formally defined as the creation of environments, scenes, scenarios, or missions in an electronic game world. Level designers create the environments that you move through and enjoy when playing video games. While the volume, complexity, and style of game levels may change between each game, designers use the same tried-and-true methods, architectural plans, and placement of obstacles to keep players consistently entertained and challenged.

Level Components

A large part of the game design document you draw up for your game will be composed of area maps and notes, and those are translated into game levels. Each level, whether it's a building interior or outdoor terrain, sets the stage for the achievement of gameplay.

Almost every single level is composed of the following:

■ Basic geometry or architecture (you know… the stuff player characters walk or jump on).

■ Details such as textures or sprite decals. Sprite decals are 2D images that can be pasted on top of 3D objects just like putting decals on a race car.

■ Stage props such as furniture, trees, rocks, and so on.

■ Environmental lighting and effects, such as sun, wind, rain, and so forth.

■ Interactive objects, such as characters, switches, pick-up items, power-ups, enemies, allies, and/or obstacles.

Levels add variety and spice to a set of gameplay mechanics. If you have a 3D shooter in which the player is an espionage agent sneaking around and shooting bad guys with tranquilizers, the places where he sneaks around and tranquilizes enemies should be different enough from one another to add entertainment, diversity, and challenge to the game.

A level designer has to make a level work in terms of fooling the player into believing that this image on the computer screen could be a real place and make it work as a stomping ground for the actions the player will take in it.

Think of every game level you create as a movie set. Some of it will only have facades, or fake fronts. Some doors may lead to nowhere. Some elements may be incomplete. All that they have to do is operate on a psychological level to make the player think that she is somewhere you want her to think she is.

A game level should do the following:

■ Set the pace of game flow, including where resources and obstacles are laid.

■ Fence the player in so she doesn't wander outside the main mission area.

■ Act as a backdrop to the action that will take place.

- May be destructible or react in interesting ways to the player's actions.
- Tease the player with glimpses of a much wider world "out there."

Level designers must also plant landmarks in these environments. Landmarks are easily recognized "set pieces" that have unique enough features to keep players from wandering lost around the game world or from going around in circles. Landmarks can be anything, as long as they stand out and get noticed.

Levels often reflect the artistic choice for the game, so if you have a cartoony style, it would work to have cartoony game worlds; and if you are making a grungy spy thriller, you will more than likely have environments based on real places that are given a darker look.

Level Designer Do's and Don'ts

The following are the best suggestions for you to keep in mind before developing a game world:

- Design your levels outside the UDK Editor first. Even if you jot down a quick blueprint on a scrap piece of paper, put your design to work before putting any work to your design. This helps you avoid wasted time and gives you purpose.
- Don't keep fiddling with a level. Build it and move on. You can always edit later.
- Save and save often. Computers crash, power can go out, and little brothers and sisters can bang the keyboards. While the game engine itself is very stable, any number of accidents can come up, losing hours of hard work if you're not careful. Be sure to save your game files as often as you can.
- Be frugal with what you build first. Design your sky, sun, and terrain before adding rivers, roads, and foliage, because if you have to adjust any of the big things, it will wreck the smaller ones and make more work for you in the end.
- Don't design a level so large that it becomes confusing and the player doesn't know where you want her to go next. Keep your levels tight.
- Don't place all your monsters, power-ups, and weapons in one single area. Spread them out and pace the game flow properly.
- Don't forget to give your player enough power-ups to survive but not so many that they make the game too easy.
- Don't make a game level so difficult it forms a "choke point" that frustrates the player. It can be easy to stump the player with puzzles, so be lenient.

- Like the theory behind *feng shui*, do always keep the action in a game level moving.

- Play your level frequently to see how your game will look from the player's perspective and to see what tweaks may be needed.

- Do try to accommodate all types of players, young and old, experienced and not so experienced.

- Always think of your game environment as an amusement park ride or a tourist vacation trap: you do want to make it interesting, fun, and an escape away from the ordinary.

On that last point, think of yourself as an amusement tycoon. You must design for the player a place to come to, play, and leave with a sense of a unique experience. The more exciting the game world you design, the less likely players are to get bored playing your game. The more games you design, the more you will discover this to be true.

No gamer has ever quit a game wishing it had been made less fun. As one reviewer said of *Mario 64* after its release, "It was simply a lot of fun just running around, not really doing anything!"

"You want your game to be convincingly real to truly inspire mood and drama—and yet you have to be inventive, without straining credulity. It's a matter of combining and synthesizing, keeping the aspirations in your head, but looking for new ways to fit it all together."

—Marc Taro Holmes, Obsidian Entertainment

CSG Brushes

BSP stands for binary space partition, but (although you may hear developers use the term a lot) it does not really mean much. BSP is more or less a way to sort out virtual surfaces in a fast way. What you will actually be using is a custom set of primitives that perform mathematical algorithms to produce surfaces. This is called constructive solid geometry (CSG).

You can use CSG for blocking out whole levels and for simple filler geometry. What I mean by this is you would not want to reconstruct the entire Taj Mahal using just CSG, but you could build the walls, floor, ceiling, and larger fixtures with CSG and then import more detailed meshes for furniture, lamps, wires, wall trim, and so on.

In general, CSG is slower to render than static meshes. You do not need every technical detail, but suffice it to say that this is the reason developers do not use CSG for everything they build for games. It is quick to build a level in CSG, but it takes longer than meshes to render, so more games these days actually use static meshes (3D models built in another program and imported into UDK) more for intricate decorations and CSG is delegated to floors and walls. In a later chapter, you will see how to use static meshes, but for now just focus on CSG.

CSG makes it a cinch to add or subtract solid shapes from your game world. You can manipulate cubes, spheres, cones, and more, and like clay, you can manipulate them into many other shapes. The process by which you would use CSG follows Occam's razor or, perhaps more succinctly, Kelly Johnson's KISS principle: "Keep it simple, stupid." Begin with elementary shapes and build off them slowly, making them more complex as you go.

Starting with the Builder Brush

When you first bring up the UDK Editor and minimize or close the welcome message and Content Browser, you will see a default interface. The red framed cube shape currently visible (as shown in Figure 5.1) is the builder brush. The builder brush gives you an approximate idea of what you will be adding or subtracting from the game world.

Figure 5.1
The builder brush.
Source: Epic Games.

Before going any further, you need to turn on mobile emulation. You only need to do this once. After that, the UDK Editor will remember you have mobile emulation executed each time you open it. This task helps you to preview your game output as it would look and behave on a mobile device (in this case, an iOS device). To turn mobile emulation on, simply click the Emulate Mobile Features button in the top-right shelf of the UDK Editor. It looks like a brown iPhone screen. Once clicked, mobile emulation will begin. Be patient and wait until it completes; this can take some time. After it has completed, the Emulate Mobile Features button should appear depressed, revealing that mobile emulation is currently on. If you ever need to turn it off, click the button again.

CSG Functions

New UDK artists often transform and position the builder brush into place and think they're done. Then they build something else and wonder what happened, where their "perfect" shape went. This is because they forgot to add or subtract the builder brush from the level. To do that, click on one of the CSG buttons in the toolbar (seen in Figure 5.2).

Figure 5.2
The CSG tools.
Source: Epic Games.

The following are the CSG tool functions:

- **CSG Add**: This will add whatever the builder brush is doing into the level as a solid chunk.

- **CSG Subtract**: This will erase, carve away, or remove the builder brush's shape from the level, affecting any geometry it touches.

- **CSG Intersect**: If you overlap your builder brush with existing geometry, it will form a new builder brush from the space where the two intersect.

- **CSG Deintersect**: Does the exact opposite of CSG Intersect. If you place the builder brush over the top of existing geometry and summon this function, it will form a new builder brush only where the two do not intersect.

Click the CSG Add button now. Notice purple and white checkerboard surfaces fill in your builder brush. Compare your screen to Figure 5.3. This is now a separate CSG shape within your level, autonomous from your original builder brush.

Figure 5.3
CSG Add.
Source: Epic Games.

Move your builder brush around. Click on one of its red edges, and watch something dramatic happen: Red squares appear at each of the corners of the brush, and a gizmo appears at its center origin. The gizmo will have handles for x, y, and z directional axes. With your cursor, grab one of the direction handles and pull in that direction. Move your builder brush up, down, and side-to-side. Note how the geometry brush you added to the level stays put, like in Figure 5.4.

Figure 5.4
Move the builder brush.
Source: Epic Games.

Switching Viewports and Modes

Click the maximize/minimize button in the top-right corner of your perspective viewport. This is the button indicated in Figure 5.5.

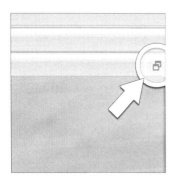

Figure 5.5
The maximize/minimize button.
Source: Epic Games.

This switches you from a typical perspective view to a four-panel view. See Figure 5.6. They are all viewports of the same scene with the same objects present. However, each one is a view from a different angle or direction, sort of like setting up a video camera in front, behind, and to the side of your scene. With these multiple views, you can see what is going on in more detail from alternate angles. The alternate angles help you so you do not miss something you cannot see from just one angle.

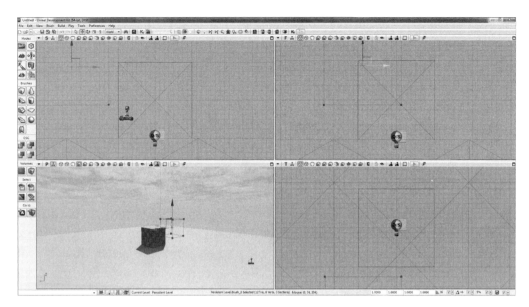

Figure 5.6

The four-panel layout.

Source: Epic Games.

The perspective is the only viewport currently in Lit view mode. This means it has lighting and surface shading. The other viewports (called "orthographic" because they each only demonstrate two directional axes, such as x and y or y and z) are in Wireframe view mode. In Wireframe view mode, you can see the skeletal outline of shapes but not those shapes' surface textures or how they look under lights.

Brush view mode subtracts the skeletal outlines and only shows the brush outlines.

Unlit view mode shows the surface shading, minus any dramatic lighting. Unlit is good to use if you have a dark or moody level you are editing and want to see all the details of your geometry as you work.

You can swap view modes by clicking on any of their shelf menu icon buttons (see Figure 5.7).

Figure 5.7

The view modes buttons.

Source: Epic Games.

I added a second piece of geometry above and touching the first, so they look like stairs.

Sometimes, in order to position shapes correctly, you have to use the other viewports, because it is deceptively difficult to do so in the perspective viewport. To move your viewport camera, you click and drag somewhere inside the chosen viewport and your camera "eye" will pan left, right, up, or down, depending on the direction you drag your cursor. You can use the mouse wheel (if your mouse has one) to zoom in and out. Typically, you want to zoom out until you can see what you are doing and where your objects lie in the scene.

Use the maximize/minimize button to restore your perspective window, so you are only looking at it for now. Move your builder's brush somewhere in between some geometry you have added, so when you are ready to subtract the brush, it will "eat away" some of the existing geometry. When you are ready, you can click the CSG Subtract button. The brush shape is added, but it deletes existing surfaces rather than create new. See Figure 5.8.

Figure 5.8
CSG Subtract.
Source: Epic Games.

Handling Mistakes

The bottom cube looks funny because I have two brush shapes placed there: the original sand-colored shape the scene opened with, and the check-patterned shape added first. To delete the sand-colored shape, click on a face where you see it and press the Delete key to remove it from the scene. See Figure 5.9.

Figure 5.9
Delete the extra brush shape.
Source: Epic Games.

At any time, even after you have added a brush shape to your level, you can go back to it and tweak or even delete it. Most of the time, you will want to switch to Brush view mode, which will just show you the brush outlines, before editing an existing piece of geometry. Usually just selecting a face and pressing Delete will not do anything to the brush itself. You have to select the whole brush by clicking on its edge or its outline in Brush view mode before you can edit or remove it.

When editing a brush that has been a part of your level geometry, you may not see your edits right away. You may have to rebuild the geometry first. To rebuild the geometry, click the Build Geometry for Visible Levels button in the shelf menu. I cover this in more detail in the "Sequence of Order" section later in this chapter.

Also, if you make a mistake, you can always correct it automatically by clicking the Undo button in the shelf menu bar, shown in Figure 5.10. All the buttons you have been using have shortcut keys, too, which you can learn to make your iteration faster. The Undo function's shortcut key is Ctrl/Cmd + Z.

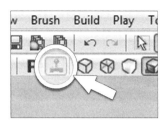

Figure 5.10
The Undo button.
Source: Epic Games.

Adding Brushes

This process is how level designers build rooms in levels. They block out the building and then subtract away the interior spaces using brushes. At that juncture, they add windows, doors, and shapes for the main fixtures.

Of course, you do not have to include rooms or make your levels appear realistic. You can use brushes to design several blocks just sort of floating in space, and have the player character jump from one to another to cross the level, if you like that kind of game.

More Complex CSG Brushes

Earlier, I said there are ways you can modify and create more complex brush shapes in your game world. Let's discuss them now.

Different Builder Brushes

First, UDK Editor offers more than a cube to use as a builder brush. As Figure 5.11 shows, you can use the following:

- Cube
- Cone
- Curved Staircase
- Cylinder
- Linear Staircase
- Sheet
- Spiral Staircase
- Tetrahedron (Sphere)
- Cards

Figure 5.11
The CSG brush shapes.
Source: Epic Games.

Editing Brush Parameters

Each one of these is a jump-off point, because you can edit the parameters or transform them after adding them to the level. To edit the parameters, simply right-click once on one of the buttons, say, for instance, the Linear Staircase. The options will pop-up with values you can set manually, such as length and width of step, number of steps, and more (see Figure 5.12). You can click Build to save your options or Cancel to close without saving. Close the dialog box by clicking the X button in the upper-right corner.

Figure 5.12
Parameters for the Linear Staircase brush.
Source: Epic Games.

Building a Round Wall

Next, build a cylinder using the following parameters: Z 512, Outer Radius 512, Inner Radius 450, Sides 8, Align to Side checked, and Hollow checked. Move it (preferably using the four viewports) to align to the floor. Make sure it is apart and beside what you have built so far. Click CSG Add when you are ready.

Compare your cylindrical wall formation to the one in Figure 5.13.

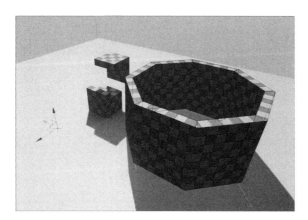

Figure 5.13
Use custom parameters of the cylinder brush to make a round wall.
Source: Epic Games.

Subtracting a Door from the Round Wall

To add a doorway to your cylindrical room, change to a cube builder brush. In the four viewports, be sure to move the brush to intersect one of the walls of the cylinder you just made. You want this new brush to touch the floor. You want the sides of the cube to stick inside and outside the cylinder walls. Imagine that it will be an arrow sticking through the target wall, with ends poking out either side. When you are confident in placement, click the CSG Intersect button. The builder brush will automatically shrink to match the thickness of the wall precisely (see Figure 5.14).

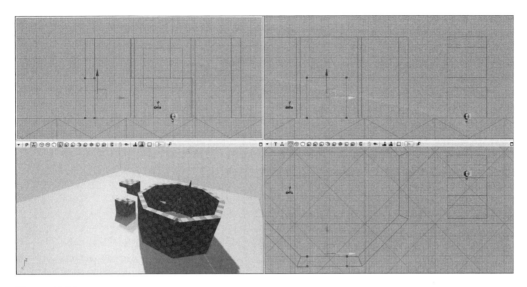

Figure 5.14
Use CSG Intersect to match your builder brush to the wall.
Source: Epic Games.

Click CSG Subtract and the builder brush will carve out a doorway from the wall, as in Figure 5.15.

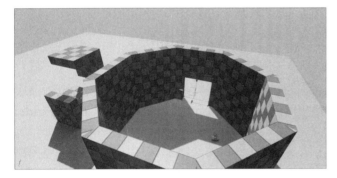

Figure 5.15
CSG Subtract will subtract away the wall, forming a doorway.
Source: Epic Games.

You would add doors, windows, shafts, and more throughout your level geometry using this process. It is a bit like puzzle pieces, really, so if you find yourself gifted at jigsaw puzzles, level design should come naturally to you.

Sequence of Order

The brushes represent sequential calculations during rendering, and you can even edit their sequence in the context menu. Just as in the history stored within programs like Adobe Photoshop, UDK stores every step you make in the development of a level. Add a cube becomes Step 1. Add another cube becomes Step 2. Subtracting a cube becomes Step 3. And so on.

Occasionally, users will get stuck wondering why their level design is not working the way they think it should, and sometimes it is because of the order of the steps they have gone through to get there.

Perhaps the easiest method for changing the sequence is to find the brush in the geometry you want to edit. Select it by clicking on its edge or wireframe (or by selecting its outline in Brush view mode). Right-click on the brush, and in the pop-up context options, select Order. There, you can move this brush's order.

Nothing will happen at first. You actually have to rebuild the geometry whenever you change the order in which you edited geometry. To rebuild the geometry, click the Build All button. The build and cook icon buttons in the shelf menu are shown in Figure 5.16. Typically, all you will need to click is the Build Geometry for Visible Levels button, unless lighting needs to be rebuilt, too. You may occasionally get an error message saying that paths need to be rebuilt. This is common but can be ignored. Usually, if you have not added any actor paths to the level, you can safely ignore this error message.

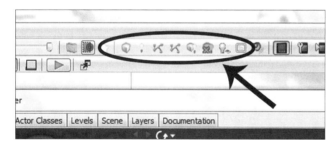

Figure 5.16
The build and cook shelf menu buttons.
Source: Epic Games.

Turning Lightmass Off

Epic built Swarm Agent into UDK to process lighting. An inherent problem with lighting can cause Swarm Agent to stop working, especially if you are using Lightmass, a volumetric lighting technique UDK offers. If you, too, get this error message a simple workaround is to go into the Build Lighting settings and deselect the Use Lightmass option. This turns Lightmass off in the current light building. Then build and see if the error message goes away.

Lightmass is an offline rendering method for calculating all global illumination for each game level. It does all the bounce and production-quality lighting for you, so you do not manually have to create any of that.

If Lightmass is becoming problematic, you can turn it off for your level permanently. To do so, go to the main menu and go to View > World Properties and expand Lightmass and deselect Use Global Illumination. You might also want to make sure your local machine Swarm Agent client is not being blocked by a firewall or anti-virus protection program.

Even if you do not get an error message, turning Lightmass off permanently may save you having to sit through rebuilding lighting for so long, because Lightmass' calculations take the longest when building (or "cooking") your level. You may get a message after building telling you that your level did not build with production-quality lighting, but you can ignore that message while you continue to work.

STATIC MESHES

Static meshes are 3D models imported into UDK from a content creation package such as 3ds Max, Maya, Lightwave 3D, Blender, or another 3D modeling and/or animation program. You import static meshes via the Content Browser.

Really, the first step in adding significant detail to your game level, static meshes provide polygon bulk to your scene. You can use them for all the grass and rocks in an outdoor scene or pillars and furniture in an indoor scene. Any decoration or fixture that goes into your game should be a static mesh.

Static meshes are technically very fast to render and memory conservative, because computer devices cache them once they are in video memory. So no matter how many times a static mesh appears, it is already in memory storage and does not have to be re-rendered.

So, say you have a rusty pipe as a static mesh. You might use that pipe 50 times in a single level, each with different scaling and positions, but the computer device only sees one rusty pipe and then places instances of it throughout the level. This speeds up the real-time rendering. Something else that speeds up real-time rendering when using static meshes is that static meshes generally use light maps to bake in pre-computed lighting created using Lightmass.

The reason you call static meshes "static" rather than "dynamic" is that static meshes do not animate. However, you can use materials to perform simple vertex-style animation on them. For example, you might have an iron shield with a material on it that glows and appears to grow and shrink, like a heart beating. The mesh itself is not animated, but the material can give the illusion that it is.

Adding Meshes

To add a static mesh to your level:

1. Open up the Content Browser from the UDK Editor.

2. Adjust the filter to show only Static Meshes.

3. Search for a static mesh you want to add to your level. UDK makes the Content Browser faster by not fully loading all the meshes completely. You might see a tiny icon in the lower left of the thumbnail images, meaning that mesh has not been fully loaded into memory. To load it, right-click on it once and it will finish loading.

Now, add the static mesh to your game level. First, click on the thumbnail image of the static mesh to select it. Return to the perspective viewport and right-click somewhere in your level and, from the pop-up options, select Add Actor; the very bottom choice should be to load your chosen static mesh (see Figure 5.17).

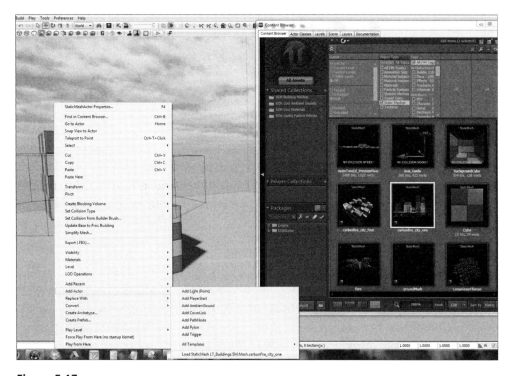

Figure 5.17
Select the static mesh in the Content Browser and then right-click to add that mesh to your level.
Source: Epic Games.

You can also just drag and drop static meshes from the Content Browser directly into your viewport, which adds it to the current scene. This makes content addition nice and easy.

Now, add some small static meshes to your level. As you can see from Figure 5.18, I added a couple barrels (specifically RemadePhysBarrel). To get the light and shading to show up, you have to rebuild lighting in your level.

Figure 5.18
Add some static meshes to your level.
Source: Epic Games.

Manipulating Objects

This applies not only to static meshes but also to brushes and other details you might add to your scenes. You can manipulate objects handily using manipulation modes. You can find the icon buttons for manipulation modes in the shelf menu, seen in Figure 5.19.

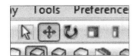

Figure 5.19
Manipulation mode icon buttons.
Source: Epic Games.

Their functions are as follows:

- **Selection Mode**: This allows you to select objects without affecting them.

- **Translation Mode**: This allows you to translate the values of a selected object by dragging the directional handles. In other words, you can move and reposition objects in Translation Mode.

- **Rotation Mode**: You can rotate a selected object around any of the directional axes.

- **Scaling Mode**: With this mode, you can resize a selected object in all directions at once, uniformly.

- **Non-uniform Scaling Mode**: This mode allows you to resize a selected object in each direction non-uniformly, if you drag one of the directional handles.

Practice with each manipulation mode. In Figure 5.20, you can see I scaled, rotated, and translated one of my barrels so it would lie on its side on the scene floor.

Figure 5.20
Practice with various manipulation modes.
Source: Epic Games.

TEXTURES AND DECALS

Textures are 2D images mapped over 3D models to provide more detail, surface texture, or color to the 3D model. Texture mapping was pioneered by Edwin Catmull in 1974.

The process of texture mapping is similar to putting patterned paper over a plain white box. Every point and edge in a 3D polygon is assigned a texture coordinate so that the texture and polygon line up correctly. You make and edit textures in 2D image editing programs, outside the 3D modeling program, and then import them into your project and lay them over your 3D models, dressing them up so they look more colorful and detailed.

You can use multiple textures even within the same 3D object. For instance, you might apply a gray texture to the head of a hammer while putting a red rubber-looking texture on the hammer's shaft.

Another way to increase details within your level, to make it appear more aesthetic or realistic, is through use of decals. Decals are 2D images or textures projected onto the surfaces of your game world. Decals are sort of like graffiti or cardboard cutouts that you can smack on walls or floors within a level to provide more detail.

In the Content Browser, up in the filters area, you might notice the current selection is Favorites. Click on the tab heading that says All Types, and then select Decal Materials from the filter list to see all available decals (see Figure 5.21).

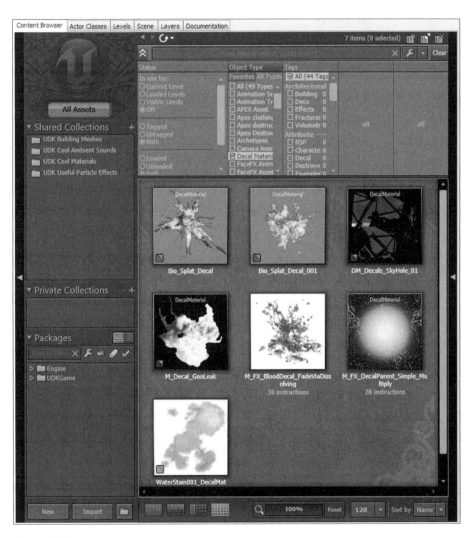

Figure 5.21

View the available decal materials in your Content Browser.

Source: Epic Games.

Just as with static meshes, you can select a decal and then right-click to load it into your scene, or you can simply drag and drop it into your scene. Decals work best if laid across the surfaces of CSG brushes or static meshes.

You can perform some interesting things with your environment using these decals, as you see from my radioactive goo splatters in Figure 5.22. I not only dragged in some decals, but I used the manipulation modes translate, rotate, and scale to create subtle changes. The more you use translate to "pull" a decal away from its surface, the more it will spray on other nearby surfaces.

Figure 5.22
Practice adding and manipulating decals in your level.
Source: Epic Games.

By now, your imagination has probably provided you with some ideas for what you could create with decals. You can use them to put burn marks on walls, add ivy creeping up the sides of pillars, create bullet holes and chips in concrete, or manhole covers in streets. Decals help you quickly and easily add many subtle details that will render quickly in game.

Decals do render fast, but if you are not careful, they can increase pixel overdraw, which will actually slow down real-time rendering. This is why it is important to mask decal materials. A decal is still a rectangular texture pattern, and often an opacity map tells the engine to hide the edges of the rectangle that you do not want seen.

A bunch of opacity maps in a centralized area can increase the pixel overdraw process and slow rendering. The trick, then, is to start with a masked material so you do not have to employ opacity mapping.

LIGHTING AND SHADOWS

As you read in the last chapter, you introduce lighting and shadows into your level via point lights, directional lights, spotlights, and sky lights. You should experiment with all of them to decide which one is right for you in each circumstance you come across.

All of these lights are dynamic lights when you first add them to your game world, but once you build lighting, UDK "cooks" the light and shading, making them static. Masked and translucent materials cast shadows correctly, which makes the game world more realistic.

In order to add a light to a level, simply right-click in your viewport and select Add Actor > Add Light (Point) from the pop-up options. This will add a point light wherever you have placed your cursor.

In the perspective viewport, make sure you are in Lit view mode. This will display the real-time dynamic effects of the light source you just added. Use the Translation manipulation mode to move the light up, just above or to the side of the rest of the objects in your scene, and watch how illumination falls on them and shadows unfurl from their crevices. Alternately, with other types of lights, you can rotate them to control their direction and the way they play rays on surfaces.

Types of Lights

So how do you add the other types of lights? One method for doing so is to right-click on your point light after you have added it to your scene and select Convert Light. There, you can convert this light into any one of the four options. If you remember from the last chapter, point lights are light sources that exist in some place in space and emit light in every single direction.

When would you want to convert a light from a point light? Say we want a light to cast illumination directly on one of our static meshes and the floor. You would not want to use a point light for this. Instead, you would convert it to a spotlight. In Figure 5.23, I converted a point light to a spotlight. I moved it above one of my barrel meshes. Then, I right-clicked and chose SpotLight Properties. A faster way, perhaps, to open the properties of any object is to double-click on that object. In the properties dialog box, I expanded Light > Light Component > Spot Light Component and set Outer Cone Angle to 20 (see Figure 5.23).

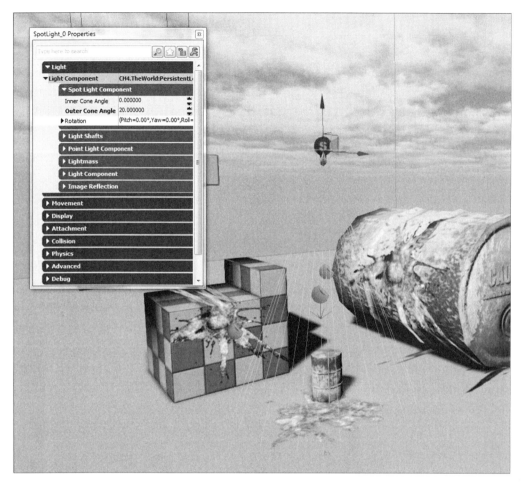

Figure 5.23
Converting a point light to a spotlight.
Source: Epic Games.

This would be useful if we also placed a static mesh of a city street lamppost in the level, and attached the spotlight directly under its lamp bulb. It would appear as if the light was spreading from a cone into a pool of light directly under the lamppost.

Directional lights run parallel rays in a single direction across the entire level, with no apparent source. They are good if you have light coming from a single direction far off. This is an easy and useful way to simulate rays from the sun or moon.

Sky lights provide general all-over illumination, like soft bounce light. If your level is too dark, or has too many shadows, you can gently lighten the whole level with a soft consistent sky light. Moreover, sky lights (as well as any other light you introduce) can be set to any color you like. Therefore, for example, you could set a green-colored sky light to tint the whole level green.

Light Color

You set color for lights by going into the light properties (double-click the light source to open properties) and expanding Light > Light Component > Light Component and adjusting the values under Light Color next to R, G, and B.

- R = red
- G = green
- B = blue

RGB is the base color composition for major computer devices. Each has a value between 0 and 255, with 0 being the absence of that color and 255 being the strongest hue and saturation.

You can adjust color by the numbers if you are good with RGB settings. Optionally, you can click the white bar next to Light Color, as it is a preview thumbnail of the chosen color of that light, and pick a different color from a Select a Color dialog box that pops up.

PARTICLE EFFECTS

Particle effects can add many dynamic little details to your level, similar to the static decals. Particle effects are often moving and animated and are thus good for things like flickering fire, smoke rising, dust clouds swirling, tree leaves falling to the ground, snowflakes falling and gathering on rooftops, and more. Particle effects can collide and interact with each other and with the level architecture if they have been set up correctly in Cascade. All of this helps the player immerse themselves in the environment, making believe the environment is real and reactive and has a life all its own.

Adding Particle Systems

Go to the Content Browser and filter by Particle Systems so only those will show for you in the browser (see Figure 5.24). Just as the other content found in the browser, you can select it and then right-click in a viewport and add that content to your level. However, you can also drag and drop items from the browser into your level, which is much simpler.

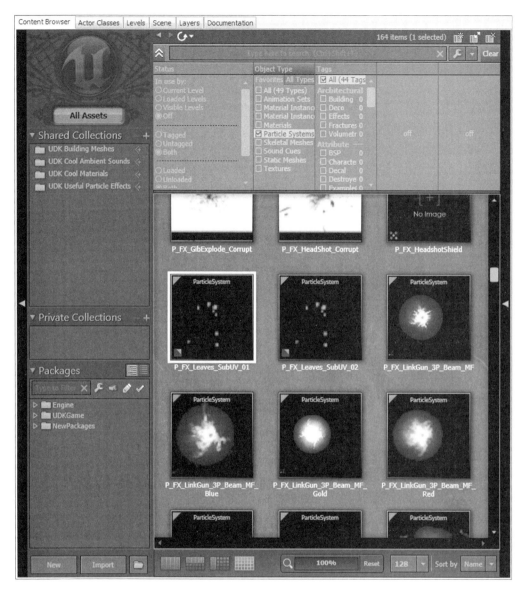

Figure 5.24
Particle systems within the Content Browser.
Source: Epic Games.

Find a particle system you like, such as falling leaves (P_FX_Leaves_SubUV_01), and drag it into your scene. Use the Translation mode to move the leaves' emitter, which appears like colored balls, high above the rest of your scene. This emitter, as shown in Figure 5.25, will be the source generator for your particle effects. You can also rotate the emitter to change the direction in which particles spawn, and scale the emitter to change how big of a spawn area you want.

Figure 5.25
Place the particle emitter within your scene.
Source: Epic Games.

Real-Time Display

You will not see the immediate animation brought on by the particle system. That is because UDK Editor does not automatically assume you want to see everything rendered in real time in your viewport. If you have an older computer, your computer may lag when rendering a bunch of particle systems at once, especially on top of any further animations or complex shaders.

Therefore, the UDK Editor has made allowance so you can toggle real-time display on (or off) by clicking the icon button in the shelf menu, shown in Figure 5.26.

Figure 5.26
Click this icon to turn real time on/off.
Source: Epic Games.

With real time on, you will see particles animate. In this case, leaves drift down. This is a great particle system to place in your level if you have tree meshes, to make it look like tree boughs are dropping leaves in an invisible breeze. With real time on, it gives you a nice indication of what your scene will look like in game.

Now add P_FX_Fire_SubUV_01 (one of the fire particle systems) to your level somewhere. I placed mine so it looks like it is inside one of my barrels. I also scaled it so it would only emit from within the barrel confines, not outside the barrel. In real time, the fire can liven up a dismal scene.

SOUND EFFECTS

Now you have built underlying geometry with CSG brushes, learned how you can add static meshes and decals to dress up your level, lit your level with various lights, and spruced your level up with animated particle effects. The last thing you will learn that will add further immersion to your game world is sound. This is vital, as audio ambience is integral to great video games.

Adding ambient sound effects that work with your visuals provides more feedback to your players as to what sort of environment they are exploring. Sounds tell them where they are and what they can expect to be around them, even what they cannot see.

Adding Ambient Sound Loops

We do this, once again, by going to the Content Browser. Change filters to All. Now, on the left side under Packages, expand UDKGame > Content > UT3 > Sounds.

From the list, click A_Ambient_Loops (see Figure 5.27). This will display all available sound loops for ambient effect.

Figure 5.27
Find A_Ambient_Loops in the Packages list.
Source: Epic Games.

The difference between looping and non-looping sound effects is that a sound loop can play continuously, always on loop, without any audible gap, while a non-looping sound is usually one-time only. Imagine a sound loop like the noise made by a babbling brook versus a non-looping sound like a shotgun blast.

You can play back any of these sounds by double-clicking their thumbnail images or by right-clicking on one and choosing Play Sound from the context options menu. To stop the noise, right-click it (again) and choose Stop Sound. Try it now. Practice with several different sound loops.

Before adding a sound to your level, it is important to be critical of its use in the scene. Currently, I have falling leaves and a burning barrel in my level and not a whole lot else. Therefore, the only sounds I need are those that would sound woodsy or like fire. I would not want to confuse the player by adding sounds that have no actual bearing on the scene they are witnessing.

Once you have found the sound or sounds you want to use, you can use the right-click or drag-and-drop method to add them into your level. The sound emitter that appears in the viewport can be moved to a location where you believe would be best for the sound source. Often, if related to a particle system, the sound emitter should go near the particle emitter, but not always. Use your best judgment.

I placed fire_medium01 (found in the Shared Collections' pane in UDK Cool Ambient Sounds) inside the barrel in the same place as my fire particle emitter, while my wind noise was placed a few units away from my falling leaves particle emitter. You can overlay ambient sounds like this to create environments that are more interesting.

Editing Sound Properties

You can also edit the sound volume. Double-click on the sound emitter to open the sound properties. In the properties dialog box, expand Ambient Sound Simple > Ambient Properties > Modulation (see Figure 5.28) and then tweak the values next to Volume Min and Volume Max from the default values.

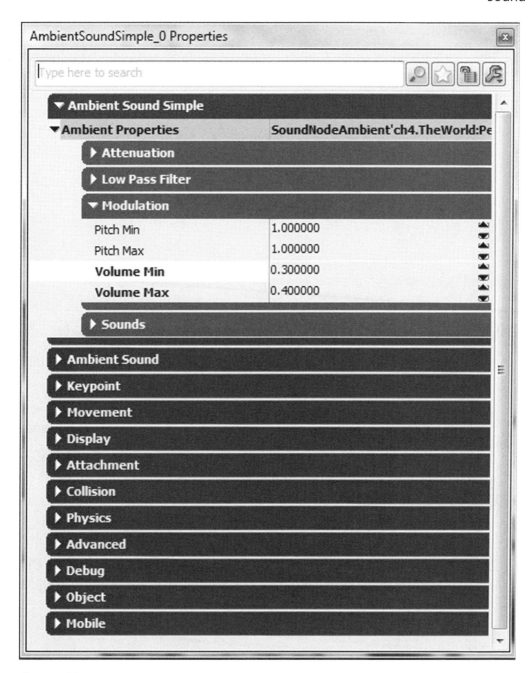

Figure 5.28
Edit the volume within sound properties.
Source: Epic Games.

Real-Time Audio

The UDK Editor assumes you do not always want to hear your sounds within your level as you are constructing it, just like with particle effects. However, you can turn sounds on in your level for testing purposes, which is great if you are editing sound volumes or falloff amounts. In the shelf menu, click the Toggle Real Time Audio icon button to turn real-time audio on/off (see Figure 5.29).

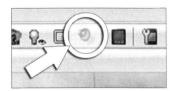

Figure 5.29
Click the Toggle Real Time Audio button to turn real-time audio on/off.
Source: Epic Games.

You can move around through the level while real-time audio is on to get an idea how the sound will carry throughout your level.

Sound Range

Every sound effect has a falloff amount, which means that the farther away from the sound emitter you are, the less you can hear of the sound, until eventually, you will not hear it at all. UDK Editor provides a spherical blue outline for this falloff amount so you, the developer, can visually see where the scope of each sound lies. This helps you plan your sound placement.

You can change the range of each sound the same way you would the volume, within the sound properties. Open the sound properties and expand Ambient Sound Simple > Ambient Properties > Attenuation. There you will find two values, Range Min and Range Max, which you tweak to edit sound range. Editing these automatically alters the blue falloff outlines.

Sound Pitch

Lastly, you can edit the sound pitch.

Know the Chipmunks? The Chipmunks voices are normal voices raised in pitch, so they sound squeakier than they really are. The same is true if you raise the pitch of any sound. If you lower the pitch of any sound, it will sound deeper.

In sound properties, expand Ambient Sound Simple > Ambient Properties > Modulation and you will see min and max values for pitch. Change these, and each time your sound loops it will do so at a random pitch between the two values you provide. This can make wind sound as though it is fading away and then coming back or fire sound like it is banking down just to flare up again.

This randomization further increases the realism of your scene.

Music

Arguably, a great game can have poor choices in music soundtrack, while a game with an amazing soundtrack can have terrible game mechanics. Regardless, music has often been touted as one of the better points of video games. Users have exclaimed they have bought soundtracks from games, although (conversely) few have purchased games for the soundtracks. Some games, however, have no music, while others (like *Rock Band* and *Guitar Hero*) may even implement music as the core gameplay.

Game soundtracks can help players focus on what their objectives are. If you play a game with missions, the music should fit the mission to help keep you on the right track. For instance, typically when a boss battle or chase scene occurs, the music will speed up and become tenser and faster tempo. This helps cue the player to pay closer attention to their actions in the game. Slower melodies are acceptable for scenes with lots of exploration or puzzle-solving.

UDK offers designers the use of looping and non-looping sound files. Looping means that a sound, once finished playing, will play over again. Looping seamless sounds can blend so well to appear to the ear to never end. You typically pick looping sound files for background music in your game.

You can set map music for specific game levels by going to View > World Properties and searching within the WorldInfo section for map music info. UDK also lets you adjust music file properties to have custom tempos for action, ambience, suspense, tension, and victory, with crossfades between each. You probably already know this, but you can get in some serious trouble for using music or sound effects intended for private home use in a for-profit production, even if it is a video game. If you pay special attention at the beginning of movies you usually see a message warning that comes up saying, "Unauthorized duplication or presentation, even without monetary gain, is punishable by law." That means that even though you may be legit and not intending to make money off your games, even if you own an original copy of the product, you could still be arrested or fined for voiding copyrights.

For educational or private usage, it may be fine to use your favorite band's MP3s, but you won't be able to make your game public without special written permission or usage license from the artist. It never hurts to ask. During one of my early game projects, I contacted five different bands to ask for use of their music within my game, and two of those were so gratified and excited, they sent me CDs and merchandise and even helped me promote my game.

If you know someone who is a freelance musician, or you are a musician on the side, then you could record your own original soundtrack for your game. Otherwise, you might want to investigate the following sites for royalty-free music in digital file format:

- **DeusX.com**: http://www.deusx.com/studio.html
- **Flashkit.com**: http://www.flashkit.com
- **FlashsoundFlashSound.com**: http://www.flashsound.com
- **GameSalad Marketplace**: http://marketplace.gamesalad.com
- **Looperman**: http://www.looperman.com
- **Shockwave-Sound.com**: http://www.shockwave-sound.com
- **Sound-Ideas.com**: http://www.sound-ideas.com
- **Sound Rangers.com**: http://www.soundrangers.com
- **The Music BakeryMusicBakery.com**: http://musicbakery.com

Volumes

Volumes, not to be confused with sound volume, are invisible brushes that define an area for localized effects. These areas can include fog banks, water pools, or lava flows. You can also use more complex mathematical formulas within volumes to conduct different effects when the player enters into those volumes.

Say, for instance, the player enters a dark tunnel. At first, you might want to dim the lighting for the whole level (lower the brightness), and then bring it slowly back up, as if the player's eyes are adjusting to the dark. Then, when the player leaves the dark tunnel, they enter another volume that amps up the brightness, so the light nearly blinds the player as their eyes adjust. This is more complicated to set up than it sounds, but you would do it using volumes.

Adding Volumes

A volume is a brush, so return to your builder brush. If you ever lose your builder brush or cannot find it on screen, you can click the Go to Builder Brush button at the bottom of your toolbar, shown in Figure 5.30.

Figure 5.30
The Go to Builder Brush button is the one on the right.
Source: Epic Games.

Set your builder brush to cube, if it is not already. The reason to use cube is that it has fewer sides and is the easiest brush to render in a game. Set the cube parameters to X 5000, Y 5000, and Z 5000. Move the brush until it is dead center and encasing your current scene.

Once placed, right-click the Add Volume button in the toolbar (see Figure 5.31). A long list of volume brush options that have been prefabricated for you will greet you. Select the one called PostProcessVolume. Once you do that, your selected volume brush appears in the level. You can move your builder brush out of the way and see the brush outline of the volume brush.

Figure 5.31
The Add Volume button is the one on the right.
Source: Epic Games.

Editing Volumes

Double-click your volume brush to bring up its properties. Expand Post Process Volume > Settings. Find the option Enable DOF and put a check next to it, as shown in Figure 5.32. What DOF stands for, in this case, is "depth-of-field," a cinematography trick where objects blur past a focal point.

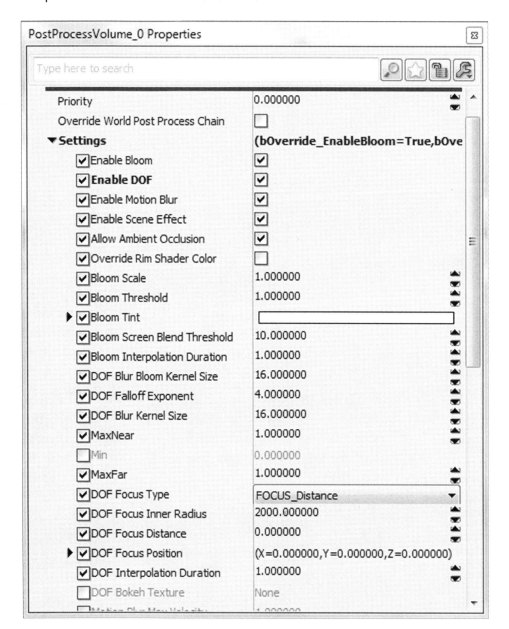

Figure 5.32
Check the Enable DOF setting.
Source: Epic Games.

Now move your viewport camera within the volume brush to see the post-processing effect DOF at work. Your perspective view should resemble Figure 5.33.

Figure 5.33
The DOF post-processing effect after it is enabled.
Source: Epic Games.

Back in the volume brush's properties settings, where you enabled DOF, you can tweak the DOF values to fine-tune your post-processing effect to your liking. You can even add color blooms. Blooms are a special type of light refraction in a scene, especially one blurred by DOF, which gives off brighter incandescence. Practice tweaking the values of these settings, as you like.

Typically, when you do not have a clue what a value will do, increasing or decreasing it by half is a general rule of thumb. That gives you a decent preview of what the value operates, and if you have to retract your change, you can easily figure what the original amount was.

You can do a lot with volumes, besides creating simple outdoor DOF and blooms.

For example, you can tint them, so that when a player character falls inside a volume brush used for water, the world turns murky and blue-green. You would do this by ramping up both DOF and blooms and tinting them aqua color. The water block would also need to have collision turned off, so the player could fall into it.

Layering Volumes

Post-process volumes alter any current post-process effect once the player enters into them.

So, say you have a large DOF volume like the one here. You might want to add a house inside your scene, that when the player enters it, you turn DOF off and maybe turn on another effect in its place. Simply add a new volume brush within your house object to do so. The volume brush within the other volume brush will take precedence during rendering.

PSYCHOLOGY OF LEVEL DESIGN

There is a lot that goes into game level design, but mostly, if you use common sense and general psychology, you will do all right. Think about when you are playing triple-A titles like *Gears of War*; anywhere you go in the level, there is a subtle, often unspoken reason why the level is laid out the way it is and why the obstacles in your path are there.

For instance, if there is a large object in the middle of the road you can run behind and use for cover, it has not appeared there out of thin air. Instead, it is perhaps a huge stone column that has collapsed. For even more realism, the designers can add debris around the general area where the column fell and some hint of from where the column fell.

Only in truly awful bargain-bin games do level items just appear where they are for no apparent reason, except to confuse the gamer.

Case Scenario

So when you are building your game, try thinking ahead.

Say you are building an underground sewer tunnel level, like the one in Figure 5.34.

Figure 5.34

A sewer tunnel level in *Amnesia: The Dark Descent.*

Source: Frictional Games® Inc.

You decide to place a few metal barrels full of radioactive slime in a corridor of your level. That would be fine, but where did the radioactive slime come from? Perhaps you have a piping system that leads to the barrels from somewhere else. Now, add some pipes and valves so they appear to flow into the barrels.

Good, but where do these pipes lead? You might add an overhead duct that leads to the next area, in which you place some large sinister-looking vats churning with radioactive goo. Now, perhaps one of those vats has a leak, and it is pooling in a splash decal under it.

With so much falling apart, this area ought to have workers busy making repairs. Maybe they have been, but they left unexpectedly and left their tools behind. Add some wrenches and buckets on the ground or even a piece of discarded hose. The workers would need light for where they are working, so now add some lamps or a switch panel for overhead fluorescent lights. This also provides places to put your point light sources in the level so they make sense.

If you want to add some machinery for players to duck and hide behind, then you have to consider what kind of machinery would normally be in an environment like this to begin with. With logic, you can improve the look and make sense of level layout.

Now you are really getting there, and your level is starting to make sense and be visually appealing. Moreover, the subtle logic behind object placement will add a sneaky depth of realism lacking in other games.

Fencing the Player

To block off areas you do not want players to go, you have to think with this logic in mind. Levels must be fenced off. You do not want your player to wander outside the play area, because there is nothing there. Every video game finds some way to fence the player.

Some outdoor levels use steep unassailable cliffs, wicked mountain peaks, or densely populated tree lines to keep players from wandering outside the game zone.

Indoor levels are easier, because you line rooms and hallways with locked doors. You can bar windows with iron or nail them shut with wood planks. You can block corridors with fallen wreckage or barricade them with piles of discarded furniture.

Just as in making a maze, you provide dead ends but only to show players, "Hey, you cannot go here. Go this way instead!" By fencing the player, you direct him where you want him to go and do it in an understated way that does not lead to the player feeling disgruntled or led by the nose.

You can also lead the player in other, subtle ways, like the trail of potion drips left behind by Daniel in *Amnesia: The Dark Descent* (see Figure 5.35).

Figure 5.35
A trail for the player to follow in *Amnesia: The Dark Descent*.
Source: Frictional Games® Inc.

Some games use sparkles, road signs, pixie dust, or other unique and unusual methods for pointing the player in the right direction. Too much, and it becomes blatant and boring, but just enough and it adds to the thrill of a game. You do not want your player getting lost in your level, after all.

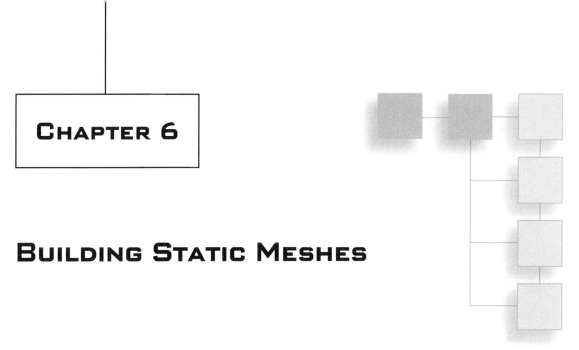

CHAPTER 6

BUILDING STATIC MESHES

Creating custom 3D models for your game world is the real meat of UDK. UDK calls 3D models without animations static meshes, so from here on you will hear them referred to as such. 3D modeling is an advanced process that will give you specific world objects that may not come as stock with the UDK download.

To create static meshes, it is recommended you have and are able to use 2D image-editing software and a 3D modeling program. As there are alternate software programs you can use, these will be discussed briefly and then the use of one will be demonstrated for creating 3D static meshes and importing those meshes into UDK.

WHAT IS 3D MODELING?

Modeling in 3D is akin to clay modeling. If you have ever created something out of clay, then you are closer to understanding how to model in 3D than someone who has not. 3D modeling is very different from 2D drawing. 2D requires an eye for line and tone, with an effective use of negative space and perspective, whereas 3D requires a mental picture of space as it exists in three coordinates (X, Y, and Z) at once and how objects would appear from various angles. X, Y, and Z are used in Cartesian geometry, so if you have covered them in school, you should be passingly familiar with how they work.

Here is a brief overview of the component hierarchy in 3D modeling:

- **Vector** (aka point, dot, or tick): A point in space defined by X, Y, and Z coordinates. You almost always see these coordinates listed in that order (X, Y, and Z), so if a program tells you to place a point at 205, 320, 0, you can infer that to mean 205 X, 320 Y, and 0 Z.

■ **Ray** (aka line, edge, or segment): A straight line between two vectors and the side edge of a plane.

■ **Plane**: A closed surface made up of connecting lines. Three lines using three vectors for their corners make up a single triangle. More than that and you have a polygon. Polygons are the typical surfaces for sub-divisional 3D modeling. They are sometimes abbreviated as polys. Often, you measure the speed of rendering 3D models in real time by how many polys a model has. In the past, 3D game artists had to be very frugal with how many polys they included in each model, which is why the older video games had such blocky-looking characters.

■ **Mesh** (aka wire mesh): A bunch of interconnecting planes folded together to make a single object are referred to as a mesh, partly because they look like a wire mesh bent and shaped to form an outline of a real object. The mesh by itself is see-through and does not have any real substance.

■ **Material** (aka shader): You can apply a material to a mesh to give it a surface. Materials are often based on a single color but have several different settings for how it reflects light, where its highlights and shadows lie, and if it has any bumps or tactile appearance.

■ **Texture** (aka map): In addition to using a single color, you can use a 2D image to wrap around the surface of a 3D model and give it more detail and a better appearance. Textures can even present fake highlights, shadows, and crevices to save the 3D artist poly count and complexity.

3D Modeling Programs

The only way to create 3D meshes is with a 3D creation tool on your computer. The list below demonstrates the most widely used and versatile 3D tools currently available that can export to file formats compatible with UDK. Most all 3D modeling programs share similarities, so if you start to pick up one and decide to switch to using another, the learning curve is a bit smaller.

■ **3ds Max** (http://www.autodesk.com/products/autodesk-3ds-max/free-trial): The Autodesk premiere software package is also one of the more costly programs. However, it has become one of the industry standards. There is a limited-time trial edition you can download, and if you are a student, you can get an educational version for free, too. 3ds Max is a hefty program, meaning that it is jam-packed with options that might be difficult to find for beginners. Reviewing video tutorials or taking a class that teaches the program would be your best bet on effectively learning 3ds Max. See Figure 6.1.

Figure 6.1

The site for Autodesk 3ds Max.

Source: Autodesk® Inc.

- **3DTin** (http://www.3dtin.com/): This is a really cool web-based program for creating 3D models. By the use of a WebGL plugin, 3DTin is built right into your web browser. You must have a browser that supports WebGL for 3DTim to work. For example, 3DTin runs just fine with the latest versions of Chrome and Firefox but may not work at all with older versions of Firefox or Internet Explorer. You can also install 3DTin as a Chrome Web App. The service is completely free. All you have to do is register an account, which you can do through your Facebook or Google profile, and agree to their terms that any models you create will be labeled with a Creative Commons license and placed in the 3DTin gallery. The gallery is a great place to find examples of what can be created using 3DTin.

- **Blender** (http://www.blender.org/): A free and open source 3D modeling and animation application that you can use for modeling, texturing, simulations, animations, rendering, compositing, and even interaction. Blender also has its own game engine technology, which you can use to make PC games. Because Blender is open source, it has been largely community based.

- **Wings 3D** (http://www.wings3d.com/): Wings 3D is a simple sub-divisional modeling program that is extremely easy to learn and use. It offers a wide range of modeling tools, lights, materials, and a built-in UV mapping facility. However, there is no support in Wings 3D for animation, so it can only be used for static meshes.

Tip

Models in Blender generally treat the positive Z axis as up, whereas UDK treats it as down. The UDK importer will automatically attempt to correct this, so the models imported from Blender will appear correctly in UDK. However, if you need a position in vector coordinates, you will have to flip the sign of Blender Y and Z coordinates to account for the correction.

2D Image-Editing Programs

Besides having a 3D program, you should also have a 2D image-editing program in your design pipeline. You can choose from several. These include:

- **GIMP** (www.gimp.org): GIMP is the GNU Image Manipulation Program and is a freely distributed piece of software for such tasks as photo touchups, image composition, and image creation. It works on a wide variety of operating systems. It is open source, therefore it is largely community driven and supported.

- **Paint.Net** (www.getpaint.net): Paint.Net is a free image and photo-editing software program for computers that run Windows. It features an intuitive user interface with support for layers, unlimited undo, special effects, and a wide variety of useful and powerful tools. The online community provides support, tutorials, and plugins.

- **Photoshop** (https://creative.adobe.com/products/photoshop): Adobe's trademark 2D art and image manipulation tool, part of its popular Creative Suite, has been an industry stay for years, with few competitors. Photoshop has all the tools you will need to draw, edit, and arrange 2D files. Unfortunately, it is also rather expensive, although you can find a limited-time trial edition for download on their site.

- **Pixlr** (http://pixlr.com/editor/): This free, web-based application requires an Internet connection but otherwise is fast and runs through your web browser. You can also install Pixlr to your mobile phone or tablet for on-the-go editing purposes. Users of Photoshop will delight in how close Pixlr resembles the Photoshop interface. The best thing about Pixlr is it is 100% free!

■ **Sumopaint** (http://www.sumopaint.com/app/): This free, web-based application requires an Internet connection but otherwise is fast and runs through your web browser. It also gives you the option to install a desktop version to your computer. The free version limits you on your choices of filters. To unlock its full potential costs less than $20. There is even an iPad app version for mobile users. See Figure 6.2.

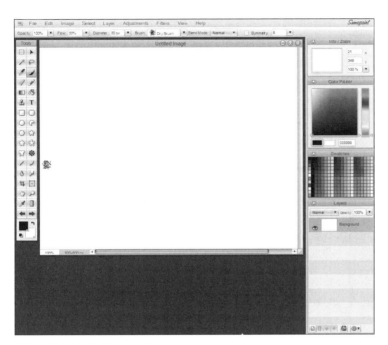

Figure 6.2
Sumopaint.
© Sumoing Ltd.

THE BASICS OF 3D MODELING

You would like to see how to make 3D models, right? The complex character models seen in games like *Gears of War* are very advanced, so you will not start there. To begin with, you can design a wood crate or box, one of the staple items in almost every video game ever made (next to the exploding metal barrel). The first lesson shows you how to accomplish this task in 3ds Max, while the second shows you how to do it online using 3DTin.

Create a Crate in 3ds Max

You can install the 3ds Max trial version from Autodesk online at http://www.autodesk.com/products/autodesk-3ds-max/free-trial. Once you have completed installation, open 3ds Max. Close the initial startup window.

Note

The Autodesk Student Community, launched in 2006, is a place for students and faculty to download select Autodesk software for free. The only requirement is that you must have a valid email address issued by a recognized university or college (high schools do not count). All the student editions of their software, including 3ds Max, have the same features and capabilities as the retail editions, except for a watermark that appears over all finished work; this is to prevent their use in commercial work. To find out more, visit the Student Community page for more information: http://students.autodesk.com/.

1. First, look to the right side of your screen for the Command Panel, as seen in Figure 6.3. This is where you have all your major design options stored for you in tabbed sections. In the Create tab, click Box from Standard Primitives to select that draw functionality. Click and drag anywhere in the middle screen to draw the base of the box, and watch as it rises with your mouse to your desired height. Click again to close the box. Compare your work to Figure 6.4. It does not matter what the particular box primitive's size is, as you will be editing it shortly.

Figure 6.3
The Create tab of the Command Panel.
Source: Autodesk® Inc.

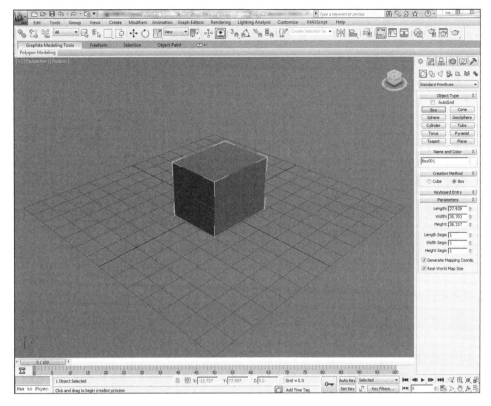

Figure 6.4
Draw a box primitive.
Source: Autodesk® Inc.

2. In the Command Panel, switch to the second tab, the Modify tab. With your
   box still selected in the viewport, change all its sizes (Length, Width, and
   Height) in the Modify tab to the same numbers to make it a perfect cube. I set
   each of my sizes to 40, as shown in Figure 6.5.

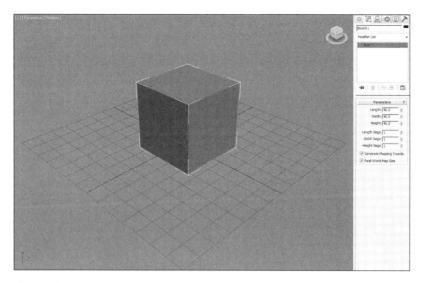

Figure 6.5
Resize your Box primitive.
Source: Autodesk® Inc.

3. Next, with your Box selected in the viewport, right-click on it to pull up the Options menu. Go to Convert to > Convert to Editable Poly, as you can see in Figure 6.6.

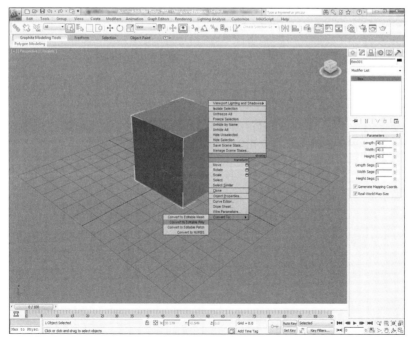

Figure 6.6
Convert your primitive to an editable poly.
Source: Autodesk® Inc.

4. Go to the Command Panel's Modify tab and in the box below where it says Modifier List, click the plus sign (+) beside Editable Poly to expand the Editable Poly list of components. Click on Polygon to enter that selection mode. Click to select one of the sides of the box in the viewport window. See Figure 6.7. Press CTRL + A to select all sides of the box at once. The whole thing should turn red; this shows you it is selected.

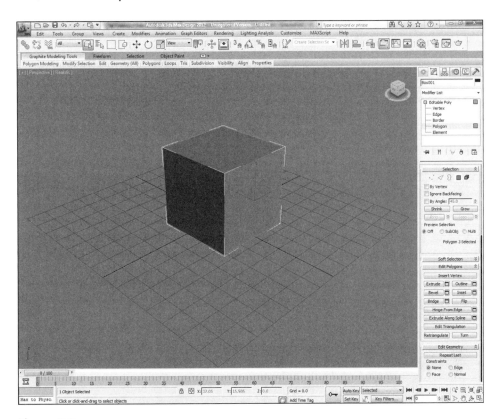

Figure 6.7
Select one poly (side) of the box.
Source: Autodesk® Inc.

5. Move your attention back to the Modify tab of the Command Panel. Look down the list below until you find the Edit Polygons section. In that section, select the small button next to the Inset tool to bring up its settings. The settings will pop up and hover over the selected object in the viewport. In the settings, click the top drop-down and choose By Polygon so Inset works on each plane separately. Then choose how far in you want to inset the poly. I put mine at 4, like in Figure 6.8. Click the green check mark button to save your edit.

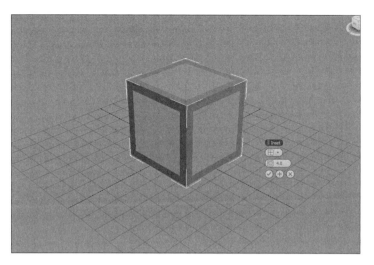

Figure 6.8
Inset the polys of your box by 4.
Source: Autodesk® Inc.

6. To make the sides go in, you will need to use the Extrude tool. So press the
   settings button beside the Extrude tool in the Edit Polygons section of the
   Modifier tab to bring up the Extrude settings. You will see that the sides are
   sticking out where you selected and not going in (see Figure 6.9), so to make it
   go in you need to change the number to a negative number. I put mine at minus
   2 (–2) (see Figure 6.10). Click the green check button to save your changes.

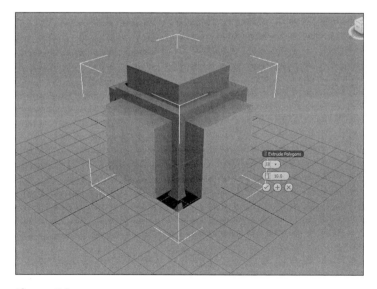

Figure 6.9
You do not want to extrude outward!
Source: Autodesk® Inc.

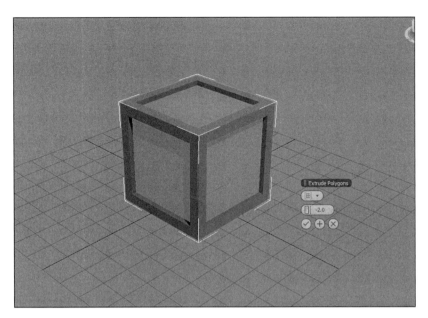

Figure 6.10
Extrude inward by using −2.
Source: Autodesk® Inc.

7. Once you have deselected the sides by clicking off the shape, you should see your finished crate. Compare your crate to mine in Figure 6.11.

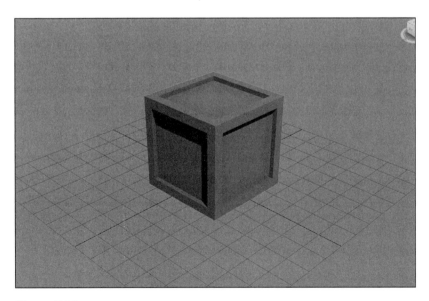

Figure 6.11
A finished crate mesh made in 3ds Max.
Source: Autodesk® Inc.

Create a Crate in 3DTin

To reveal the innate similarities and differences between the 3D modeling software, you should attempt to create the same 3D model in 3DTin. After experiencing both, you can decide which one would appeal more to you.

You do not have to install any software to use 3DTin, but it is required that your web browser be WebGL-enabled. To double-check and make sure your browser is WebGL-ready, and to download WebGL if it is not, go to http://get.webgl.org. When you are ready, go to www.3dtin.com.

1. On the right side of the screen, follow the onscreen options to register an account with 3DTin, so that you can save and export your project.

2. Once you have finished registering an account, start with a new sketch (see Figure 6.12).

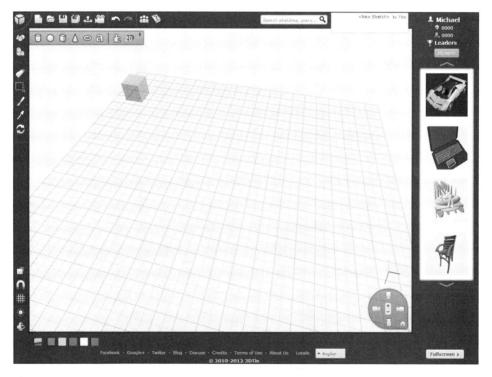

Figure 6.12
Start with a new sketch in 3DTin.
© 2010-2012 3DTin.

3. Click the Create New Geometry button (it looks like a jigsaw puzzle piece) at the top middle toolbar. This will open the Geometry Builder shown in Figure 6.13.

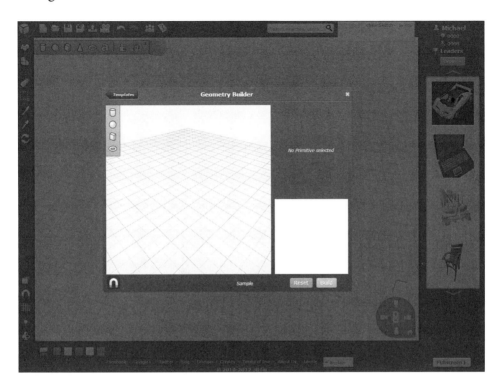

Figure 6.13
Open the Geometry Builder.
© 2010-2012 3DTin.

4. Click the cube primitive button on the left. This places a see-through cube block in your viewport, which will follow your mouse around. Click to add it to your viewport. It will appear solid.

5. On the right, toggle your X, Y, and Z dimensions to each be 10, or a perfect cube. Note that, as seen in Figure 6.14, the preview window below the dimensions settings updates as you change these numbers and shows you a preview of what your finished box will look like.

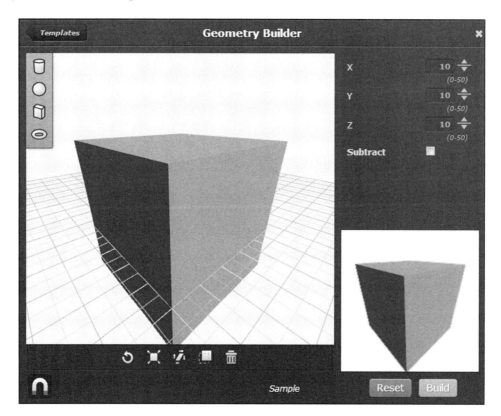

Figure 6.14
Resize your box into a perfect cube by adjusting its settings.
© 2010-2012 3DTin.

6. Add a second cube, but set it to be 8 all the way around. Check the Subtract box beneath the dimension settings, so that it will subtract from other primitives it might touch. Now maneuver it into place so that it overlaps just one side of the original block, creating an inset groove. See Figure 6.15. Sometimes, you will have to move your cursor to an empty space and click-drag to move your camera around, so you can get a better view of what is going on in your viewport window. Moving your objects in the Geometry Builder is, unfortunately, not very specific and requires a lot of trial-and-error.

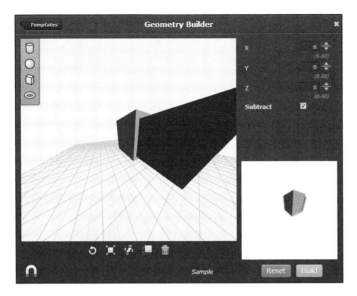

Figure 6.15
Overlap the first cube with your duplicate to subtract from the first.
© 2010-2012 3DTin.

7. With the second cube still selected, click the Clone button, found beneath the viewport and beside the Delete (trashcan) button, to create a duplicate of your 8 × 8 × 8 cube. Maneuver this clone to another side of your cube, so that the indent in the original cube appears similar to your first indentation you made. See Figure 6.16.

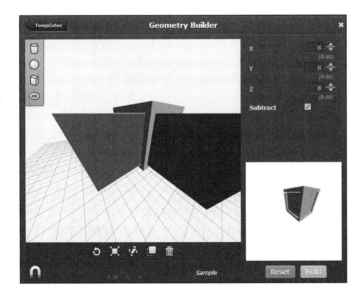

Figure 6.16
Add another subtractive cube to create another indention in the side of the original box.
© 2010-2012 3DTin.

8. Repeat step #7 until you have every side of the original box inset. When you are satisfied, click the Build button to save your work and return to the main editor. Click anywhere to add your original geometry.

9. To change its color, click the rainbow-colored square at the bottom left of your screen and pick a brown color. Then, switch to the Change Color (hotkey S) tool, which looks like a paintbrush, and with the brown color selected below the viewport, click on your box. Now it is brown. Compare your work with Figure 6.17.

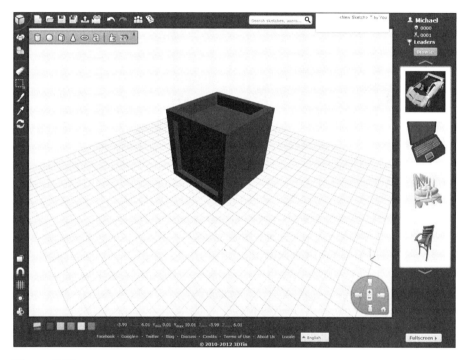

Figure 6.17
An example of what your finished 3DTin crate might look like.
© 2010-2012 3DTin.

10. Alternatively, instead of using the Geometry Builder, you could create the object cube by cube. If you are familiar with the game *Minecraft*, then you already know how you can accomplish this. By using the Add Cubes button (hotkey A), you can start with a large block and then place little blocks around the sides to create your indentions (see Figure 6.18). As each new cube is added, it becomes an indivisible part of the whole. Be ready to click Undo as needed, and use the View Rotate or Pan tool (hotkey R) to change your viewing angle so you can see every side of your box as you work to construct it.

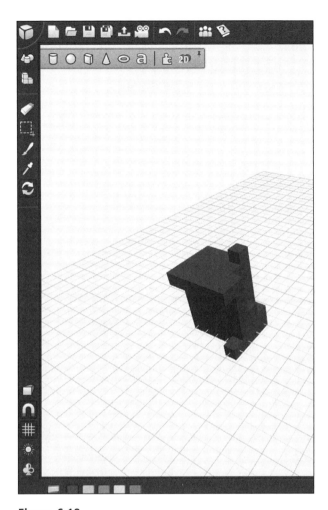

Figure 6.18
You could also build your crate bit by bit, cube by cube in 3DTin similar to how you would in the game *Minecraft*.
© 2010-2012 3DTin.

ONLINE RESOURCES

What follows are some sites where you can download assets for your game project.

Free 3D Models for Download

You do not have to be a whiz 3D artist to make static meshes for your game. There are many online sites offering free-for-download models that you could use in your game project. Be sure to check the copyrights and user restrictions of each. Some sites prefer that you only use their 3D models for non-commercial or educational projects only, while others will allow you to use their 3D models as long as you credit the original author(s). If you are uncertain about their usage policies, browse their site carefully for this information or check the notes that the original author(s) have left with their 3D models. It is not recommended to steal another artist's work for use in a game you want to publicize and make money from, because that would be illegal.

The following are some suggestions for online sites where you can get 3D models:

- **3D Total** (http://www.3dtotal.com/): 3D Total provides free stuff in categories of human characters, household items, body parts, vehicles, weapons, alien characters, cartoon, and more.

- **3Delicious** (http://www.3delicious.net/): Only "the most delicious" free 3D models offered.

- **3DModelFree** (http://www.3dmodelfree.com/): Free 3D models for download.

- **3DXtras** (http://www.3dxtras.com/3dxtras-free-3d-models-list.asp): Download high-quality 3D models for 3ds Max, Maya, Softimage, and Lightwave.

- **Archive 3D** (http://archive3d.net/): Free 15,000-plus 3D models for download without any registration required.

- **Artist-3D** (http://artist-3d.com/): An exchange directory of royalty-free 3D models. 3D artists and graphic designers submit 3D models or download ones for personal and non-commercial use.

- **Blender Models** (http://www.blender-models.com/): The Blender model repository is a resource for Blender artists to learn and share with other Blender artists.

- **BlendSwap** (http://www.blendswap.com/): Blend Swap is a proud community of 3D artists sharing their work and building the largest Blender-based 3D assets library, all of which is free for download.

- **Exchange 3D** (http://www.exchange3d.com/Free-3D-Models/cat_35.html): An online exchange directory of Blender and 3ds Max 3D model files.

- **Mr. Furniture** (http://www.mr-cad.com/Free-3D-Models-c-19-1.html): Over 5,000 free 3D models for furniture in .3DS, .MAX, and .DXF format.

- **Rocky3D** (http://www.rocky3d.com/free3d.html): Rocky3D specializes in providing useful 3D models for your scenes, with thousands of models (many of which are free) to choose from.

- **TF3DM** (http://tf3dm.com/): TF3DM is a vast library of free 3D models and 2D textures for your modeling and animation needs, with a clever minimalistic search interface. See Figure 6.19.

- **Top3D.net** (http://www.top3d.net/3d-models/): Free download site for 3D animation and models in .MAX, .C4D, and .3DS format.

- **Turbosquid** (http://www.turbosquid.com/): Turbosquid is a large library of free 3D models for download. Registration is required for download.

Figure 6.19
The TF3DM website.
© tf3dm.com

Free 2D Textures for Download

Besides 3D models, you might also want to build up a library of textures over time. Textures are the flat 2D images you wrap around 3D meshes to give them the appearance of solid objects. The better the texture is the more realistic detail you can give to the mesh without clustering memory-intensive polygons together.

- **Archive Textures** (www.archivetextures.net): A social network–friendly texture repository, featuring all sorts of free textures for download. Categories include mosaics, brick, bark, textile, stone, paving, and more.

- **3DModelFree.com** (http://map.3dmodelfree.com/): Free downloadable 3D textures, especially for walls and floors.

- **CGTextures** (http://www.cgtextures.com/): A repository of textures.

- **Dave Gurrea's Textures** (http://www.davegh.com/): A collection of textures, both non-edited photographs and digital game-ready images. You can use the majority of these to make seamless tileable textures. See Figure 6.20.

- **Free Seamless Textures** (http://freeseamlesstextures.com/): Download seamless textures, tileable background images, and repeating patterns.

- **Good Textures** (www.goodtextures.com): Free high-quality textures and photographs that can be cropped and edited to become textures.

- **Mayang's Free Textures** (www.mayang.com/textures/): A texture library with over 4,350 free-to-download, high-resolution textures.

- **Texture Warehouse** (http://www.texturewarehouse.com/): High-resolution textures for graphic designers and 3D artists.

- **Texturer** (http://texturer.com/): A large library of free-for-download textures and reference images.

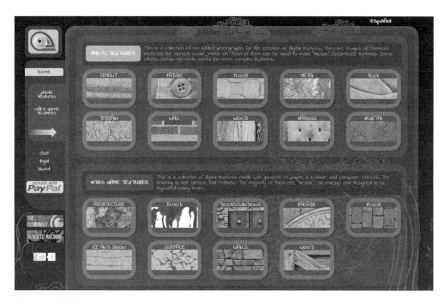

Figure 6.20
Dave Gurrea's website.
© Dave Gurrea.

Note

What does "tileable" mean when talking about textures? It means you can line a texture up next to itself, running both horizontally and vertically, to make a single overall pattern. You consider the repeated "tile" texture to be "seamless" when you cannot tell where one image ends and the next begins.

This book does not include any lessons on using 2D image-editing programs, or creating textures. You can discover how to make seamless textures quickly by searching online for "how to make seamless textures." Depending on the image-editing program you decide to use, you can also find documentation and tutorials online fairly easily by performing a web search.

IMPORTING A MESH YOU DOWNLOAD

Say you use one of the free online resources found above. You have a 3D model file and need to get it into UDK. What do you do?

1. Go to http://www.turbosquid.com/ and register for an account. You can browse all you want, but to download a 3D model from the Turbosquid website, you must have a registered account and be signed in.

2. Once logged in with your account, search for the 3D model you want. You can find free 3D models by going to Sort By > Lowest Prices in the filters bar near the top of the page (see Figure 6.21). I typed "crate" into the Search field to find only those 3D models with "crate" in the title. Then I picked Free Crate by user Charnel; you can go directly to it by using the URL http://www.turbosquid.com/ 3d-models/free-3ds-model-wooden-crate/597590 (if it is still available at the time you read this). You can see the Free Crate model I chose in Figure 6.22.

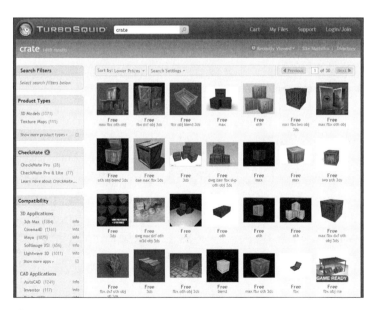

Figure 6.21
Sort your 3D models list by lowest prices (starting with free).
© 2013 TurboSquid.

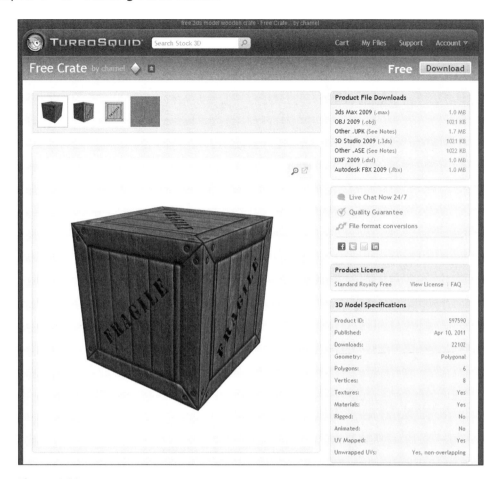

Figure 6.22
Pick an .FBX 3D model, such as Charnel's Free Crate (shown here).
© 2013 TurboSquid.

3. When you click the Download button, Turbosquid adds your 3D model to your Purchases & Downloads page. This, as shown in Figure 6.23, is essentially an online shopping cart. Download your archive file. Most 3D models you pick from Turbosquid will have more than one file format to choose from. If you are lucky, you can find a .UPK or an .ASE file that is UDK-ready. Otherwise, you can attempt to work with an .FBX file; as long as it is a 3D model made compatible with your version of UDK, it should work.

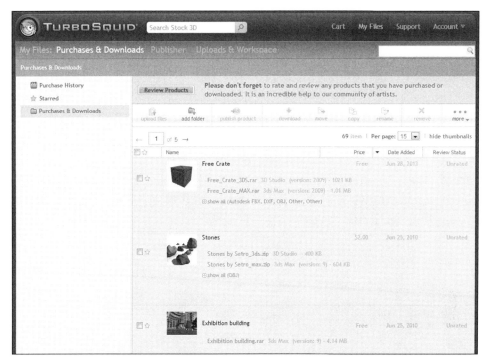

Figure 6.23
Download your chosen file from the Purchases & Downloads page.
© 2013 TurboSquid.

Note

In order to import into UDK, the file type must be .ASE or .FBX for the 3D static mesh and .TGA for the texture. These are the formats UDK accepts.

To convert a .JPG, .PNG, or other image file into a .TGA file, you can open the file into Photoshop (if you have Photoshop installed on your computer) and, through Photoshop's main menu, go to File > Save As and save in the .TGA format. Or you can use the online image conversion tool at http://image.online-convert.com/convert-to-tga to convert your selected file to the .TGA format.

To convert any 3D file format into an .ASE or .FBX file, open the file in 3ds Max and export as an .ASE or .FBX.

4. Extract/unzip your archive folder you just downloaded. To unzip an archive folder, you need decompression software like WinZip, WinRAR, or B1 Free Archiver. Personally, I prefer B1 Free Archiver for its minimal interface and ease of use. B1 can also handle .7Z archive folders, which the others do not. Once you have decompression software installed on your machine, unzipping is as simple as right-clicking the zip folder and selecting to extract its contents to the directory of your choice.

5. Once the file contents have been extracted, open UDK and, starting within a new untitled level, go to the Content Browser. Click the Import button at the bottom left, beneath your packages list. Browse to the place you extracted your 3D model's files. Import your 3D model file (.ASE or .FBX). Although the Free Crate model I picked came as a .UPK (Unreal package) file format, expressly ready for installation into UDK, I will import the .ASE file to show you how it works.

6. In the Import dialog, create a new package for your static mesh by typing in a new name for it, or leave it at default (MyPackage). If you want to add your new imported object to a specific group, you could add it now, but you do not have to. Make sure you give the object an appropriate name. See Figure 6.24. Click OK when you are done.

Figure 6.24
Import your 3D model file.
Source: Epic Games.

7. Click Import again, and this time browse to and select the 2D texture file that accompanies your 3D model. For my crate, I picked Diffuse.bmp, as shown in Figure 6.25.

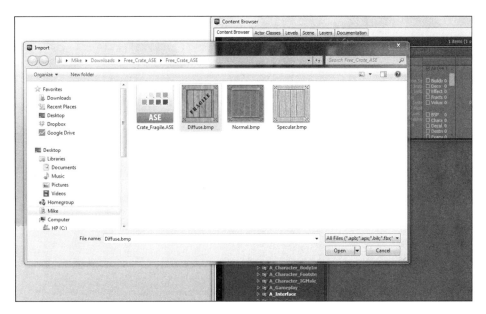

Figure 6.25
Import your 2D texture file.
Source: Epic Games.

8. Right-click your new Texture2D in the Content Browser window and select Create New Material from the pop-up options list. Leave the defaults as-is (see Figure 6.26) and click OK.

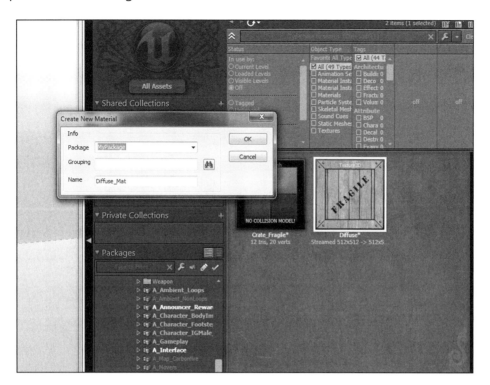

Figure 6.26

Create a new material based on your 2D texture file.

Source: Epic Games.

9. Double-click your new blank material. This opens the Material Editor. Note that, in the center panel, there are two nodes covering up one another. Press and hold down the CTRL key while clicking to drag the Texture Sample node from the stack to the right side of the middle panel, just so you can see it separate from the material node, like in Figure 6.27.

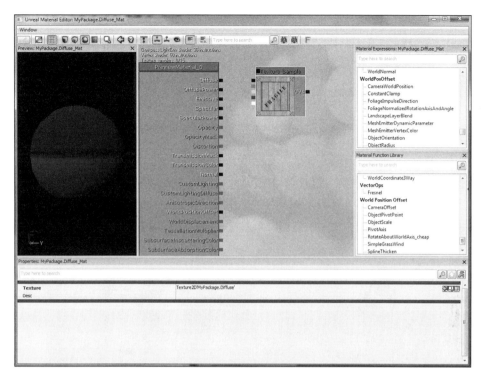

Figure 6.27
Drag the Texture Sample node off the material node so you can see them side-by-side.
Source: Epic Games.

10. As you are working with a box, you can alter the material preview (left side of the screen) by clicking the Cube icon button just above it. In the middle panel, click and drag a connector from the Diffuse property of the material node (left) to the black connector of Texture Sample node (right), as shown in Figure 6.28.

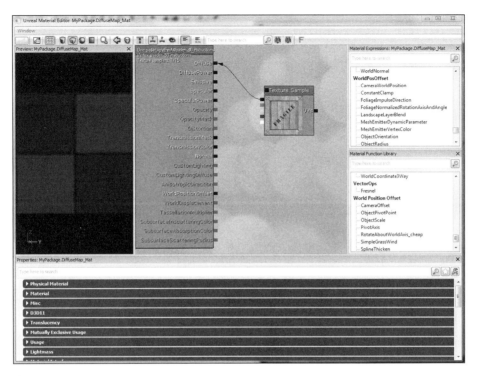

Figure 6.28
Connect the texture sample to the material by the Diffuse property.
Source: Epic Games.

11. You may notice how the material preview did not change automatically when you added the connector, which would normally bind the texture to the material. This is because you are working in mobile emulation, and mobile games use a separate texture for all the normal ones. At the bottom of the Material Editor, scroll down and expand Mobile to find Mobile Base Texture. This is where you should add your 2D texture image. To do so, return your attention briefly to the Content Browser and click once to select your 2D texture file. Then, back in the Material Editor, click the green arrow button to the right of Mobile > Mobile Base Texture to bind the texture file to the material (again). Now you should see a change in your material preview! See Figure 6.29. Close the Material Editor dialog. It will ask if you want to apply changes to the material. Click Yes to save.

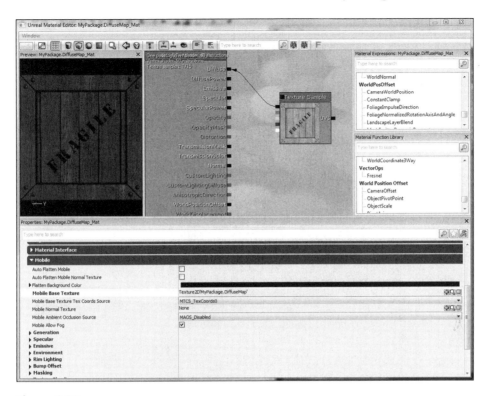

Figure 6.29
Attach the texture file to the material by the Mobile Base Texture property.
Source: Epic Games.

12. Double-click on your static mesh to open the Static Mesh Editor dialog. Search for "material." Select your Material in the Content Browser and click the green arrow beside the Material input field in the Properties panel of the Static Mesh Editor to bind the material to your mesh.

13. Drag your static mesh from the Content Browser into the UDK Editor. Using the Scaling Mode, scale the mesh up if required.

14. Currently, your object has no collision set, which means the player character could walk straight through it. Return to the Static Mesh Editor. From the main menu's drop-down list, set Collision to 6DOP simplified collision. See Figure 6.30. Right-click your static mesh in your game world and select Set Collision Type > Block All. Alternatively, you could Select All (press F4), then go to Collision > Collision type and select COLLIDE_Blockall from the options.

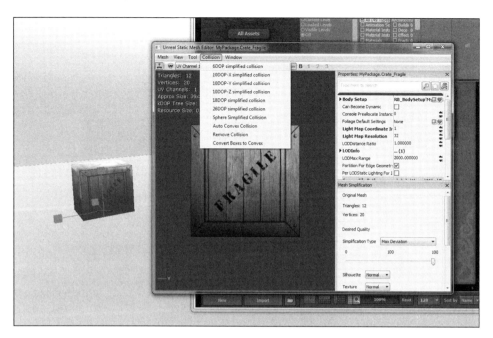

Figure 6.30
Add a collision model to your static mesh to give it substance.
Source: Epic Games.

15. That is all it takes to import a downloaded model. If you want, you can save your current level and open a new one for more experimentation.

Collision Models

What follows are the most prevalently used collision models applied to meshes in UDK.

- **6DOP simplified collision:** A six-sided box. Surprisingly effective in most cases.
- **Sphere simplified collision:** A sphere. Rolls smoothly unlike many polygonal shapes.
- **26DOP simplified collision:** Generates a polygonal shape that does a fair job in many cases.
- **Auto convex collision:** If all else fails, use this option and mess with the values of the three sliders. Generally, set Allows Splits low (around 4), Max Hull Verts high (around 24), and leave Depth at the default setting.

IMPORTING A MESH FROM 3DS MAX TO UDK

If, however, you want to import a static mesh you made yourself, it really is quite simple. If you use 3ds Max for your 3D art, you can follow along with these steps to import the finished mesh (.ASE) into UDK:

1. Open the UDK Editor, if it is not already open.

2. Go to the Content Browser and click the Import button (bottom left).

3. Find the exported mesh you have ready for import. If exporting from 3ds Max and you are using Windows, it will generally appear in the 3dsmax/exports folder inside My Documents. Locate the mesh and select OK.

4. In the dialog that comes up, check the following:

   i. It is being saved in the desired package (defaults to MyPackage).

   ii. The mesh name has no spaces or wild characters in it. If you must have a space, use underscore (_) or camel case notation. Camel case notation is where all the words used run into one another, but where the first letter of each word is capitalized and the rest is lowercase. For instance: ThisIsCamelCaseNotation.

   iii. Also check that the following are selected before pressing OK:

   - Override Full Name
   - Import Mesh LODs
   - Import Morph Targets
   - Import Animations
   - Import Materials
   - Import Textures
   - Create groups automatically

5. Once you click OK, the static mesh should appear inside the package with its materials. Be sure to save the package before continuing. To do so, right-click the package and select Save.

The following are the steps you would use to import your texture(s):

1. Go into the UDK package where your mesh resides. Import your 2D texture file. In the dialog that comes up, check the following before clicking OK:

   i. You are saving it in the desired package (defaults to MyPackage).

   ii. The texture name has no spaces or wild characters in it. If you must have a space, use underscore (_) or camel case notation.

2. Back in the Content Browser, right-click on your new Texture2D file in your package and select Create New Material.

3. Name the material (it should end in "Mat") before clicking OK.

4. The Material Editor will pop up. Hold down CTRL while dragging the Texture Sample node to the right of the material node, so you can see both.

5. Click and drag a connector from the black square next to the Texture Sample node to the Diffuse property of the material node beside it.

6. Do not forget to select the material node and scroll down to go to Mobile and, with the Texture2D file selected in the Content Browser, click the green arrow button beside Mobile Base Texture to apply your texture for mobile emulation, too.

7. Close the Material Editor and select Yes to save your changes.

When to Use Meshes

UDK, as you read in Chapter 5, "Level Construction in UDK," has a wide variety of tools that allow you to build geometry for your level. The blocks you build become a solid part of the overall level architecture, and the player character can traverse across them to reach the game's goals. So when would you need to add static meshes?

First of all, static meshes are typically used as part of set design, like window dressing. They can include trees, flowers, rocks, boulders, bridges, windmills, towers, and so much more. These are objects not normally created as part of the UDK level architecture but are important regardless.

Secondly, you can use static meshes as tokens within the video game. They can be player tokens, such as power-up items and breakable objects such as exploding barrels. They can be enemy tokens as well, such as dangerous objects that hurt upon impact or spring a trap on the unsuspecting player.

So there are many reasons why you would use 3D models instead of basic geometry in your game world. However, you cannot go hog wild with it. With each new mesh added to your game, the more complex the game becomes and more memory reserves it will use to render the game on the end user's device. Since that device might very well be a mobile one, like the iPad platform, you have to be frugal with the amount of reserves it uses.

Therefore, it is imperative you have a plan for each new mesh you want to add to your game. Make sure it is not going to be a waste of system resources but an integral part of the game. Either it should add to the game's ambience in some meaningful way or exist to support the game's rules.

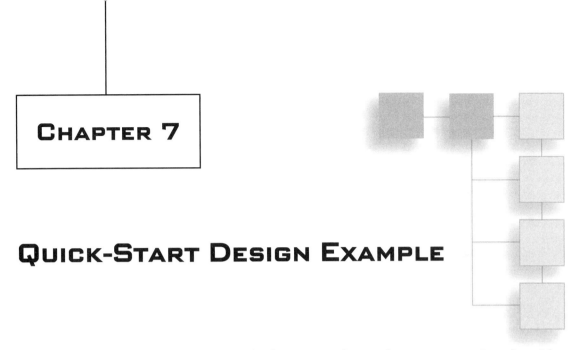

CHAPTER 7

QUICK-START DESIGN EXAMPLE

You could begin a new game entirely from scratch. To do so, you need a clear idea of what content you'll include from the beginning and work your way up, first designing sketches and then more formalized art assets such as 2D texture maps and 3D models and animations. Later, you'll begin designing the level itself. Keep in mind that iPad games have to be kept minimal in their approach to level design due to the performance limitations of the device. After designing the level and importing the base resources, you then add your special touch through Kismet and Matinee, effectively bringing the artificial world to life. All this is doable but takes a lot of skill and time. It would be hard to do as a beginner.

To whet your appetite, and to prove how easy and effective UDK is for designing iPad games, you could instead start with one of the sample projects included with the UDK download. Practice with it would help springboard your own original ideas later. This method of game creation is precisely what this chapter aims to show you.

OPEN TEMPLATE

You will use the Kismet tutorial file found within the downloadable UDK as a basis for this lesson.

1. First, open the Unreal Editor. Make sure Emulate Mobile Features is on (the iPhone icon button in the top right shelf of your UDK Editor should appear depressed); this is something you executed in Chapter 5.

2. When your initial screen comes up, select the option to start editing an existing map (see Figure 7.1). This option allows you to choose an existing .udk map file to open up in the Editor window.

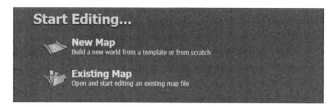

Figure 7.1
Start editing an existing map. Choose KismetTutorial_Start.udk from the Mobile folder.
Source: Epic Games.

3. From the Maps directory, enter the Mobile folder and pick KismetTutorial _Start.udk. The .udk files in the Mobile folder are saved iOS map files you can inspect at your leisure. The KismetTutorial_Start.udk file was created as a basis for the *Jazz Jackrabbit* third-person action game. It is used freely as part of Epic's tutorial for learning how to create mobile games only and should not be used for commercial projects without express permission of Epic. Also, if you cannot find the KismetTutorial_Start.udk file in your Mobile folder, you can download the project from Epic's website at http://download.udk.com/showcase/ JazzTutorial.zip. The following lesson uses Epic's tutorial as a basis.

4. Go to the main menu and select File > Save As. Browse to your UDK directory to UDKGame\Content\Maps. Create a new folder there using your name or personal tag. For instance, I would use Mike_Duggan. Within that folder, save your project as Start.udk.

Player Model

Next, add the player's character to the virtual world. This character will be the manner by which the player will interact with that virtual world. For this lesson, you will be using a rabbit that looks a little like Rambo. He is the titular character of Epic Games' *Jazz Jackrabbit* game, Jazz.

1. Open the Content Browser and navigate to the Actor Classes tab.

2. Uncheck Show Categories, the third option from the top.

3. In the list, expand Pawn and GamePawn. You should see the object MobilePlaceablePawn listed, as shown in Figure 7.2.

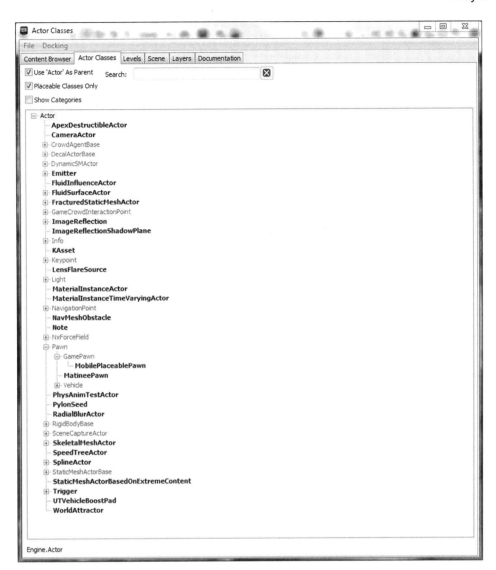

Figure 7.2
Expand the list of Pawn categories until you find MobilePlaceablePawn.
Source: Epic Games.

4. Click and drag the MobilePlaceablePawn object from the list into the game world, like Figure 7.3 shows. If you have trouble clicking-and-dragging, or prefer not to, you can select MobilePlaceablePawn from the list and then right-click within the game world and choose Add MobilePlaceablePawn Here from the pop-up options. It will look like a cutout of a dinosaur's head for now.

Figure 7.3
Put your MobilePlaceablePawn on your map somewhere.
Source: Epic Games.

5. Where you place your avatar in the game world is totally up to you. You can use the axis handles to change its position on the map. If you move it where you cannot see it very well, remember you can click the Go To > Actor icon button at the bottom of the toolbar.

6. Double-click the MobilePlaceablePawn object that is in your map and you will see its properties open up.

7. Expand the Pawn property.

8. Now expand the Mesh and Skeletal Mesh Component, as you can see in Figure 7.4.

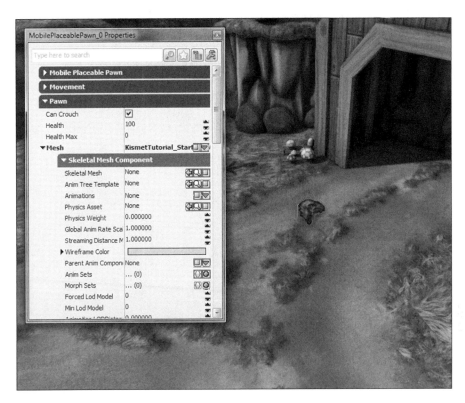

Figure 7.4
In the Object Properties window, expand Pawn > Mesh > Skeletal Mesh Component.
Source: Epic Games.

9. Before going any further, you will need to browse to find the art asset you will use for this next step. Without closing the properties window, return to the Content Browser.

10. In the Packages panel, expand the following: UDKGame > Content > Mobile > Misc. Click to select KismetGame_Assets. Wait for the Content Browser to show all the KismetGame_Assets.

11. In the search field in the upper middle of the Content Browser, type in "jazz" to filter the assets so they only show the assets with those characters in their names.

12. Scroll down until you find the SK_Jazz SkeletalMesh object, as displayed in Figure 7.5. Click to select it. Note that assets with names starting with "SK_" are generally SkeletalMesh objects. This is a designer choice for staying organized.

Figure 7.5
Search for and select SK_Jazz SkeletalMesh from the KismetGame_Assets package.
Source: Epic Games.

13. Return to the MobilePlaceablePawn_0 Properties dialog box.

14. Under Skeletal Mesh Component, where you see the line item Skeletal Mesh, click the green arrow beside it to assign the currently selected object (SK_Jazz) to the pawn. Compare your screen to Figure 7.6. Save your project when you are done.

Figure 7.6
Assign SK_Jazz to the pawn's Skeletal Mesh.
Source: Epic Games.

ANIMATION

A player character with a mesh is still just a static model. It can be moved by player input controls, but it will not look animated until you give it some animations. Not all characters need animations. Characters made to look robotic, such as floating spheres or cylinders, would not need any animations.

Many developers, in fact, use dummy models in place of the final rendered and animated models during level building, and once the game is nearly complete, they swap the models. This makes iterative development fast and easy. Therefore, there is no shame in using models that lack animations for characters in your game, and if you want, you can replace them later.

The following section shows you how to get your character moving:

1. In the Content Browser, scroll until you find the Jazz_AnimTree object. Click to select it.

2. Return to the MobilePlaceablePawn_0 Properties dialog and assign Jazz_AnimTree to the Anim Tree Template line item under Skeletal Mesh Component by clicking the green arrow. The Anim Tree should always point to an

AnimTree object in the game package. BeginPlay on the Skeletal Mesh Component will instance (copy) the tree and assign the instance to the Animations pointer.

3. Last but not least, you have to add the animation set. Browse the Content Browser to find and select the SK_Jazz_Anims AnimSet object.

4. In the properties window, look for Anim Sets under Skeletal Mesh Component. Currently there are none (0). To add an Anim Set, click the green plus icon beside the line item.

5. Assign the SK_Jazz_Anims AnimSet to the new Anim Set, as shown in Figure 7.7. Anim Sets is where UDK will look to find a particular animation sequence, as specified by name in the AnimNodeSequence. So if your avatar is just sitting there, doing nothing, the Anim Set defines the "idle" animation set to display.

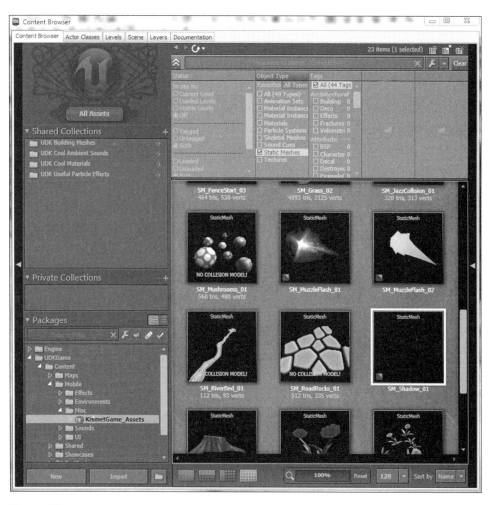

Figure 7.7
Assign SK_Jazz_Anims to the pawn's Anim Set.
Source: Epic Games.

6. Now your character model has all the essential elements needed in order to animate: an imported, animated skeletal mesh; an AnimTree; and an AnimSet. If your character still refuses to animate with all these in place, review the steps to find what went wrong or search for "create custom animated character in UDK" online. At the time of this writing, a decent tutorial could be found at http://forums.epicgames.com/threads/717339-Guide-Custom-Character-with-Custom-Animation.

COLLISION

Currently, the player can move an animated character around the virtual world. However, every believable character or object within the virtual world must also have a definition for collision, so that they do not pass through other characters or objects.

Virtual objects are not solid and never can be without collision parameters. You have probably experienced games where one model brushes up against another and some or whole parts of them may go through the other. A character model may even disappear through a wall or sink into the terrain briefly. This is because 3D worlds are based entirely on make-believe and mathematical algorithms. They do not have any real substance. Collision parameters give 3D meshes the appearance of substance by not allowing them to go right through each other.

1. Within the virtual world, make sure you have Jazz Jackrabbit selected. Click the Go to Actor button at the bottom of the left toolbar, if you need to find and view the player character up close. Press ALT + C (or just C if you are using an older version of UDK) to reveal the bounding boxes, or visual collision parameters, for objects within your scene. The bounding box for the character is currently visible as a cylinder.

2. To broaden the collision cylinder, return to the MobilePlaceablePawn_0 Properties dialog box. Scroll down to find and click the left-side arrow to expand the Collision > Collision Component properties. Beside the Collision Radius input field, click the up arrow to increase the number incrementally, while viewing the changes in the collision parameters on screen as you do so (see Figure 7.8). Find a good setting that encompasses Jazz Jackrabbit. I set mine at 45.

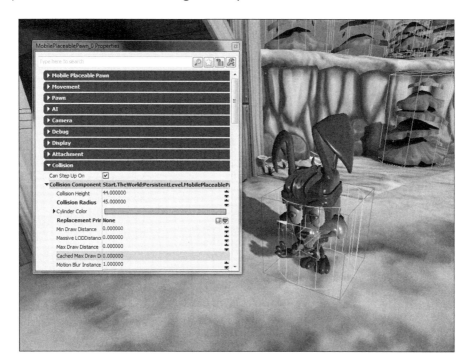

Figure 7.8
Increase the Collision Radius until it surrounds your model.
Source: Epic Games.

3. Close out of the MobilePlaceablePawn_0 Properties dialog box when you are done, and save your game project.

CAMERA PLACEMENT

You have a character placed in your virtual world but no way for the player to bear witness to it without an eye into that virtual world. This is what camera actors are for in UDK. Camera actors are actors separate from player or enemy actors. Camera actors watch the activity and report it by video display to the player.

1. Open the Content Browser and navigate to the Actor Classes tab. Make sure that Show Categories is deselected.

2. In the list, find the CameraActor object. It should be second from the top. Click and drag the CameraActor object from the list into the game world, like Figure 7.9 shows. Alternately, you can select CameraActor from the list and then right-click within the game world and choose Add CameraActor Here from the pop-up options. Either way will bring the actor into your virtual world. Close the Content Browser when you are done.

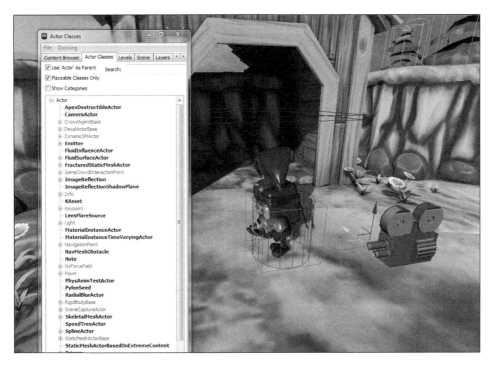

Figure 7.9
Drag a CameraActor object into your world.
Source: Epic Games.

3. Double-click the camera after it has appeared in the virtual world. This will bring up its properties dialog. Go to its Attachment properties; click the left-side arrow to expand them, if necessary. Click the lock icon in the upper right of the CameraActor's properties dialog to lock this dialog for now (so you do not inadvertently switch to another object's properties).

4. Click on the player model in the game world, and in the CameraActor's properties dialog, click the green arrow to the right of the Base input field in the Attachment properties. This will use the player model as the base for this camera. In other words, you have now linked the camera to the player's avatar. See Figure 7.10.

Figure 7.10
Use the player model as the base attachment for the camera.
Source: Epic Games.

5. Place a check beside Hard Attach and Ignore Base Rotation, because you do not want the camera to rotate with the player model. You could allow it to, but that means any time the player decides to turn left or right or spin 360 degrees, the camera would move and spin too, which would not suit this game. Hide the bounding boxes by pressing ALT/Option + C (or simply C if using an older version of UDK).

6. Right-click on the camera and select Snap View to Actor from the pop-up options list. Above the world screen, click the eyeball icon button (Lock Selected Actors to Camera) to turn on viewing for this camera. Now, you should be able to move the camera anywhere you like at a decent distance from the player model. Move the camera up in the air, off to one side or the other, and rotated so it is looking down at the player character, as shown in Figures 7.11 and 7.12. When you are satisfied, leave the camera control view by clicking the eyeball icon again.

Figure 7.11
The view the camera sees (taken while the actor is snapped to camera).

Source: Epic Games.

Figure 7.12
The view from the side, showing the angle of the camera.

Source: Epic Games.

7. In the CameraActor's properties dialog, turn off Constrain Aspect Ratio by removing the check mark next to that property (found under CameraActor). You will also want to change FOV/Angle to 65.

8. At the top menu, click the Open UnrealKismet icon button, which looks like a letter K. Wait for the UnrealKismet dialog to open.

9. Look in the gray middle panel of the UnrealKismet dialog to find the box area named Setup Camera. Right-click in an empty area inside this box and select New Event > Level Loaded from the pop-up options list. Use the mouse to zoom in, out, and pan as necessary, the same as you would within the game world. Zoom in until you can clearly read the node you just added, like in Figure 7.13.

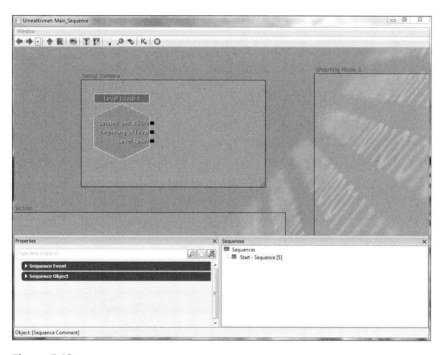

Figure 7.13
Zoom in until you can read the wording on the Level Loaded node you placed.
Source: Epic Games.

10. Beside the Level Loaded node, right-click in an empty space and select New Action > Camera > Set Camera Target from the options list. If you need to move any nodes to organize them better or make them look more like the figures given here, select the node and press and hold down CTRL while dragging them. Let go of CTRL and the mouse to stop moving a node. Click and drag a connector from the Level Loaded node's Loaded and Visible property to the Set Camera Target node's In property (click and drag from the black square to the other black square). This links the two nodes together. See Figure 7.14. Click to select the Set Camera Target node when you are through.

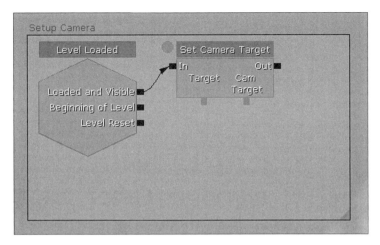

Figure 7.14
Connect two nodes by dragging a connector between properties.
Source: Epic Games.

11. Return your attention to the game world for a moment and click to select the camera you just finished setting up. Back in the UnrealKismet dialog, right-click on the pink square below the Set Camera Target node's Cam Target property and select New Object Var Using [name of camera object].

12. Hold the P key down and click in an empty space to the left of the camera object variable you just added for Cam Target. This adds an All Players object variable node to your Kismet. Click and drag a connector from the pink square below the Set Camera Target node's Target property to the All Players object variable. See Figure 7.15.

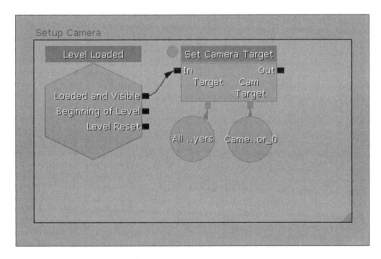

Figure 7.15
Add an All Players object variable and connect it to Set Camera Target's property.
Source: Epic Games.

13. Right-click in an empty space beside the Level Loaded node and select New Action > Toggle > Toggle Input from the options. Click and drag another connector from the Level Loaded node's Loaded and Visible property to the Toggle Input node's Turn Off property.

14. Drag a connector from the Toggle Input node's Target property to the All Players object variable you added earlier. This turns off the default player spawns and enables only the player character selected.

15. Click to select a node and, while pressing down the CTRL key, move the node so you can see each of the nodes and their connectors more easily, as in Figure 7.16. This is optional and does not change the way any of them work but makes your screen more organized and code easier to read.

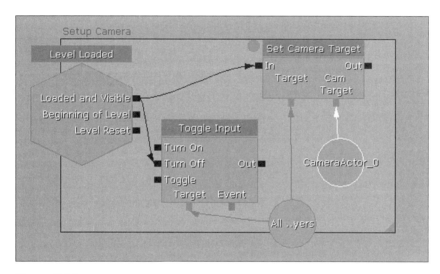

Figure 7.16
Rearrange the nodes so you can see them better.
Source: Epic Games.

16. Save your game project before continuing.

PLAYER CONTROL

With the player character set up to animate, and the camera set up to watch the player character, it is time to give the game some player controls, so the gamer has some input in the game world. You will add this via Kismet.

1. In the UnrealKismet dialog, look for the box beneath Camera Setup that says Right Stick = Rotation/Shoot Direction. These container boxes have been arranged specifically for the purposes of this tutorial. It is fine to work without them, to arrange nodes at will, but the boxes help you understand what similarly grouped nodes do at a glance.

2. Right-click in an empty area inside the Right Stick = Rotation/Shoot Direction box and select New Event > Input > Mobile Look from the pop-up options list. Mobile Look is basically a thumb-stick controller for touchscreen mobile devices. The default in UDK is to have two thumb-sticks on one touchscreen. You are going to use one thumb-stick for the character's look direction and the other for the character's movement direction.

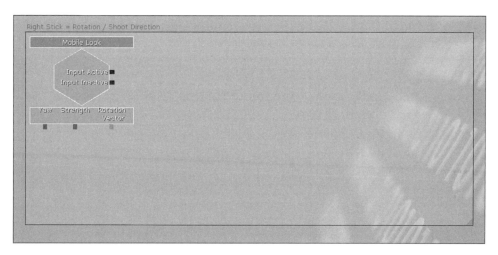

Figure 7.17
Add a Mobile Look input event.
Source: Epic Games.

3. In the Properties panel of the UnrealKismet dialog, expand the Seq Event Mobile Zone Base to find Target Zone Name. Type "UberStickLockZone" in the input field, as you can see in Figure 7.18.

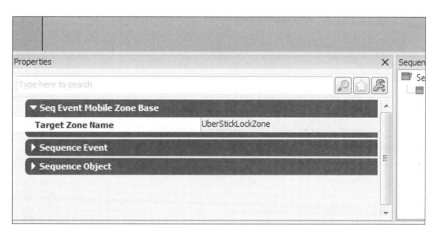

Figure 7.18
Give the Target Zone Name the name UberStickLockZone.
Source: Epic Games.

4. Go up to your Mobile Look node in the middle panel and right-click the blue square beneath its Yaw property and select Create New Float Variable. The Yaw is basically the direction the stick is pointing toward. Leave this new float variable set to zero.

Note

There are roughly three types of numbers you will use prominently throughout Kismet. Kismet refers to these three as floats, integers, and vectors. Floats are decimals. Integers are just that: hard numbers, without decimal values. Vectors are X, Y, and Z coordinates. For instance, a vector might be X = 30, Y = 205, and Z = 0. By triangulation, you could pinpoint a spot in 3D space using a vector. In Kismet, you can only connect floats to floats, integers to integers, and vectors to vectors. They are not interchangeable.

5. Right-click in an empty area of the middle panel (somewhere beside your Mobile Look node) and select New Action > Math > Set Vector Components. When Set Vector Components appears, click and drag the blue square beneath its Y property to the float variable you created coming off Yaw, so the two are connected by an arrow (see Figure 7.19).

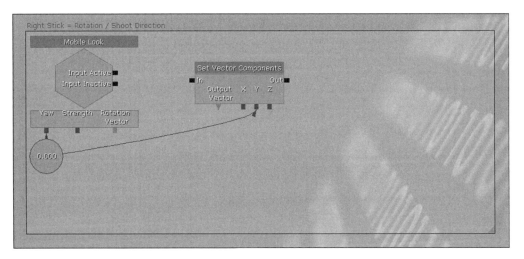

Figure 7.19
Connect the Y to the Yaw.
Source: Epic Games.

6. You can now right-click on the yellow square beneath the Set Vector Components node's Output Vector and select Create New Vector Variable from the options list.

7. Click and drag from the Mobile Look node's Input Active property's black square to the black square beside Set Vector Components node's In property. This connector sets the output vector to come from the player's right thumb-stick input.

8. Right-click in an empty area of the middle panel again and select New Action > Actor > Set Actor Location.

9. Click and drag a connector between the Set Actor Location node's Rotation property and the Output Vector's variable. Click and drag another connector between the Set Vector Components node's Out property and the Set Actor Location node's In property, so the two are linked together. Compare your screen to Figure 7.20.

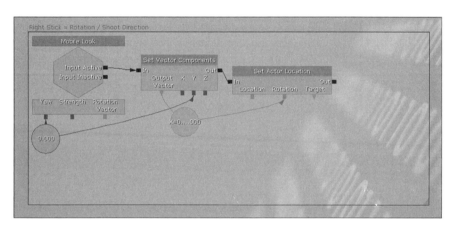

Figure 7.20
Use Set Actor Location to change the actor's Rotation based on Output Vector.
Source: Epic Games.

10. Select the Set Actor Location node and, in the Properties panel, expand the Seq Act Set Location properties and remove the check mark beside Set Location (see Figure 7.21). You only want to set rotation, not the whole location, for this actor.

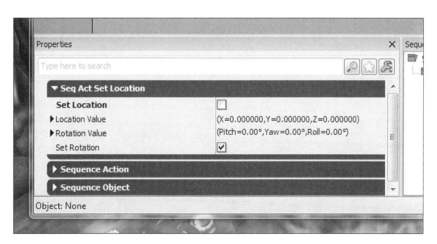

Figure 7.21
In the Set Actor Location's properties, uncheck Set Location and make sure Set Rotation is checked.
Source: Epic Games.

11. Select your player character in the game world, and then return your attention to the UnrealKismet dialog. Right-click on the pink arrow below Set Actor Location's Target property and select New Object Var Using [name of the player character model; it is the one currently selected in the scene]. An object variable representing the player model, displaying a dinosaur head, will appear. This concludes the rotation direction of the camera.

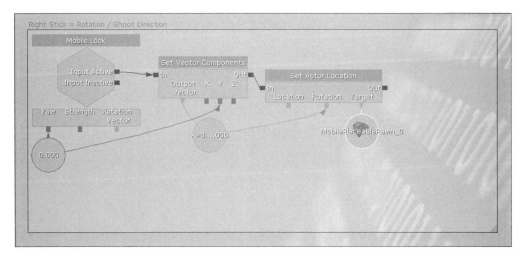

Figure 7.22
Give Set Actor Location's Target property an object variable of the player character model.
Source: Epic Games.

12. Select the Mobile Look node. Press CTRL + C to copy it and CTRL + V to paste it. Hold down the CTRL key while you drag your duplicate down to the Left Stick = Movement panel for ease of organization.

13. Right-click on your duplicate Mobile Look node and select Break All Links to Obect(s) from the pop-up options. This will remove the connections to the earlier nodes.

14. In the Properties panel, select Seq Event Mobile Zone Base and change the Target Zone Name for this node to UberStickMoveZone instead of UberStickLookZone, as this node will be used for movement.

15. In the middle panel, you should right-click on the blue square below your new Mobile Look node's Strength property and select Create New Float Variable from the pop-up options. Strength handles how far away from the center of the thumbstick the player's thumb has moved, and how fast, so Strength will handle both our player character's speed and movement direction.

16. Right-click on the Rotation Vector property's yellow square and select Create New Vector Variable from the options list. Compare your work to Figure 7.23.

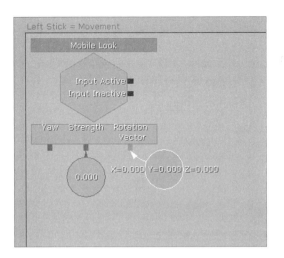

Figure 7.23
Add a float variable to Strength and a vector variable to Rotation Vector.
Source: Epic Games.

17. Right-click an empty area beside the Mobile Look node and select New Action > Math > Multiply Float from the options list. Click and drag a connector between the Multiply Float node's A property to the Strength's float variable you created earlier. Right-click on the Multiply Float node's B property and select Create New Float Variable from the options list. Do the same for the Float Result property.

18. Drag a connector from the Mobile Look node's Input Active property and the Multiply Float node's In property, so the two are linked. Compare your work to Figure 7.24.

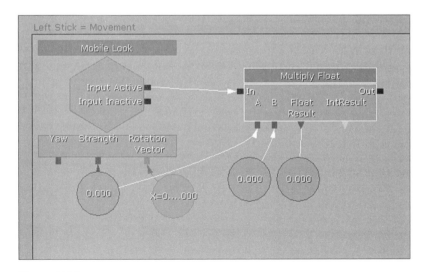

Figure 7.24
Add a Multiply Float action node like so.
Source: Epic Games.

19. Select the float variable for Multiply Float node's B property. In the Properties panel, expand Seq Var Float and set the Float Value to 3.0 in the input field. See Figure 7.25. You are using this variable as a separate, non-static variable, so if you wanted to program the character to move faster or slower, all you have to do is return to UnrealKismet and edit this variable.

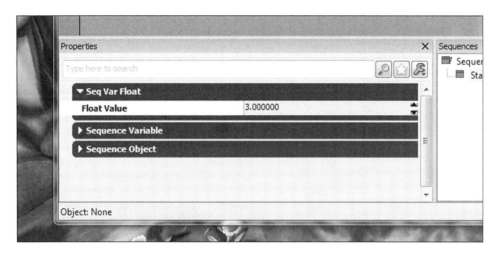

Figure 7.25
Edit the Float Value for Multiply Float's B float variable.
Source: Epic Games.

20. Right-click in an empty area beside your other nodes and select New Action > Actor > Set Velocity from the options list.

21. Drag a connector from the Multiply Float node's Out property to the Set Velocity node's In property.

22. Drag another connector from the Set Velocity node's Target property to the Target property of your other thumbstick's nodes, which is the player character model. You can identify that node pretty easily, because it looks like a dinosaur head. See Figure 7.26.

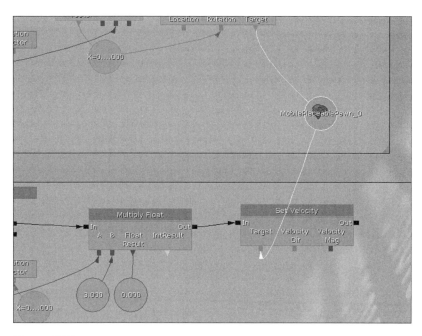

Figure 7.26
Connect the Set Velocity's Target property to the player model object variable of the Set Actor Location's Target property from earlier.
Source: Epic Games.

23. Drag a connector from the Set Velocity node's Velocity Dir(ection) to the Mobile Look node's Rotation Vector property's float variable you created earlier.

24. Drag a connector from the Set Velocity node's Velocity Mag(nitude) to the Multiply Float node's Float Result's float variable you created earlier (see Figure 7.27). This orchestrates the speed at which the player character actually moves, based on the player's thumb input multiplied by 3.0.

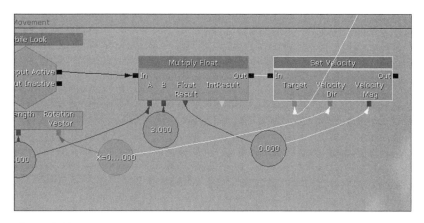

Figure 7.27
Finish placing the connectors for the Set Velocity node.
Source: Epic Games.

25. You have set up everything needed for the player character to move in a certain direction based on player input (which is what the Input Active property entails), but what about when the player stops the input or lets off the touchscreen with his thumb? You want the player character to slow down and finally stop, so he is not moving any longer. Input Active is a continuous stream of data sent while the player has his thumb on the touchscreen, but the Input Inactive is a one-time trigger, so you need to set up a logic loop that tells the program to slow down the velocity until it reaches zero. To do so, start by right-clicking in an empty space below your other nodes and select New Condition > Comparison > Compare Float from the options.

26. Drag a connector from the Mobile Look node's Input Inactive property to the Compare Float node's In property, to link the two.

27. Drag a connector from the Compare Float node's A property (at the bottom of the node) to the Multiply Float node's Float Result property's float variable. Then, right-click on the Compare Float node's B property and select Create New Float Variable from the options. Leave this new variable set to zero. Compare your work to Figure 7.28.

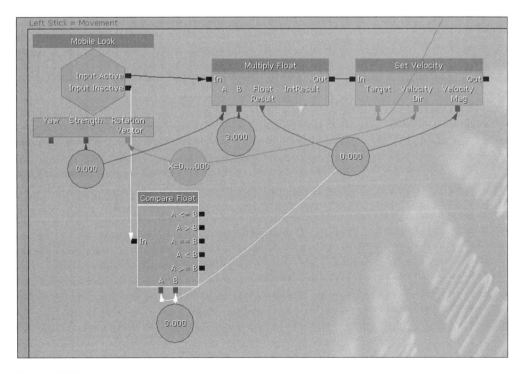

Figure 7.28
Your Compare Float should look like so.
Source: Epic Games.

28. Right-click in an empty space beside the Compare Float node and select New Action > Math > Subtract Float from the options. Drag a connector from the Subtract Float node's A property to the Multiply Float node's Float Result property's float variable.

29. Right-click on the Subtract Float node's B property and select Create New Float Variable. In the Properties panel, expand (if necessary) Seq Var Float. Set the Float Value to 20.0.

30. Drag a connector from the Subtract Float node's Float Result property to the Multiply Float node's Float Result property's float variable.

31. Drag a connector from the Compare Float node's A > B property to the Subtract Float node's In property. Compare your work to Figure 7.29. This tells the program that, if variable A (the movement strength) is greater than variable B (zero), continue to subtract 20 from A.

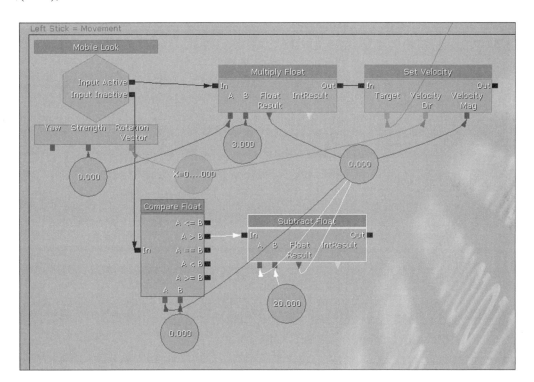

Figure 7.29
Your Subtract Float should look like so.
Source: Epic Games.

32. You also want to set the velocity within this loop. Select the Set Velocity node from earlier and press CTRL + C to copy and CTRL + V to paste. You do not want to break the connections to this new node; you will want to leave it the

same. Drag this duplicate node down beside your Subtract Float node. Drag a connector from the Subtract Float node's Out property to the In property of this duplicate Set Velocity.

33. Right-click on the duplicate Set Velocity's Out property and choose Set Active Delay from the options. Set the Delay variable to .01. Drag a connector from this Out property to the In property of the loop's Compare Float node. See Figure 7.30. This closes the loop, so that the variable comparison between A and B will continue until the player character's movement comes to a complete stop.

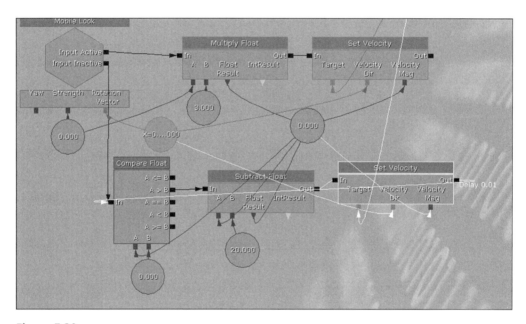

Figure 7.30
Close the loop after the Set Velocity action.
Source: Epic Games.

34. You do not want the number for the A variable to go below zero, so you will need to add another node that stops it before it does. Right-click in an empty space below your other nodes and select New Action > Set Variable > Float from the options.

35. Drag a connector from the Compare Float node's A < B property to the Float node's In property. Right-click the Float node's Value property and select Create New Float Variable. Leave this new float variable set to zero.

36. Drag a connector from the Float node's Out property to the second Set Velocity's In property, and drag another connector from the Float node's Target

property to the Multiply Float node's Float Result property's float variable. This will conclude the movement controls.

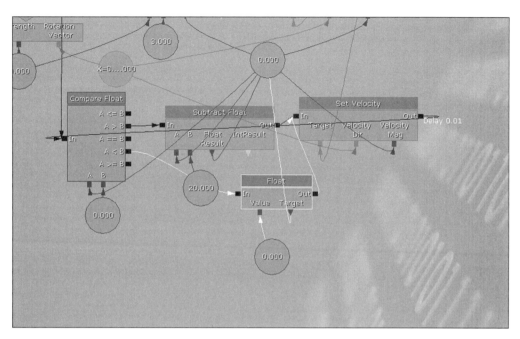

Figure 7.31
Add a Float action that sets the float to zero if Compare Float's A ever drops less than B.
Source: Epic Games.

37. Close the UnrealKismet dialog for now, and save your game project.

PLAYER WEAPON

The player can see that he has a player character set in the game world, and he can move that character around inside the game world. The last bit of interaction you will add will be to give the player character a gun, so he can shoot at obstacles.

1. Select your player model in the current scene. Zoom in and pan around to see the front of the player model. His hands are open, as if he would be holding a rifle, as you can see in Figure 7.32. However, a rifle is not apparent. To give him one, go to the Content Browser and search for SK_JazzGun. When you find it, drag this skeletal mesh into the scene. Do not close the Content Browser yet.

Figure 7.32
The character is ready for but missing a weapon.

Source: Epic Games.

Figure 7.33
Drag the SK_JazzGun into your game world.

Source: Epic Games.

2. Go up to the main menu and select View > Enable Socket Snapping. You should see what looks like little red or pink diamonds appear in both Jazz's hands and in the muzzle of his gun. These are sockets created by the model artist for these items.

3. Click to select the socket within the player character model's right hand, in the crux between his thumb and forefinger. A dialog might appear, asking you which weapon socket you wish to use for the hand socket you just clicked on; if so, choose Weapon_R (see Figure 7.34). His gun should automatically jump into Jazz's hands. Now he has his weapon.

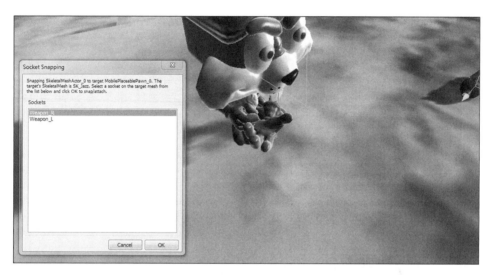

Figure 7.34
Give Jazz his gun by snapping sockets together.
Source: Epic Games.

4. To make his weapon shoot, you will have to go back to Kismet. Click the Open UnrealKismet icon button in the menu bar at the top and wait for the UnrealKismet dialog to open. In the middle panel, find the Shooting Mode 1 box area that has been added. This is somewhere you can place your shooting logic nodes.

5. Right-click in an empty space and select New Action > Actor > Projectile Factory from the options list. In the Properties panel, go to and expand Seq Act Actor Factory to find Factory and click the blue arrow out beside it. Select ActorFactoryArchetype from the options list.

6. Without closing the UnrealKismet dialog, return to the Content Browser and search within for the package KismetGame_Assets > Projectile. Clear any previous filtering you may have set. Search for and click to select the Blaster_01 archetype.

7. Go back to the UnrealKismet dialog and, in the Properties panel, go to and expand Factory until you see the Archetype Actor you just added. Type "Blaster_01" into the name field and press Enter. The name field should change to show the full directory path of your Blaster_01 archetype, as shown in Figure 7.35. Blaster_01 has now been bound to the Projectile Factory.

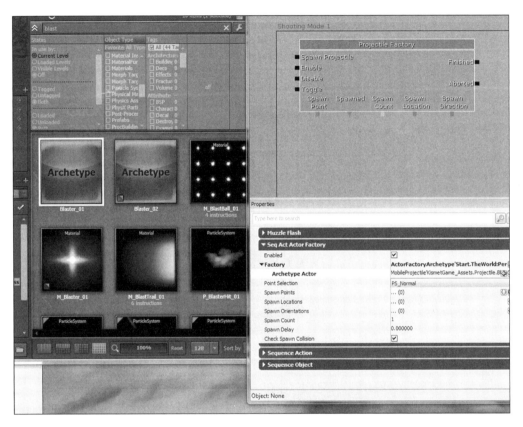

Figure 7.35
Bind the Blaster_01 archetype to the Archetype Actor of the Projectile Factory.
Source: Epic Games.

8. Now add a muzzle flash. Scroll up the Properties panel to Muzzle Flash and expand it. In the Content Browser, find and select the P_BlasterMuzzle_02 ParticleSystem. Back in the Properties panel of UnrealKismet, you could click the green arrow beside Muzzle Flash > PSTemplate to bind the ParticleSystem to the gun's muzzle flash, or you could type the name for the ParticleSystem file (P_BlasterMuzzle_02) in the input field and press the Enter key; as long as the file of that same name is found somewhere within your available assets, it will detect and load the file directory name and bind it for you. See Figure 7.36.

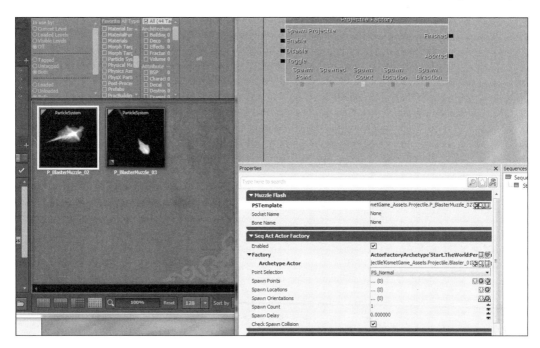

Figure 7.36
Bind the P_BlasterMuzzle_02 particle system to the Muzzle Flash > PSTemplate of the Projectile
Factory.
Source: Epic Games.

9. The Socket Name refers to the socket on the gun from where you want the
   muzzle flash to spawn. There is already a socket on Jazz's gun, and that socket is
   named Muzzle. So in the Socket Name input field, type "Muzzle."

10. Close the Content Browser and revisit your scene. Select the gun in the game
    world, and then, within the middle pane of the UnrealKismet dialog, right-click
    on the Projectile Factory node's Spawn Point property and select New Object
    Var Using [object's name]. This locks the place where shots are fired from the
    gun to the gun itself.

11. Now you need to set up a way to launch this Projectile Factory. You will want
    to use the Mobile Look from the right thumbstick. It is a continuous stream of
    data, however, so you will want to limit how often the player character shoots.
    Below the Projectile Factory node, right-click in an empty space and select New
    Action > Switch > Switch.

12. In the Properties panel, go to Seq Act Switch and set Link Count to 2. Drag a
    connector from the right stick's Mobile Look node's Input Active property to
    the new Switch node's In property. Compare your work to Figure 7.37.

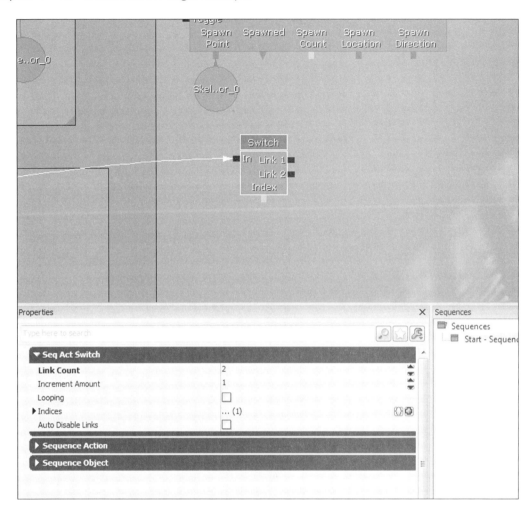

Figure 7.37
Add a Switch with two links and an In property rising from the first Mobile Look's Input Active property.
Source: Epic Games.

13. Drag a connector from the Switch node's Link 1 property to the Projectile Factory node's Spawn Projectile property. Right-click on the Switch node's Index property and select Create New Int Variable from the options list. This adds an integer variable to Index.

14. Right-click in an empty space beside the Switch node and select New Action > Set Variable > Int from the options. Drag a connector from the Target property of the new Int node to the integer variable under the Switch node's Index property. Drag another connector from the Link 1 property to the Int node's In property.

15. Right-click on the Value property of the Int node and select Create New Int Variable. With this new variable selected, expand Seq Var Int in the Properties panel and set Int Value to 2. Compare your work to Figure 7.38.

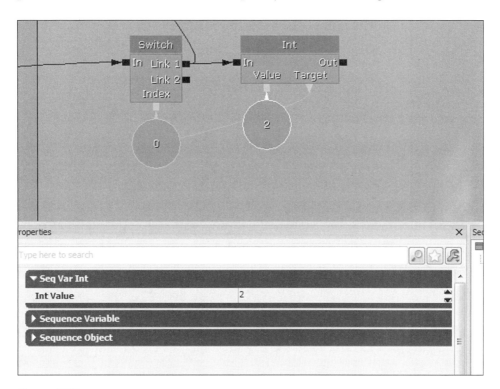

Figure 7.38
Add connectors to your Switch and Int nodes as you see here.
Source: Epic Games.

16. Right-click in an empty space beside the Int node and select New Action > Misc > Delay from the options. Drag a connector from the Int node's Out property to the Delay node's Start property.

17. Right-click on the Duration property of the Delay node and select Create New Float Variable from the list. With this new float variable selected, expand (if necessary) Seq Var Float in the Properties panel and set Float Value to 0.2.

18. Select the Int node and press CTRL + C to copy it and CTRL + V to paste it. Move the copy to the right of the Delay node. Right-click on the Out property of this duplicate Int node and select Break Link To > Delay (Start) from the options. Drag a new connector from the Delay node's Finished property to the duplicate Int node's In property.

19. Right-click the connector below the Int node's Value property and select Break Link To > Switch (Index). Right-click on Value's square again, and this time select the option Create New Int Variable. In the Properties panel, go to Seq Var Int and set it to 1. See Figure 7.39.

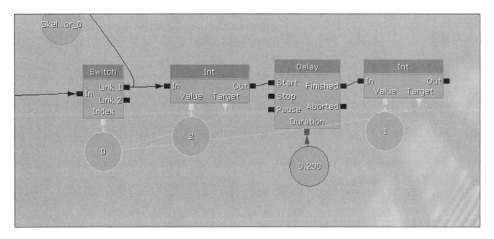

Figure 7.39
Close up your connectors between the Switch, Int, Delay, and other Int.
Source: Epic Games.

20. This concludes the shooting logic. Basically, every 0.2 seconds, the gun will fire a shot accompanied by a muzzle flash. Close UnrealKismet and save your game project.

PREVIEW

You are done with the initial setup of your action game for an iPad. Now all you have to do is preview your game. To do so, run your play test on mobile preview. You can do this by clicking the Play in Viewport icon button (the blue play arrow; hotkey is ALT + F8) or the Play in Editor Window icon button (the green play arrow; hotkey is F8), either of which can be found in the menu bars at the top of your screen. The former will run a game preview in the main editor panel, while the latter will open a separate window for play testing.

You will see left and right thumbsticks appear faintly on the preview windows, as in Figure 7.40. You can use your mouse to drive the left or right thumbstick and see what each does. Unfortunately, this preview does not accurately mimic mobile device usage, in that you cannot click and drag both thumbsticks at once, as you could if you were using your mobile.

Figure 7.40
Play test your game project.
Source: Epic Games.

The easiest way to mimic mobile device usage, then, is to use the UDK Remote, which is a free app in the App Store. UDK Remote lets you use your iOS device as a remote controller for UDK mobile game projects. These two work great together and allow you to iterate your game quickly.

1. Using the App Store on your iOS device, search for UDK Remote and click the Install button. Alternately, you could go to the following web address to install the app through iTunes (in other words, install this app just like you would any other app!): https://itunes.apple.com/us/app/udk-remote/id398375618?mt=8.

2. UDK Remote uses networking to communicate with the PC on which you have UDK installed, so you may need to set up the WiFi on your iOS device to be the same network as your PC.

3. After installing UDK Remote, run it. When you first open the app, it will take you to a Settings screen. Otherwise, simply click the *i* button to go into Settings (shown in Figure 7.41). Click the first line to enter the name (for instance, MyComputer) or IP address (such as 183.112.1.24) of your PC. If you do not know this information, contact whoever set up your computer or network to

help you. Here's a hint: If using a Windows OS, go to Start and right-click on My Computer or Computer and select Properties from the options. A system control panel that displays your computer's name will appear.

Figure 7.41
UDK Remote's Settings.
Source: Epic Games.

4. If you entered a network name and not an IP address, UDK Remote will attempt to resolve the name into an IP address, and it will display the results at the bottom left. If it was unable to find the network name, it will tell you, "Unable to send data…" At this point, you will need to go back into Settings and add a new computer name or IP address. You can use Edit to remove old or wrong computers from the list and click the plus sign (+) button to add new computers to the list.

5. If you entered an IP address, the app will not attempt to resolve the address to make sure it connects. UDK Remote uses a connectionless model, and there is currently no indication UDK Remote is able to send data to a PC when using the IP address alone. If you have the IP address, therefore, it is recommended you use it in the UDK Remote's Settings, as setup is faster.

6. For multi-touch and tilt information to be usable on the PC, you should run your UDK game in Mobile Previewer mode. To do so, click the Mobile Previewer button located in the menu bar at the top of your UDK Editor screen, as you can see in Figure 7.42.

Figure 7.42
The Mobile Previewer button.
Source: Epic Games.

7. Once you are on the main screen and have a valid address set up, and your PC is running in Mobile Emulation mode, simply touch and tilt the device to send the data to the PC. The game should respond to the touch and tilt just as if it were running on an iOS device, depending on how you set your game up to use touch and tilt, of course.

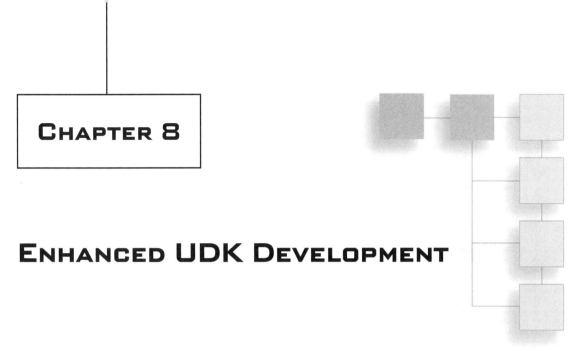

CHAPTER 8

ENHANCED UDK DEVELOPMENT

You have learned the basics of making an iPad action game in UDK, using a template to start from. This chapter seeks to enlighten you as to how you can do different, more advanced things within an action game, including general themes from the video game genre, such as monsters to fight and pickup items that help you score points or regain health.

SPAWN ENEMY BOTS

Perhaps one of the more prevalent aspects of action games, especially shooters, is the existence of enemies that try to harm the player character. Without enemies to avoid and/or vanquish, an action game may seem to be missing something. Here is one method, using Kismet's drag-and-drop interface, which you can use to add enemy bots to your game.

1. Open the UDK Editor. Start from an existing map. Open SimpleCourtyard.udk. As the title suggests, it contains a single medieval courtyard with nothing else in it. Save it as SpawnEnemyTest.udk in the same folder. If you were to play this level as it stands, you would see that the left mobile thumbstick controls player movement and the right mobile thumbstick controls the look up/down action. The game is in first-person camera mode.

2. There are some path nodes in this level. You will want to remove them in order to add your own. A path node is a point in a network of lines that will determine where AI (a computer-controlled bot) can and will travel. Essentially, the bot will search for the nearest path node and proceed to its location and

then go to the next closest one, and so on. Path nodes appear as apples in the editor. Select one of the apples you see in the level and right-click on it. Go to Select > Select All Pathnode Actors. UDK Editor will select all four existing path nodes for you. See Figure 8.1. Press the Delete key to remove them.

Figure 8.1
Select the path nodes that are already in your level.
Source: Epic Games.

3. Now add your own path nodes. Open the Content Browser and go to the Actor Classes tab. You find the path node under Navigation > Pathnode (if you have Show Categories checked). See Figure 8.2.

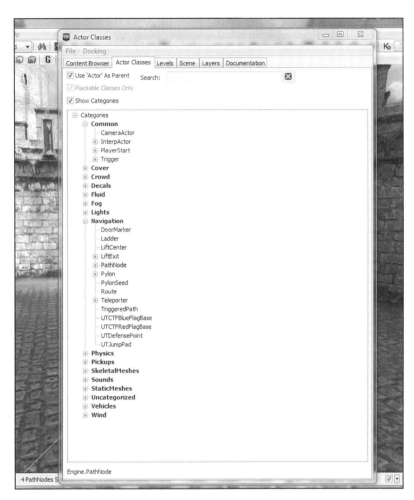

Figure 8.2
Create path nodes to replace the ones you deleted.
Source: Epic Games.

4. You can right-click in your viewport and select Add Actor > Add Pathnode, or you can drag and drop each path node from the Actor Classes tab into the current level. Place six path nodes along the inside wall of your courtyard. Position the path nodes so you have them equally dispersed throughout the area you want the bot to navigate. Compare your work to Figure 8.3, which shows you the courtyard from a top-down angle. You only really need one path node, the one used for spawning, but the more the merrier, as they can help direct the bot's patrol patterns.

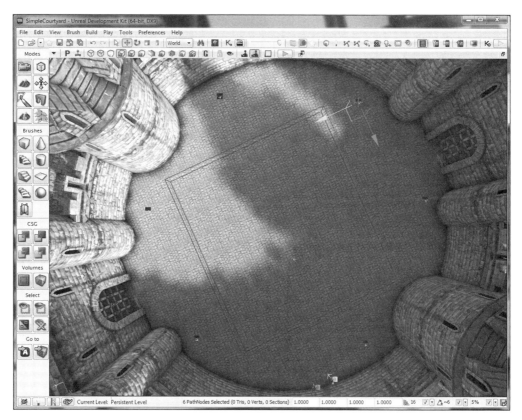

Figure 8.3

Disperse your path nodes around the inner wall of your courtyard.

Source: Epic Games.

5. Remember to click the Build Paths button in your level (shown in Figure 8.4) before continuing.

Figure 8.4

Use the Build Paths button to rebuild your paths.

Source: Epic Games.

6. Next, select the path node that you want the bot to spawn from initially in the level. Open Kismet with this path node selected.

7. Right-click in an empty space (you do not have an organization box pending for this function, so use any empty space) and select New Event > Level Loaded.

8. Beside the Level Loaded node, right-click and select New Action > Actor > Actor Factory.

9. As you can see in Figure 8.5, drag a connector between the Level Loaded node's Loaded and Visible property to the Spawn Actor property of your new Actor Factory node.

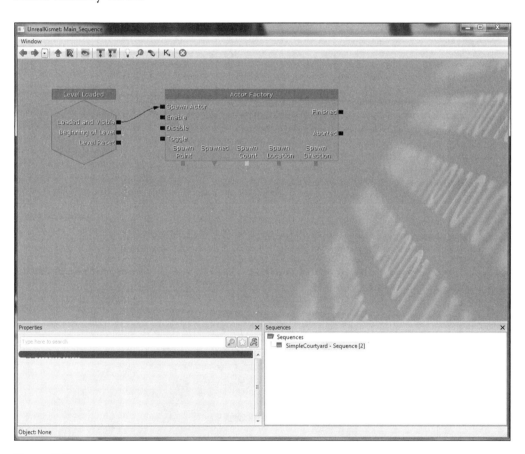

Figure 8.5
Connect the Actor Factory to Level Loaded.
Source: Epic Games.

10. Right-click on the Spawn Point of the Actor Factory node and select New Obj Variable Using [path node's name] to assign the path node you have selected in the viewport to that property.

11. In the UDK Editor, go to View > World Properties from the main menu.

12. Expand Game Type. Set both Default Game Type and Game Type for PIE to UTDeathmatch, as you can see in Figure 8.6.

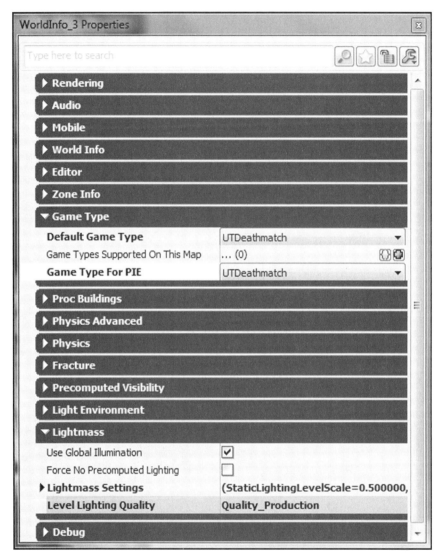

Figure 8.6
Set your game type to UTDeathmatch.
Source: Epic Games.

13. Select the Actor Factory node. In the Properties panel, expand Seq Act Actor Factory. Click on the blue arrow beside the input field for Factory and select

UTActorFactoryAI. Once added, expand to see all the properties of UTActorFactoryAI.

14. Check the box next to Force Deathmatch AI.

15. Leave Controller Class set to None. Set Pawn Class to UTPawn. Give this pawn the Pawn Name of Enemy. This defines what team the enemy spawned is on, and it will display as the bot's name in game.

16. Check the box next to Give Default Inventory. Click the green plus sign button beside the Inventory List to add a new inventory item, and use the drop-down beside this new inventory item ([0]) and assign the bot a weapon. For this example, give the enemy a UTWeap_ShockRifle.

17. Scroll down to Spawn Count. Set Spawn Count to 8. Over the course of a single game, eight enemies will spawn. The Spawn Delay is how long of a delay there will be between each enemy spawning. Set this value to 12.5 (seconds). Compare your screen to Figure 8.7.

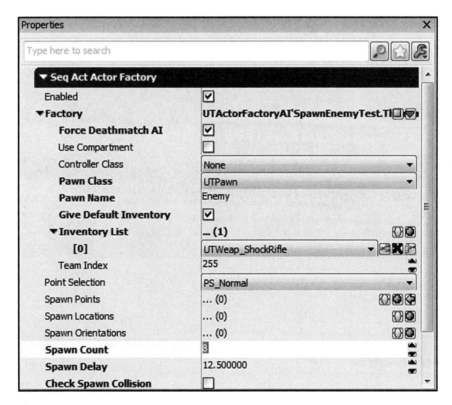

Figure 8.7
Edit the Actor Factory's properties like so.
Source: Epic Games.

18. You may want to reposition the player start position (the actor known as PlayerStart). I prefer to set the player as far away from the enemy spawn point as possible, to give the player more time to defend himself. This is merely a preference during testing. Normally the enemy spawn points will be scattered throughout a game level, in convenient nooks and crannies that are out of the way of prying eyes.

19. Save your level. Play test it to see if everything works correctly. You may avoid the enemy shooting at you long enough to see multiple enemies spawn, and watch how they will actually stop to attack each other before the victor returns his attention to you. Shoot them to destroy them. Watch the onscreen heads-up displays (HUDs) to gauge your ammo and health, as well as to see the position of the enemies on your radar. See Figure 8.8.

Figure 8.8
Preview the play of your game.
Source: Epic Games.

ADD PICKUP ITEMS

Perhaps the next most common item to the action genre of video games is the pickup item, which is any object the player can pick up during play that gives that player some kind of benefit. Typical pickup items include health, ammunition, weapons, armor, and so on. This lesson will show you how to add pickup items to your game using Kismet.

1. Open the UDK Editor. Open SimpleCourtyard.udk. Save it as PickupItemTest.udk in the same folder.

2. Open the Content Browser. Click to select the UDKGame package on the left. In the Tags section at the top, select Deco. In the package that appears, find and select a mesh. You may want to use a custom mesh object you created in your third-party 3D modeling program, but for the purposes of this lesson, I will choose one of the standard-issue meshes. To be clear, I picked S_LT_Mech_SM_Techcylinder01 from the package list (as shown in Figure 8.9). Once you find your mesh, click to select it.

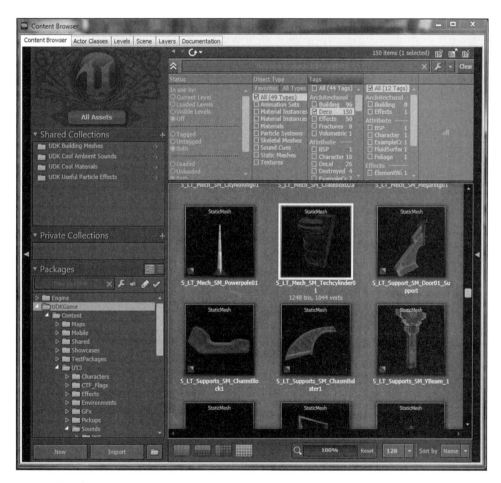

Figure 8.9
Find and select a suitable mesh.
Source: Epic Games.

3. In the perspective viewport, right-click in an out-of-the-way spot on the floor of your courtyard and select from the options Add InterpActor: [name of your mesh], like in Figure 8.10. An InterpActor (interpolating actor) is a special version of a static mesh that supports a variety of physics and dynamic lighting, and can be controlled in a variety of ways within Unreal Kismet and Matinee.

Figure 8.10
Add an InterpActor based on your chosen mesh.
Source: Epic Games.

4. Press F4 to open the InterpActor's properties. Go to Collision and select COLLIDE_TouchAllButWeapons from the drop-down list (see Figure 8.11). You could use COLLIDE_TouchAll, but if you do and your player accidentally shoots the pickup item, it will respond as if the player had walked upon the pickup item, and you do not want that.

Figure 8.11
Set your InterpActor's collision accordingly.
Source: Epic Games.

5. Close the InterpActor's properties dialog and open Kismet.

6. Find an empty space in the middle panel and right-click. Select New Event Using [InterpActor name] > Touch from the pop-up options listed. Now you have the default setup for any pickup item you can think of. You can run all sorts of actions off the Touch property of this action, from entering/exiting vehicles, teleporting to distance locations, hurting the player (which might be useful for lava flows or electric fences), giving infinite ammo, and much more.

7. Right-click in an empty space beside the Touch node you just added. Select New Action > Actor > Modify Health from the options (see Figure 8.12).

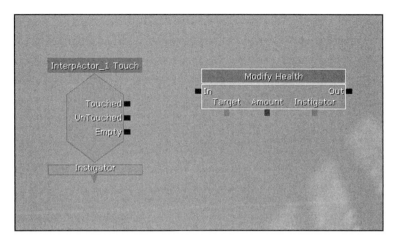

Figure 8.12
Add a Modify Health node.
Source: Epic Games.

8. Drag a connector from the Touch property of the Touch node to the In property of the Modify Health node to bind the two.

9. Beneath the Modify Health node, press and hold down the P key while clicking to create a Player object variable. By default, UDK sets this to All Players. You do not want it to modify all the players in your game. So, with the new object variable selected in Kismet, go to the Properties panel and expand Seq Var Player (if needed). Uncheck All Players so that the only player controlled by this object variable is Player 0.

10. Drag a connector from the Target property of the Modify Health node to this new object variable, as you can see in Figure 8.13.

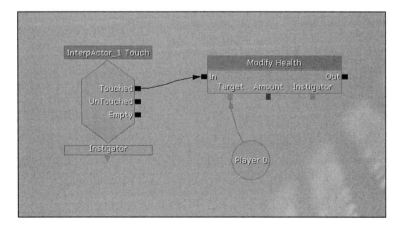

Figure 8.13
Add the player as the Modify Health's target.
Source: Epic Games.

11. Select the Modify Health node and look within the Properties panel. Under Seq Act Modify Health, you will see all the major properties governed by this node.

12. The drop-down list beside Damage Type can demonstrate what sorts of damages this item could do the player, if you wanted it to be a dangerous object. As this will be a health pickup item, you do not want this item to be dangerous, so leave Damage Type set to None.

13. Check the Heal option and give it the Amount of 50. See Figure 8.14.

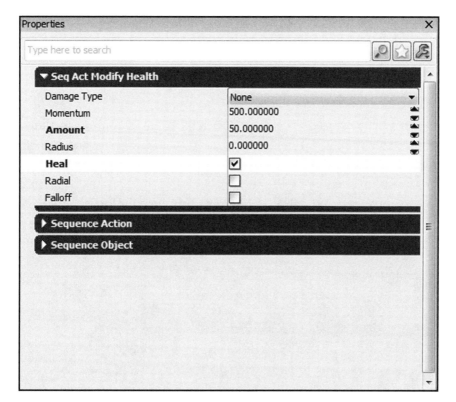

Figure 8.14
Set your Modify Health to heal the player 50 points.
Source: Epic Games.

14. Now, you want to remove the pickup item after the player has picked it up. This is not always necessary. It depends on the type of pickup item. You might want a health pad that consistently restores player health on touch, or opposite that, a dangerous object that remains to cause the player more damage no matter how many times they touch it. But for this item, which restores the player's health by 50, you want to remove the item after the player has used it.

Right-click an empty area to the right of the Modify Health node and select New Action > Actor > Destroy.

15. Select the InterpActor in the perspective viewport, if you do not already have it selected. Back in Kismet, right-click on the Destroy node's Target property and select New Obj Var Using [InterpActor name].

16. Drag a connector from the Out property of Modify Health to the In property of the Destroy node.

17. In the UDK Editor, go to View > World Properties from the main menu. Then Expand Game Type. Set both Default Game Type and Game Type for PIE to UTDeathmatch. This adds the heads-up displays (HUDs), so you can preview the changes to player health.

18. Save your level and run it to see what happens.

19. It is nearly impossible to see what adding 50 health points would do in the preview, because your maximum health is set to 100, and there is not a present danger to lower the player's health. So exit the play test and, in Kismet, select the Modify Health node, and go to its Properties. Uncheck the box next to Heal and then play your game again. This time, when you run over the pickup item, you should see your health go down 50 (see Figure 8.15). This just verifies that your pickup item is working correctly. You can set it back to Heal when you are satisfied.

Figure 8.15
Note that your player's HUD shows the health go down when Heal is unchecked.
Source: Epic Games.

ADD REACTIVE OBJECTS

Many games, including the popular *Penumbra* series and *Amnesia: Dark Descent*, allow the player to knock over and move objects based on their actions in game. You, too, can add reactive objects to your level.

1. Open the UDK Editor. Continue with or reopen PickupItemTest.udk. Save it as RigidBodyTest.udk in the same folder. You could combine all of these short test examples in one map, if that is your wish, but it might be easier to manage if you separate them for now.

2. Open the Content Browser. Select the UDKGame package and Decos from the Tags panel to show just Decos group items found in the UDKGame package. Search for RemadePhysBarrel, which looks like a rusty oil barrel (see Figure 8.16). Click to select it.

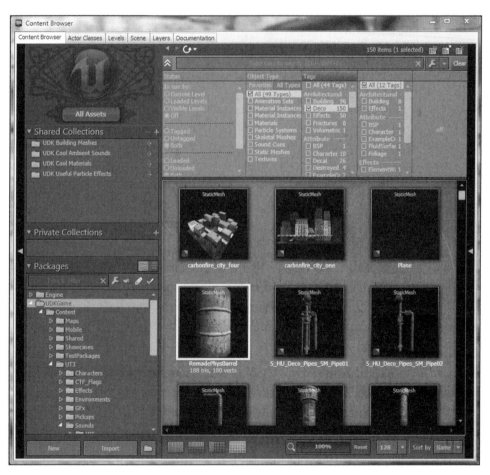

Figure 8.16

Find the RemadePhysBarrel object you want to add to your scene.

Source: Epic Games.

3. In your viewport window, find a nice area off to itself and away from your other work, perhaps next to the courtyard wall. Right-click and choose Add RigidBody: [name of your selected mesh].

4. If you open the KActor's properties (by pressing F4), you will see that under KActor, you can limit the velocity by which this item will move upon impact. You would lower the velocity and even limit this velocity for heavier objects, such as giant steel crates, or raise the velocity and not limit it for lightweight objects. For now, leave these at default. Go to the KActor's Collision and set Collision Type to COLLISION_BlockAll.

5. Save your level and play it. Now, you should be able to walk up to and shoot the barrel to make it fall over. You can also roll it along the ground, as you can see in Figure 8.17. Do this with other items to make your game world more convincing.

Figure 8.17
You have added an object that can react to the player.
Source: Epic Games.

Open Doors and Gates

So many games have doors and gates that react to the player character (opening and/ or closing for him). To recreate this operation in UDK, follow this lesson.

1. Open the UDK Editor. Continue with or reopen RigidBodyTest.udk. Save it as OpenGates.udk in the same folder.

2. You should navigate your camera in the perspective viewport to focus on the center of the courtyard.

3. Next, you will start by adding a door and a doorframe to your level. For this example, you should select the UDKGame package and type "door" into the search field at the top of the Content Browser. All available doors will appear in the list below. Find S_LT_Doors_SM_Door04 and S_LT_Doors_SM_DoorWay04. These two go together. See Figure 8.18.

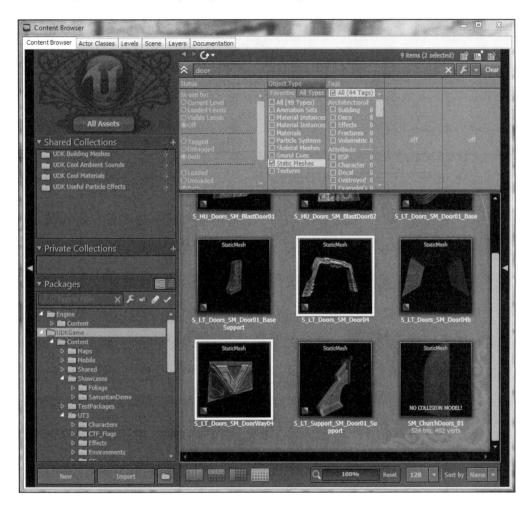

Figure 8.18
Select your door and doorframe static meshes.
Source: Epic Games.

4. Drag and drop the door and doorframe into your scene. Position them to fit one within the other, as in Figure 8.19.

Figure 8.19
Place the door and doorframe within your level.
Source: Epic Games.

5. Right-click on the S_LT_Doors_SM_DoorWay04 static mesh and select Convert > Convert Static Mesh to Mover from the options. This should turn your door from green, the static mesh color, to pink, the InterpActor color, in your viewports.

6. With your mover door still selected, press F4 to enter its properties. Go to Collision and change No Collision to Block All. See Figure 8.20.

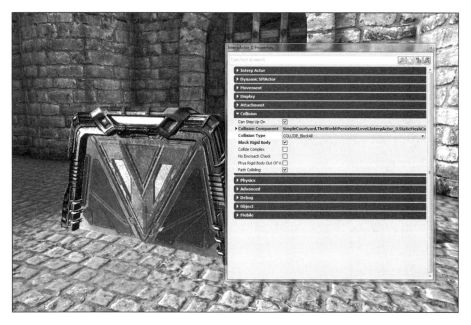

Figure 8.20
Use a Block All collision on the InterpActor door.
Source: Epic Games.

7. You will also need to place a trigger volume around the door. To do this, place the red builder brush so that it is large enough to encompass the door. Then, click the Add Volume button in the toolbar and select Trigger Volume from the options. Select the green wireframe volume and reposition as needed. Again, it just needs to be large enough to surround the door, like in Figure 8.21.

Figure 8.21
Add your trigger volume to your door.
Source: Epic Games.

8. With the green wireframe trigger volume selected, open Kismet and, in the middle panel, find a blank area to right-click in and select New Event Using [trigger volume name] > Touch.

9. Return to the viewport and click to select the door. Go back to Kismet. Right-click inside the middle panel, beside your last node, and choose New Matinee. Matinee is a tool used in UDK for keyframing the properties of actors in your scene over time, including their positions. You can even use Matinee to make cinematic sequences within your level.

10. Double-click the Matinee node in Kismet to open the Matinee Editor.

11. Right-click in the dark gray area to the left of Matinee and select Add New Empty Group (see Figure 8.22). You can name this group whatever. For this example, I named mine Door. Make sure your group is a green color and that when you select and deselect the group it selects and deselects your door in the level. If it does not, redo the previous steps until it works.

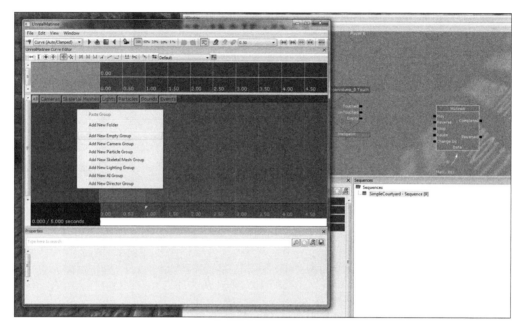

Figure 8.22
Select Add New Empty Group to your Matinee.
Source: Epic Games.

12. Right-click on the door group and select the option Add New Movement Track.

13. Use your scroll bar along the bottom of the Matinee Editor window to move the time slider (or loop end marker, as Matinee calls it) to 2 seconds (or however long you want your Matinee sequence to be). You can also use the toggle snap button, which looks like a red magnet icon, at the top of the Matinee window.

14. There is a scrollbar at the bottom of the time slider to help you move back and forth along the timeline. Click and drag the ending red triangle to match the ending green triangle at the 2-second marker. This sets the end of the sequence at the end of the movement action. See Figure 8.23.

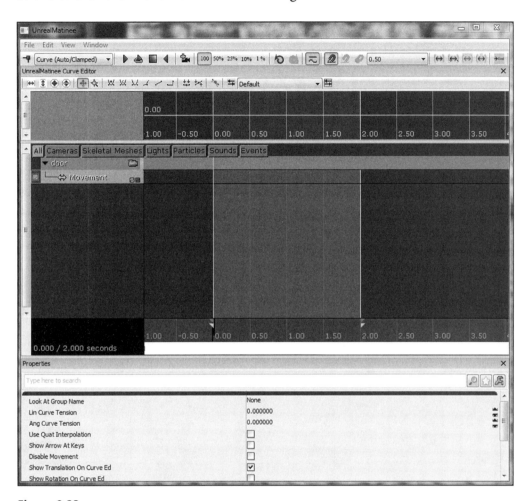

Figure 8.23

Change your Matinee sequence to be 2 seconds long.

Source: Epic Games.

15. Your current key is the first in the timeline. Go ahead and press the Enter or Return key or click the Add Key icon button (top left of the Matinee window) to add a key to your movement track. See Figure 8.24.

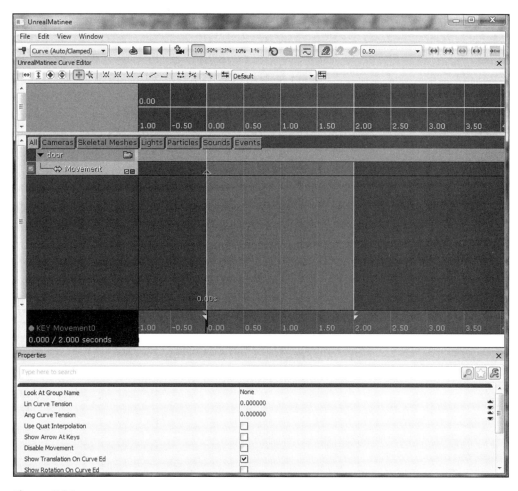

Figure 8.24
Add a keyframe to the start of the movement track.
Source: Epic Games.

16. Click in the gray area at the 2-second marker. The horizontal black bar, which shows you the current key position, should move there. After it does, press Enter/Return or click Add Key to add another key here. This key will be the open position of your door.

17. So, with this key on the track selected (highlighted), in your perspective viewport, move the door up to an open position. See Figure 8.25. You can move objects in all sorts of ways and directions in the movement track to create various cinematic events, but the door going up (last frame) and down (first frame) is all we need for now.

Figure 8.25
Raise the door up, as it would appear when in the open position.
Source: Epic Games.

18. You can preview your animation using the play control buttons at the top of your Matinee Editor.

19. Close the Matinee Editor and return to Kismet. Drag a connector from the Touched property of your Trigger Volume Touch node to the Play property of your Matinee node.

20. Save your level and give the door a test run. As you can see in Figure 8.26, once you approach the door, it should open automatically. It does this for any player pawn. If you want to restrict usage, you could add an object variable to the Instigator property of the Trigger Volume Touch node in Kismet. For instance, you may not want anyone but the first-person payer (Player 0) to open the door, using it to block access to enemy bots.

Figure 8.26
Play through your level to see how your door works.
Source: Epic Games.

Use a Switch to Open Doors and Gates

You could also use a switch or lever to open certain doors or gates within your level.

1. Continue with OpenGates.udk, but save it as OpenGates2.udk in the same folder.

2. In the Content Browser, find S_NEC_Lights_SM_WallLight01_arm_B static mesh in the UDKGames package. Drag it into your level and place it beside and a little in front of your doorway you just made. See Figure 8.27.

Figure 8.27
Add the wall light arm to pose as your door switch.
Source: Epic Games.

3. Right-click next to the wall light arm you just added and select Add Actor > Add Trigger. Position the trigger so it fits over the wall light arm static mesh in your level, as you can see in Figure 8.28.

Figure 8.28
Put a trigger on top of your wall light arm.
Source: Epic Games.

4. Open Kismet. Right-click an empty space and select New Event Using [trigger name] > Used. Previously you used a Touch control, but this trigger will use the Used control.

5. Deselect the Aim to Interact property under Seq Event Used in the Properties panel. Change the Interact Distance to 200, like in Figure 8.29.

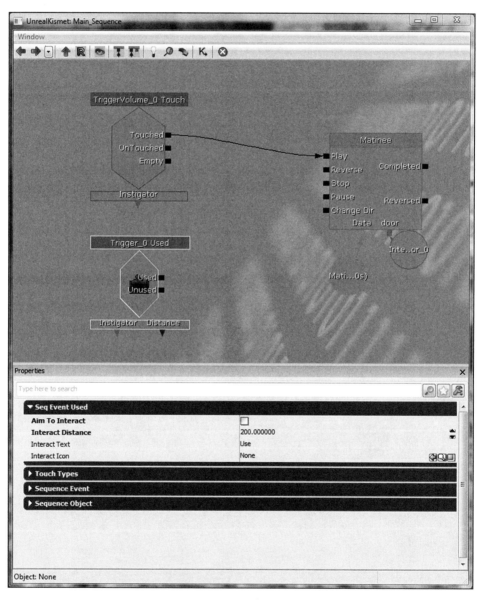

Figure 8.29
Edit the Used node's properties like so.
Source: Epic Games.

6. Break the link between the Touch node and the Matinee node. Between the Used node and the Matinee node, right-click and select New Action > Switch > Switch from the options. Select this Switch node and change Link Count to 2 and put a check next to Looping. Drag a connector from the Used output of the Used node to the In property of the Switch node. Connect Switch's Link 1 to the Play property of the Matinee node, and connect Switch's Link 2 to the Reverse property of the Matinee node. Compare your Kismet to Figure 8.30.

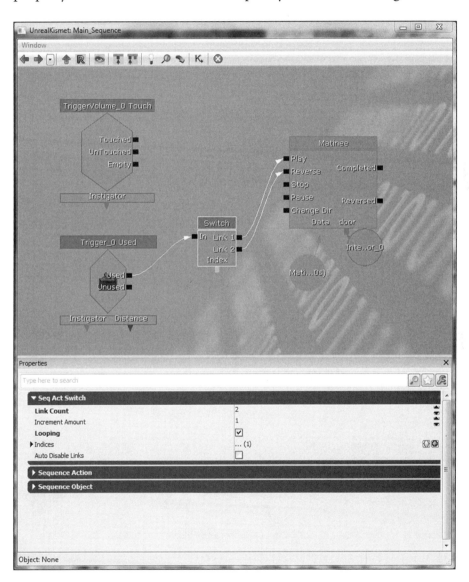

Figure 8.30
The way your connections should look between your nodes.
Source: Epic Games.

7. With the Used node selected, expand Sequence Event in the Properties panel and set Max Trigger Count to 2.

8. Close Kismet and return to the viewport window. With the trigger still selected, press F4 to open its properties dialog. Scroll down and expand Mobile. Put a check next to Enable Mobile Touch (shown in Figure 8.31). This will allow touch interaction with the trigger through your mobile touchscreen interface.

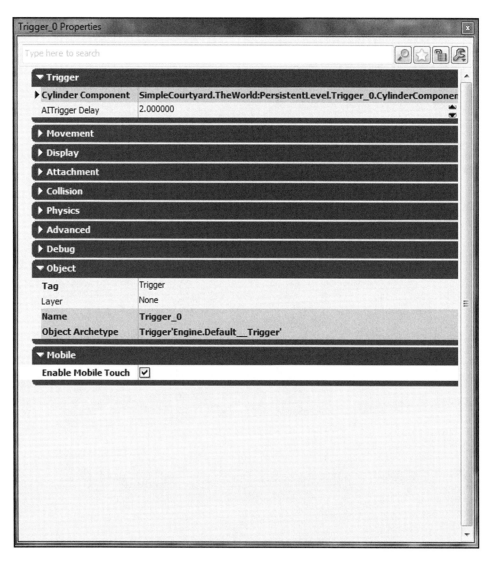

Figure 8.31
Enable mobile touch on the trigger.
Source: Epic Games.

9. Save your level. You can play through it, but on the PC, you will have to activate the light arm's switch by pressing the E key.

Note

There are multiple ways to capture and track touchscreen input from an iPad (to read more, go online to http://udn.epicgames.com/Three/MobileInputSystem.html). In order to have a trigger like the one above activated by input on an iPad, you would have to set it up in Kismet differently. The easiest way would be to use an InterpActor and a new event node based on Touch, like you did for the pickup items in the "Add Pickup Items" section earlier in this chapter, to trigger the Marquee action, instead of using a trigger and an event node based on Used, like you do here. Best yet, you could use both sorts of input to derive the same Marquee action, and then, based on whether the gamer is playing on a computer or iPad, they could find some way to trigger actions in game.

CHAPTER 9

TAKING YOUR GAME TO MARKET

Eventually, either you will reach the end of your game project development and want to advertise your home-brewed iPad game or you will have a decent start but need more help or cash flow to continue with the development process. When you get to that point, you may have some friends you can show, but to really get your game out there, you will have to be savvy. Whatever your intentions are to get the world to notice you and your game, this chapter shows you how.

DEVELOPING A PROPOSAL

If you have a decent start of a game but feel you could do much better with a whole team of developers (besides your club of friends, who may be willing to help for free) or a bigger budget, you might consider developing a game proposal and seeking out people to help you or investors to give you money.

A game proposal is similar to and often based on your game-design document. When working on a game proposal, keep in mind the differences between those materials intended for internal use and those you want non-developers to see. When writing game proposals, most designers do not include every detail.

The most important details non-developers needs to understand are as follows:

- You know what you are doing and have the skills to pull off the project you propose.
- The game you propose looks good. Notice I said "looks." You can talk a good game, but until you have a demo (especially a playable prototype) to show someone, they usually won't give you the time of day. Why is that? Because

ideas are a dime a dozen in the game industry. Almost everyone has an idea for a game. Making a game demo is a proper foot in the right direction.

- Your proposed game has all the earmarks of a best-selling game (for example, it sounds fun to play, appears to have an original premise, has some amazing audio and/or graphics, and so on).

- You have set your design above all the rest by being fresh, innovative, and appealing. You have a clear identity and a clever gimmick (more about this in a moment).

If you go before a publisher or investor, try to secure a face-to-face meeting to deliver and review your proposal. This way, you can elaborate on specific points that you think are important. You can also answer clarifying questions more quickly. Just remember to go in prepared, collected, and dressed nicely. Your proposal can be on paper, but it is recommended you use visual media. You can use Microsoft Power-Point to develop a slideshow presentation. You could set up a demo of the game right there or show them a pre-recorded demo of gameplay. Remember, you'll want the freedom to discuss and evolve your game description while also answering questions. In most cases, the publisher or investor's willingness to listen will be directly related to the energy you impart, so go in pumped and excited about your game.

Also, if you're under the age of 18, most people will want to work with someone older as an intermediary (if they give you the time of day at all). Some of the reasons are legal, such as the fact that minors cannot enter into legally binding contracts.

Be forewarned that snagging a publisher is not an easy row to hoe. In fact, it is a whole lot easier to self-publish and self-promote your games, which is a possible strategy in this cyber age of garage game development. iPad development is truly a godsend in this matter, because it makes indie game submission via the App Store relatively painless and levels the playing field, so depending on the quality of the game you make, you can actively compete next to veteran game designers.

Crowd funding is another method for gaining funds to complete your game design and requires little to no physical contact with publishers. Crowd funding describes the collective effort of individuals who network and pool their money via the Internet to support efforts you initiate. Nowadays, many people are getting funds to birth their projects through online crowd funding sites. The following sites have more information and will actually help you get started if you are interested in crowd funding.

- **Kickstarter**: http://www.kickstarter.com
- **RocketHub**: http://www.rockethub.com

- **Indiegogo**: http://www.indiegogo.com
- **GoFundMe**: http://gofundme.com

ADVERTISING YOURSELF

Some people find it difficult to promote themselves. If you place yourself in this category, believe me, you are not alone. As a reclusive shut-in myself, I know how difficult it can be to put yourself out there and get noticed. Even the sensational singing legends Madonna and Lady Gaga have admitted to being prone to self-doubt, and they have been recognized the world over as some of the best self-promoters. You may be plagued by insecure feelings and doubts, or you may be self-confident but feel selfish or that you have to be humble. When it comes to advertising your game-making abilities, don't be! If you want people to notice you and play your game, you cannot act like a fly on the wall. You have to be as noticeable as possible.

Now, I'm not advocating dressing like Marilyn Manson when you stroll down the streets of your hometown. And if you plan to visit with a publisher or conduct yourself in a business atmosphere, you'd best wear nice clothes. You are expected to dress the style of the environment you are entering; as the adage goes, "When in Rome, do as the Romans do." If you hang around a game-design company where everyone's wearing sloppy T-shirts and blue jeans, you can wear a sloppy T-shirt and blue jeans. But if you go into a boardroom to negotiate a contract with a potential investor, you had best put on a decent outfit.

What I am telling you to do is to stop being vague, colorless, wishy-washy, or the amazing invisible man or woman. People will never notice you if you do not want to be noticed—and that is a downright shame, because you deserve to be noticed. You might say, "It's my game that I want people to notice, not me," and there is some truth in that. But if you are an unnoticeable person used to evading comment and keeping to yourself, then there is a great possibility your game will never get the notice it deserves.

DEVELOPING A CLEAR IDENTITY OR GIMMICK

Many game companies use gimmicks to help sell their games. A gimmick is a clear idea or image that represents and helps sell your product, and in this case your product is your game. You have probably noticed gimmicks all around you. Some can be very transparent or clumsy, but most often, a gimmick is purely an understandable image of an idea that takes too long to explain. Think about your game for a moment. Can you express your game in a single, clear sentence? Can you express it in a single image or avatar? If you can, this can be turned into a gimmick to help you advertise your game.

Taking time to write down your game idea helps you sharpen and clarify your idea. If you started making your game before taking time to simplify your core concept, you should stop and take a moment to work it out now, before going any further. After you've simplified your game idea, consider the following and find one thing that would serve as a possible gimmick:

- **Character**: Do you have a cute, sexy, strong, or mysterious character that is different and exciting enough to serve as an icon for your game?

- **Place**: Is the setting for your game adventurous, glorious, beautiful, or mysterious enough to serve as an icon for your game? Think of *Alice in Wonderland*, where Wonderland becomes an iconic place.

- **Prop**: Does your character wield an interesting, powerful, cool, or different sort of weapon or artifact that looks neat enough to serve as an icon for your game? Think of the dragonlance in the fantasy novels by Tracy Hickman and Margaret Weis or the dark crystal in the Jim Henson movie by the same name.

- **Enemy**: Do you have a scary, awesome, powerful, or mysterious enemy that is enthralling enough to serve as an icon for your game?

- **Element**: Is there some gameplay element so infusive that it's found everywhere in your game and looks different and exciting enough to serve as an icon for your game?

Let me give you just a few examples of gimmicks other games have used, in case you're still confused.

- In *Tomb Raider*, the gimmick is Laura Croft. In *Super Mario Bros.*, it is Mario. In *Donkey Kong Country*, it is Donkey Kong. In *Zelda*, it is the green-clad elf Link. All these games have the main character as a gimmick.

- In *Prince of Persia*, the gimmick is a combination of the main character (the prince) and the place (a romanticized ancient Persia).

- In the games *Diablo* and *Rayman: Raving Rabbids*, the gimmicks are the enemies that are constantly thrown at you.

You have to find just the right look for yourself and the right gimmick for your game, and you want people to notice you and play your game. Because you worked hard at creating a fun game, which people will like, you know you are not offering empty promises. You are only giving players excellent entertainment.

So how do you get the world to notice you and your game? How do you clue folks in that you have something for them to play? One of the best ways in this beautiful cyber age is through the use of the Internet.

MARKETING YOUR GAME ON THE WEB

These days, the easiest way to market yourself, what you do or make, is to build a website, put your art on it, and get people to come to your website to see it, something anybody can do for little or no cost.

Finding a Web Host

It all seems simple. You click, and a new page appears on your screen. But where do these pages live while not being viewed? Where are webpages stored?

Websites and their pages are stored on special computers called servers. A server is a computer hooked up to the Internet 24/7 and might have one or more websites stored on it at any given time. The number of sites and pages that can reside on a single server depends on the server's memory capacity. When you enter a webpage address in the Address bar of your browser, the server responds by sending a copy of that page to your browser.

To publish your website, you don't need to set up your own personal server. You can borrow someone else's server to put your files on. This type of server is called a web host. There are countless choices in finding web hosts: some free and others at a cost. What follows is a list of free web-host services:

- **110 MB**: 110mb.com
- **AtSpace**: www.atspace.com
- **Byet Internet Services**: www.byethost.com
- **Freehostia**: www.freehostia.com/hosting.html
- **Webs**: www.webs.com
- **Tripod**: www.tripod.lycos.com

When choosing free hosting, go with a reputable host. Some free hosting sites add bulky code to your page, which increases the loading time or speed at which your page displays. Others place advertisements on your page. Avoid these types of hosts if you can.

Companies with dedicated servers cost you more, but as in everything in life, you get what you pay for. The top web hosts with dedicated servers you can pay for at the time of this writing are listed here:

- **BlueHost**: bluehost.com
- **Dot5Hosting**: www.dot5hosting.com
- **HostMonster**: www.hostmonster.com
- **HostPapa**: hostpapa.com
- **StartLogic**: www.startlogic.com

Building a Website

Think of your website as a neighborhood. Just as a city planner would, you need a clear concept of what kind of stuff you want to include in your site before you start building it.

Mainly, you want your site to describe your game and include a link to the App Store page for your iPad game once you have uploaded it (more on this later in this chapter). You can also include screen grabs of your game, concept artwork, and behind-the-scenes notes of everything that went into making your game.

Prepping Your Text

Before you build your site or update it with new material, take time to write all your text beforehand. Your best bet is to use a word-processing program like Microsoft Word, because it enables you to check your spelling and it even makes suggestions relating to grammar and usage.

Prepping Your Images

Images must be small enough for transmission over the Internet. When I say "small," I am referring, of course, to the size of the file, not the dimensions of the image itself.

Unlike images you prepare for print, which must have a resolution of 150 to 300 dots per inch (dpi), an image bound for the Web needs to have a resolution of 72 dpi. To achieve this file size, you will likely need to compress your images. This reduces redundancy in image data, often without a noticeable loss in image quality. Compressing your images not only makes it more convenient for upload, it also benefits your visitors because it enables them to download your site more quickly. Use an art or photo-editing software application to compress your images. Note that some sites where you upload images, such as Facebook, auto-compress images as they are uploaded, so you do not have to do it before uploading.

You can find several online apps to help edit and improve your digital image files, which I recommend. Here are some of the more popular ones:

- **Photoshop Express Editor**: www.photoshop.com/tools/expresseditor
- **Pixlr.com**: pixlr.com/editor/
- **Pixlr-o-matic**: pixlr.com/o-matic/

You can also store your finished digital image files online using Photobucket (photobucket.com), which also has a built-in editor to spruce up your images.

Putting It Together

You could code all your webpages by hand, using HTML. HTML is a simple markup language that tells the browser how to display code on the page. It's so simple, in fact, anyone can learn it. There are numerous HTML tutorials online that can get you up to snuff in hand coding in no time. To find them, search Google for "HTML tutorial."

Note, too, that you don't need special software to hand-code webpages in HTML. You can use a text editor such as Notepad (Win) or BBEdit (Mac) to type your code and then save your resulting file with the .html extension. When you open it later, it will launch in your default browser to preview.

Cascading style sheets (CSS) is a computer language used to describe the presentation of structured documents that declares how a document written in a markup language such as HTML should look. CSS is used to identify colors, fonts, layout, and other notable aspects of web document staging. It is designed to facilitate the division of content and presentation of that content so that you can actually swap out different looks without having to alter the content at all. CSS can thus be kept separate from the HTML coding.

Save all your web files to a single folder, with index.html for your home page. Once you have your pages created, upload them to your hosting server by way of file transfer protocol (FTP) or another upload option. This is usually dependent on which host you go with.

Using Dreamweaver for Web Building   Adobe Dreamweaver, shown in Figure 9.1, is the premier website construction kit for professionals. It allows pros to work in either a WYSIWYG (what-you-see-is-what-you-get) or code environment, or both simultaneously. Dreamweaver comes with several built-in site templates. All you need to do is add your content and create your custom logo. In addition, there are many free templates available online.

Note

Dreamweaver can be fairly complicated to work with. As such, you will probably need to read a book that focuses on teaching you its inner workings, such as Sherry Bishop's *Adobe Dreamweaver CS5 Revealed* (Cengage Learning). You can learn more about Dreamweaver and how to use it from Adobe's site at www.adobe.com/products/dreamweaver.

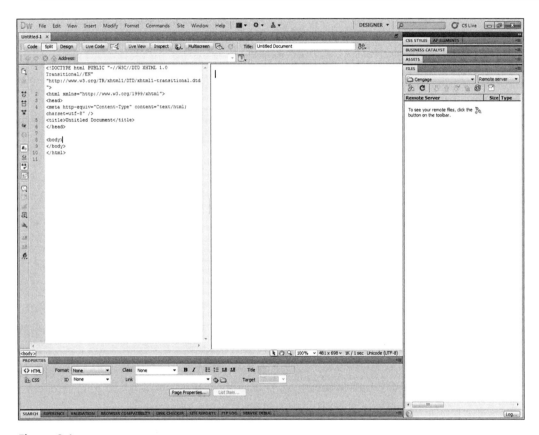

Figure 9.1
Adobe Dreamweaver CS5.
© Adobe Systems Incorporated.

Using Nvu for Web Building An alternative, especially if you don't have the budget for Dreamweaver, is Nvu (pronounced "N-view"), which is available online at www.nvu.com. Nvu is an open-source web-authoring application for Windows, Mac, and Linux users. This free program provides a great WYSIWIG editing environment and built-in file transfer system to satisfy most designers' needs. If you've always wanted to get your feet wet building websites but don't have much in the way of disposable income, consider Nvu (shown in Figure 9.2).

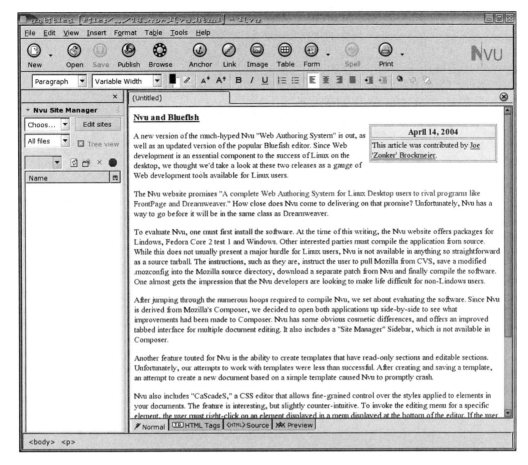

Figure 9.2
Nvu.
Source: Nvu.

Using Free Online Web Builders If you feel completely out of place trying to code your own website by yourself, or you would prefer whipping something together with very little effort and don't have to possess the most amazing or customized site, you can make use of one of several free online web builders.

Some of these kits create websites for you on a trial basis, asking you to pay money for adequate hosting or maintenance, while others are free if you agree to use their hosting service. Be sure to read the fine print of any web builder that says it is "free" because too many people have been disappointed before from using them.

Personally, I currently use the free version of Moonfruit and am very satisfied with all the editing tools and built-in shopping cart system.

- **DoodleKit**: doodlekit.com/home
- **Handzon Sitemaker**: www.handzon.com

- **Moonfruit**: www.moonfruit.com (see Figure 9.3)
- **Wix**: www.wix.com
- **Yola**: www.yola.com

Figure 9.3
The home page of Moonfruit's site.
Source: Moonfruit.

Making Use of Social Networks   Do you keep a blog or community profile, such as a Facebook, Google+, Tumblr, Blogger, or Twitter page? These are all other reputable ways to get your games noticed. You don't have to learn anything about HTML, and the blog or community service editors are nowhere near as complicated as Dreamweaver can appear.

What follows are instructions for making a Facebook page that advertises your game.

1. Log in to Facebook with your current Facebook account. If you do not have one, you can register for one.

2. Click the Like Pages link in the left navigation bar. On the Recommended Pages page that comes up, click the Create Page button near the top.

3. On the Create a Page page, click Brand or Product as your main topic (see Figure 9.4). In the options dialog box that appears, type the name of your game or the name you want to give your game company. From the drop-down category list, choose Games/Toys. Read the Facebook Pages Terms before selecting the checkbox that says you have read them.

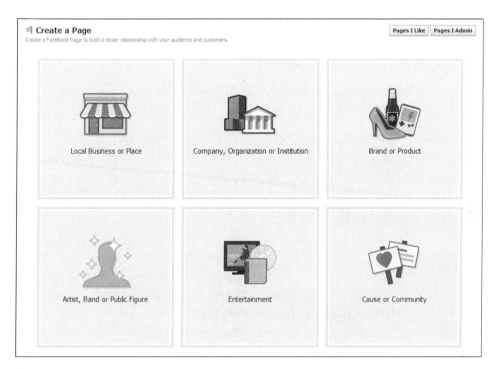

Figure 9.4
Pick Brand or Product.
Source: ® Facebook, Inc.

4. Add a square (1:1 ratio) avatar image for your game. Continue, and you will be directed through the steps to add a description, a cover image to go at the top of the Facebook page, and more.

5. When finished, you can send invitations to people you might have on your Friends list to "like" your page. From this point forward, you can use your Facebook page as a place to point people to when advertising your game.

Submitting Your Site to Search Engines

Now that you have some cyber real estate and you're confident in your overall design abilities, it's time to open the doors wide and let gamers in. For them to find you, your first step is to submit your site to search engines so that it can be indexed with them.

A search engine is a web program that searches the Web for specified keywords and phrases and returns a list of documents in which those keywords or phrases are found. Popular search engines include Google, Bing, Yahoo!, AOL, Alta Vista, Dogpile, and Ask.com. What follows is a list of search engines to which you should consider submitting your site:

- **Bing**: Visit www.bing.com/toolbox/submit-site-url to submit your URL.

- **Google**: Visit www.google.com/addurl.html and follow the onscreen instructions.

- **Open Directory Project**: A bunch of search engines use Dmoz.org for their search material, and you can submit to Dmoz.org, too. Go to www.dmoz.org /add.html and follow the onscreen instructions.

- **Yahoo!**: Visit search.yahoo.com/info/submit.html and follow the onscreen instructions.

Creating a QR Code

A QR code is a two-dimensional barcode that can be scanned easily using any modern mobile phone. After scanning, this code is then converted into a piece of text and/or a hyperlink. For instance, if you walk into a grocery store and notice a poster for an event that seems interesting, you can take out your mobile phone, scan the QR code, and instantly get more information about the event and/or a link to a website where you can book tickets. QR codes are typically small, square images and thus save a lot of space on the advert or product, making it a clever and ideal marketing strategy.

You can link to your game's page in the App Store or to the website you built to advertise your game by use of a QR code. QR codes are easy to make using Visualead's QR Code Generator online. Follow these steps:

1. Go to www.visualead.com/qurify2/en/ and type or copy and paste the URL of your game or website into the blank field. Then, click the Generate QR Code button.

2. A prompt will appear, asking you to choose a graphic for the background of your QR code. There are many to choose from (see Figure 9.5), and you can click the More button at the bottom of the list to show more. You could also

select the blank white one to get the QR code by itself, without a background, or click the Browse Your Files and Folders button to upload your own background image.

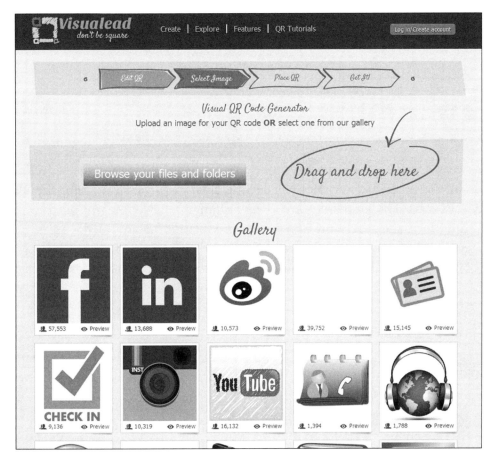

Figure 9.5
Pick a background graphic.
© Visualead.

3. After you have chosen the image, the next prompt will show you where you can place your QR code on the background image. Click the Generate Silver button when you are satisfied with the placement of the code and wait for the code to be generated. When it is finished, click Next.

4. Register or log in with Facebook or Google to download your QR code for free. You can also keep track of all your generated QR codes, see how many visitors have scanned them, and re-download them as needed. Using an image editor, you can paste your QR code onto signs, flyers, posters, and more.

DISTRIBUTING YOUR APP TO iPADS EVERYWHERE

The next section will show you how to use Apple's App Store to distribute and share your game app. Distribution requires jumping back and forth between Apple's developer site and applications on your computer. Once you have your game uploaded to the App Store and have a visible store page, you can link to it from your social network site or website.

Note

You must have a Mac with Application Loader installed in order to complete the App Store submission process.

Apple has very specific guidelines for app approval. Your fart app will be declined. It states this in the guidelines. Apple will decline a fart app because there are already too many fart apps. The guidelines are always changing, and you will need to review them carefully to make sure your app is not in violation of any of the rules. Also, I strongly recommend staying on the up and up and being legal in everything you do when it comes to making and distributing your games. Only use programs that you are licensed to use.

CREATING A DISTRIBUTION IPA

You can play-test your iPad game from within the UDK Editor interface, but before publishing a finished game to the App Store, your game map(s) will need to be packaged into an IPA to be used by iOS devices and to submit your app to the App Store. Packaging your game is done through the Unreal Frontend application (see Figure 9.6). In Windows, you open this application by going to Start > All Programs > Unreal Development Kit > UDK [version date] > Tools > Unreal Frontend.

Figure 9.6
Unreal Frontend.
Source: Epic Games.

1. Once Unreal Frontend is opened, click the MobileGame on PC … Cook/Make/ Sync button at the top to open the configuration settings and set them as MobileGame, iPhone, ReleaseScript, and Shipping_32. Click OK to save your settings, as shown in Figure 9.7.

Figure 9.7
Configure your settings like so.
Source: Epic Games.

2. In the mobile section, which should now have appeared, change the Packaging Mode to Distribution.

3. Next, add all the maps that need to be packaged into the application. This is done in the Maps section. Set the map you want loaded by default. This should be the starting level.

4. Once done, click the Cook button and select Clean and Full Recook. Wait for the cooking process to complete. After it has, click the Package button and select Package iOS App. Wait for the packaging process to complete.

5. When the package setup is done, you should have a file with the file extension .IPA in your directory. This is the file to be uploaded to the App Store for distribution.

Becoming an Apple Developer

You cannot upload apps to the App Store without first having a registered Apple developer account. To do so, follow these steps:

Note

This entire setup is performed through and dependent on Apple's developer website. As this is a winding, complex process, and one that is most definitely subject to change if Apple reorganizes their development process (which they do a lot), the best thing to do is to follow the instructions step-by-step from Apple's iOS developer center.

1. Apply for and become a registered iOS developer. Go to Apple's iOS Developer Center (shown in Figure 9.8) at https://developer.apple.com/programs/ios/.

Figure 9.8
The Apple iOS Developer Center.
Source: Apple, Inc.

2. Standard registration at the time of this writing costs $99 for a year's membership. Registration gains you access to the iOS SDK (software development kit), which is used to build applications for iPad, iPhone, and iPod Touch, as well as videos, sample code, documentation, and various forums. This price is the same, whether you are a student or a pro. You will also need to sign in or create an Apple ID. If you do not already have an Apple ID, the registration process will allow you to create one.

3. If you need to, upgrade your operating system and iTunes installation. Apple suggests you use the very latest version of Mac OS and iTunes.

4. Download the iOS SDK. The iOS SDK contains the code, information, and tools you need to develop, test, run, debug, and tune applications for iOS. Go to the iOS Developer Center and log in. After logging in, download and install the latest iPhone SDK. Do *not* download the beta version of the SDK. Note that downloading and installing the iPhone SDK will also install Xcode, which has a complete development environment of its own, including a source editor and graphical debugger. Xcode also provides the launch point for testing your applications on an iOS device and in iOS Simulator, which is a platform that mimics the basic iOS environment on a Macintosh computer.

5. Upgrade your device (iPhone/iPod Touch only). This could require you to purchase a $9.99 upgrade if you are using iPod Touch.

6. Get your device identifier. Using the USB cable, plug in your iOS device, and launch Xcode. Xcode will detect your device as new. When it does, press the button labeled Use For Development. If that doesn't open the Organizer window, go to Window > Organizer. You should see your iOS device in the Devices list at left (see Figure 9.9). Select it and write down your device's unique identifier code. This code should be about 40 digits long.

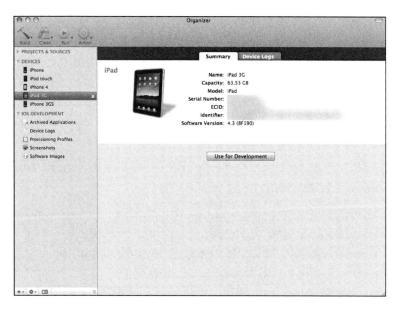

Figure 9.9
The Organizer window.
Source: Apple, Inc.

7. Add your device. Log in to the iOS Developer Center and enter the program portal. Go to the Devices page. Once there, click the Add Device button. Enter a name for your device (alphanumeric only) and your device's identifier code, which you wrote down in the last step. Click Submit when done.

8. Create a certificate. Within the iOS Developer Center, click the Certificates link and follow the instructions to generate a certificate (see Figure 9.10).

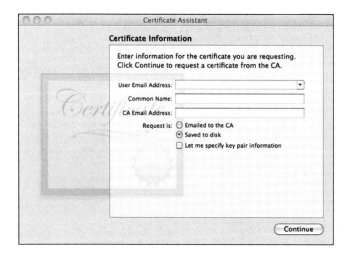

Figure 9.10
Create a certificate.
Source: Apple, Inc.

9. Create a provisioning profile. The easiest way is within the iOS Developer Center. Go to Certificates > Development and click the Request Certificate button. You can then upload the certificate you just created. Provisioning profiles are a little more advanced than that. They are set up differently depending on how you've organized your team. Since there is no case that fits all circumstances, you can read up on how provisioning works on iOS Developer Central at http://developer.apple.com.

Creating a Provisioning Profile

Submitting your app to the App Store is a lengthy process. Information telling you how to distribute your app to the App Store can be found on Apple's iOS Developer Center, specifically in the Distribution section of the iOS Provisioning Portal (see Figure 9.11). This information changes and is updated often, so you should start there, wherein you will find step-by-step instructions for the first task, which is to obtain your iOS Distribution Certificate.

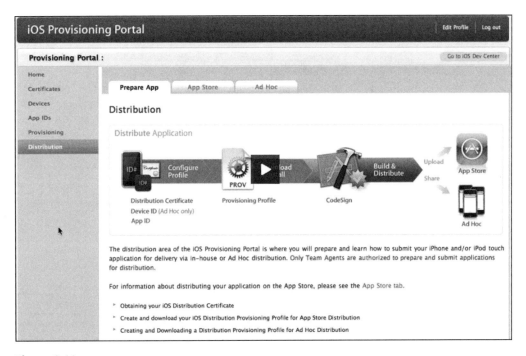

Figure 9.11
The iOS Provisioning Portal is where you go to create provisioning profiles, especially for distribution purposes.

Source: Apple, Inc.

Once you've gotten your iOS Distribution Certificate, you will have to create and download your iOS Distribution Provisioning Profile used for App Store distribution. To successfully build your app with Xcode for distribution via the App Store, you need this App Store Distribution Provisioning Profile; this is different from the Development Provisioning Profile in that Apple *only* accepts apps built with an App Store Distribution Provisioning Profile.

This requires you to log into the iOS Developer Center as your Team Agent, which is typically the account you created when you first joined the iOS Developer Center. You create your Distribution Provisioning Profile by navigating to the Provisioning section of the iOS Developer Center and clicking on the Distribution tab. Click the New Profile button to start creating a new iOS Distribution Provisioning Profile (see Figure 9.12). Make sure the App Store radio button is selected, and give your profile a unique name like "AppStore Provisioning Profile." Then load your App ID. If you don't already have an App ID, which is an integral part of iOS development and is a unique ten-character string, you can create one in the App IDs section of the Provisioning Portal.

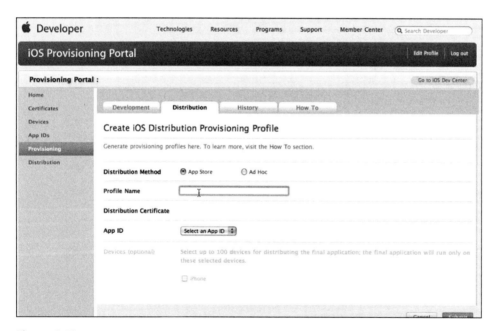

Figure 9.12
Creating a new distribution provisioning profile.
Source: Apple, Inc.

After creating your App Store Distribution Provisioning Profile, click the Download button (see Figure 9.13). Once installed, open it in Xcode by double-clicking on it from whatever directory you installed it to. Now that you have an iOS Distribution Certificate and an App Store Distribution Provisioning Profile, you need to build your application with Xcode for distribution. Refer to the step-by-step guide in the Distribution section of iOS Developer Center's Provisioning Portal if you get lost or confused.

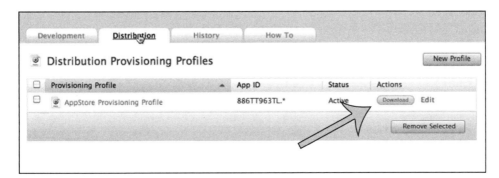

Figure 9.13
Download your App Store Distribution Provisioning Profile.
Source: Apple, Inc.

Submitting an App to the App Store

Now you should be prepared to add your app to Apple's App Store.

1. To submit your app to the App Store, go to itunesconnect.apple.com, or within the Member Center of the iOS Developer Center, click the iTunes Connect link.

2. Here (as seen in Figure 9.14), you may need to log in again. Once in, click on Manage Your Apps to manage your applications and click on Add New App to begin (see Figure 9.15).

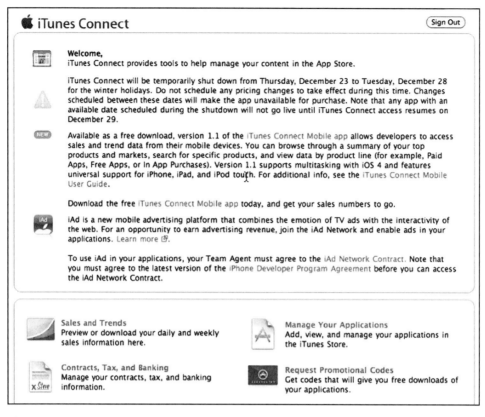

Figure 9.14
Go to iTunes Connect.
Source: Apple, Inc.

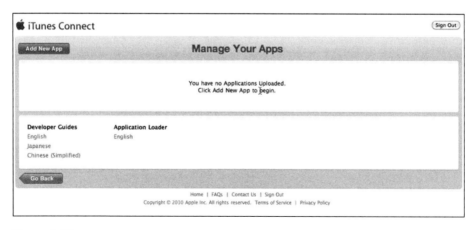

Figure 9.15
Then enter Manage Your Apps.
Source: Apple, Inc.

Tip

When filling out the submission information, be as transparent as possible, because Apple reviewers must verify your application in detail and providing the information required ahead of time will enable your application to get through the review process quicker.

3. For the SKU Number that Apple requests in the form, use any unique identifier. The SKU Number is simply a reference number you will use to track your own games later. For instance, your first game could be called MYGAME-00001, and your second would be called MYGAME-00002, and so on.

4. Next to each field you are asked to fill out will be a question mark that will give you further details about each option. If you have specified an App ID for this profile, add it as your Bundle ID.

5. You don't know for certain when Apple will approve the app, so set the Availability Date out for some time in the future. You can choose what pricing tier you want your app to belong to, but for your first time out, you should select Free. Continue to fill out the form as accurately and fully as possible. When you get to Apple Content Descriptions (shown in Figure 9.16), be honest as you can in describing your app content.

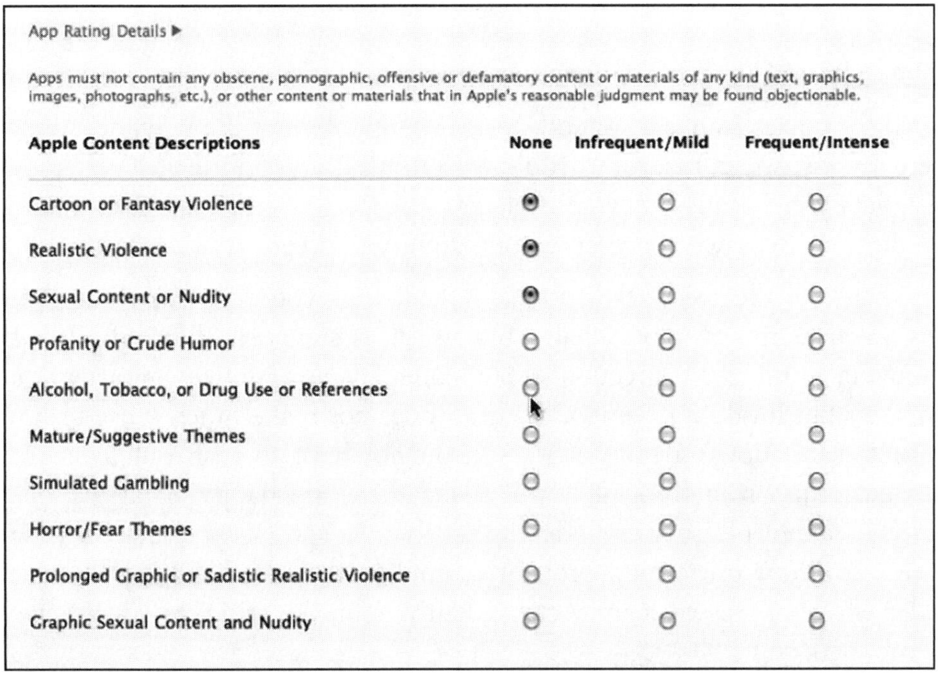

App Rating Details ▶

Apps must not contain any obscene, pornographic, offensive or defamatory content or materials of any kind (text, graphics, images, photographs, etc.), or other content or materials that in Apple's reasonable judgment may be found objectionable.

Apple Content Descriptions	None	Infrequent/Mild	Frequent/Intense
Cartoon or Fantasy Violence	●	○	○
Realistic Violence	●	○	○
Sexual Content or Nudity	●	○	○
Profanity or Crude Humor	○	○	○
Alcohol, Tobacco, or Drug Use or References	○	○	○
Mature/Suggestive Themes	○	○	○
Simulated Gambling	○	○	○
Horror/Fear Themes	○	○	○
Prolonged Graphic or Sadistic Realistic Violence	○	○	○
Graphic Sexual Content and Nudity	○	○	○

Figure 9.16

Be as transparent and honest as you can when entering information about your app.

Source: Apple, Inc.

6. Next, you'll need to select a 512 × 512 pixel icon and iPad screenshots for your app. If you don't have these, go ahead and make them. You can use any image-editing program to paint or modify an image for your icon, keeping the image size at 512 × 512 pixels. You can capture screenshots from in-game using Command + Shift + 4 + Spacebar and clicking on the window pane you want to capture or, if using Windows, use the Print Screen key or Windows Snipping Tool found at Start > All Programs > Accessories (Windows 7 or better).

7. You don't use any encryptions, so skip that section of the form. Go ahead and finish the form, saving your app description. Afterward, you can check the status of your app. The status should tell you it's waiting for app upload.

8. To upload your app, return to Xcode and navigate to and run the Application Loader (found in Utilities). Here, you'll need to log in again with your iOS developer account. Select the app you want to upload and choose the zipped app file you built previously. Hit Send, and watch it upload.

9. All you have to do now is await Apple to review your app, and if successful, Apple will add it to the App Store. You can return to Manage Your Apps on iTunes Connect to check the status of your app until then. When your app appears in the App Store, you can advertise it online by providing links on your website, blog, or social network site.

WHAT'S NEXT?

Be prepared for player feedback—good, bad, and ugly. Ignore the ugly, because sometimes there are just weak, insecure people who think it a good idea to attack amateur game designers just because they can. Never take it personally. I know that can be harder to do than to say, but preserve your dignity and ego by trusting me on this.

However, there will be feedback, good and bad, that you *should* pay attention to. Again, do not take any of it personally, but use it as signposts that indicate whether you are moving in the right direction. If someone tells you he likes the way you have brick platforms but thinks a disembodied head does not make much sense to him as a player character, jot down a note of it. You do not have to rush out to change the player character into something that will make the critic happy. That was just one critic, and you cannot please everybody all the time. As soon as you altered the disembodied head, someone else would probably complain that she liked it the way it was and wonder why you messed it up. Act prudently upon the criticism you receive.

Some of the feedback you receive from others will be dire and necessitate edits to your game. For example, you might have thought you tested all your game levels, but perhaps you missed the fact that one platform physically blocked another, and now players are stuck and cannot continue. If you receive glitch information like that from your players, you are obligated to fix it as soon as possible and release a new version of your game.

While mulling over the feedback you get from your first game, start planning your next project. Now that you have at least one game finished, what is to stop you from making another? Just as they say, "Practice makes perfect," so too does frequent creativity. The next game you make will be even better, and the next one after that, and the next one after that, and so on. Eventually, you will have a stellar portfolio you will be proud to show off!

Appendix A

Resources

Herein you will find all the websites mentioned within this book and online resources you might find useful.

Main Resources

- **Unreal Development Kit:** www.udk.com
- **Epic Games:** epicgames.com
- **This book's companion site:** www.cengageptr.com/downloads

Game Design

- **GamaSutra:** www.gamasutra.com
- **GameDev:** www.gamedev.net
- **David Freeman Group on Creating Emotions in Games:** www.freemangames.com/idea/

2D Image Editors

- **GIMP:** www.gimp.org
- **Lunapic Editor:** www151.lunapic.com/editor/
- **Paint.Net:** www.getpaint.net
- **Photoshop:** https://creative.adobe.com/products/photoshop

- **Picmonkey:** www.picmonkey.com
- **Pixlr:** http://pixlr.com/editor/
- **Sumopaint:** http://www.sumopaint.com/app/

2D Textures

- **Archive Textures:** www.archivetextures.net
- **3DModelFree.com:** http://map.3dmodelfree.com
- **CGTextures:** www.cgtextures.com
- **Dave Gurrea's Textures:** www.davegh.com
- **Free Seamless Textures:** http://freeseamlesstextures.com
- **Good Textures:** www.goodtextures.com
- **Mayang's Free Textures:** www.mayang.com/textures/
- **Texture Warehouse:** www.texturewarehouse.com
- **Texturer:** http://texturer.com

3D Modeling Programs

- **3ds Max:** http://www.autodesk.com/products/autodesk-3ds-max/free-trial
- **3DTin:** www.3dtin.com
- **Blender:** www.blender.org
- **Wings 3D:** www.wings3d.com

3D Models

- **3D Total:** www.3dtotal.com
- **3Delicious:** www.3delicious.net
- **3DModelFree:** www.3dmodelfree.com
- **3DXtras:** www.3dxtras.com/3dxtras-free-3d-models-list.asp
- **Amazing 3D:** www.amazing3d.com/free/free.html
- **Archive 3D:** http://archive3d.net
- **Artist-3D:** http://artist-3d.com

- **Blender Models:** www.blender-models.com
- **BlendSwap:** www.blendswap.com
- **Exchange 3D:** www.exchange3d.com/Free-3D-Models/cat_35.html
- **Mr. Furniture:** www.mr-cad.com/Free-3D-Models-c-19-1.html
- **Rocky3D:** www.rocky3d.com/free3d.html
- **TF3DM:** http://tf3dm.com
- **Top3D.net:** www.top3d.net/3d-models/
- **Turbosquid:** www.turbosquid.com

Music/Sound Effects

- **DeusX.com:** http://www.deusx.com/studio.html
- **Flashkit.com:** http://www.flashkit.com
- **FlashSound.com:** http://www.flashsound.com
- **GameSalad Marketplace:** http://marketplace.gamesalad.com
- **Looperman:** http://www.looperman.com
- **Shockwave-Sound.com:** http://www.shockwave-sound.com
- **Sound-Ideas.com:** http://www.sound-ideas.com
- **Sound Rangers.com:** http://www.soundrangers.com
- **The Music Bakery:** http://musicbakery.com

Sound Editors

- **Audacity:** audacity.sourceforge.net/
- **Audio Expert:** www.audioexpert.com/
- **ClubCreate:** remixer.clubcreate.com/v2/musiclab/launch.html
- **Musicshake:** eng.musicshake.com/create/
- **Soundation:** soundation.com/

Free Web Hosts

- **110 MB Hosting:** 110mb.com
- **Atspace.com:** www.atspace.com

- **Byet Internet Services:** www.byethost.com
- **Freehostia:** www.freehostia.com/hosting.html
- **Webs:** www.webs.com
- **Tripod:** www.tripod.lycos.com

Paid Web Hosts

- **Bluehost:** bluehost.com
- **Dot5Hosting:** www.dot5hosting.com
- **HostMonster:** www.hostmonster.com
- **HostPapa:** hostpapa.com
- **StartLogic:** www.startlogic.com

Web Editors

- **Adobe Dreamweaver:** www.adobe.com/products/dreamweaver
- **NVU:** www.nvu.com

Web Builders

- **DoodleKit:** doodlekit.com/home
- **HandzOn:** www.handzon.com
- **Moonfruit:** www.moonfruit.com
- **Wix:** www.wix.com
- **Yola:** www.yola.com

Search Engine Submission

- **Bing:** www.bing.com/toolbox/submit-site-url
- **Google:** www.google.com/addurl.html
- **Open Directory Project:** www.dmoz.org/add.html
- **Yahoo!:** search.yahoo.com/info/submit.html

SOCIAL NETWORKS

- **Facebook:** www.facebook.com
- **Blogger:** www.blogger.com
- **Tumblr:** www.tumblr.com
- **Twitter:** www.twitter.com
- **Wordpress:** wordpress.org

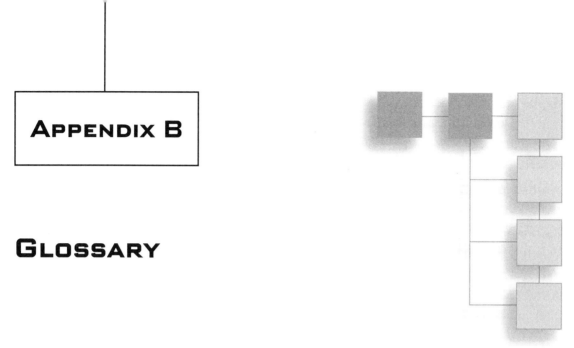

APPENDIX B

GLOSSARY

This glossary defines terms used within this book and other terms you might encounter in your use of the software found herein.

A

Accelerometer   As it refers to the iPad's accelerometer, this is a device like a gyroscope that measures proper accelerations of frames of reference to detect the position of the device and provide for screen display (portrait or landscape).

Action games   Games where the player's reflexes and hand-eye coordination make a difference in whether she wins or loses. Most action games feature such common tropes as enemies, weapons, and health pick up items.

Actor   An object that can be placed or spawned in the world. This includes such things as the Players, Weapons, StaticMeshes, Emitters, Infos, Sounds, etc.

Additive BSP   BSP space that has been added to a subtracted BSP space. Additive BSP is solid, impenetrable space within the game environment. *See also* BSP.

Adventure games   Games that traditionally combine puzzle-solving with storytelling; what pulls the game together is an extended, often twisting narrative, calling for the player to visit different locations and encounter many different characters.

AI (Artificial Intelligence)   A term used to describe the behavior and apparent thought process of computer-controlled characters. This can include things as simple as non-interactive scripted sequences to things as complex as computer characters that learn from player actions and adapt.

Algorithm   A set of instructions, listed out step-by-step, issued to your computer, to make it do what you want it to do.

Alpha channel   An extra channel in a texture that allows for not only transparency but also translucency in a texture.

AmbientSound   An actor that when placed in the level will loop a sound file selected from the Sound Browser.

Animated sprite   A 2D rectangular image that will be animated, like a character walking across the screen or a waving flag on a pole. *See also* Sprite.

Animation   Movement created for a 3D model with bones that allows it to move in game. The animations are stored in .PSA files and several can be imported for a single skeletal mesh.

AnimTree   An animation setup applied to a skeletal mesh, containing multiple animations, blends, and skeletal bone controllers.

Antagonist   Another word for the villain or dark force at work in a story. *See also* protagonist.

App Store   As it refers to the iOS App Store, this is Apple's official online distribution platform for iPad, iPhone, and iPod Touch mobile devices.

Application   In computer science terms, this can stand for any computer program with a user interface or one that has been designed for a specific task.

Archetype   An original model of a person, ideal example, or a prototype after which others are copied, patterned, or emulated.

Audio compression   A process that restricts the range of sound by attenuating signals exceeding a threshold.

Avatar   The player's character in a game; often the hero or protagonist of the game narrative. Some games offer player expression by providing avatar customization.

B

Backstory   The events that take place before the game narrative actually starts.

Bit   The smallest measure of digital data that comes from the phrase "binary digit," and is either a 1 or a 0. *See also* Byte.

Bitmap   A fixed-resolution image, generally a scanned painting or drawing, composed of tiny squares of color information called pixels. *See also* Pixel.

Blocking volume   A volume that can be created in the UDK Editor that will block players as well as other actors, but it will not block zero extent trances.

Boss encounter   A more difficult enemy battle that represents a major shift in the game narrative.

Bot   A computer-controlled player that has its own AI.

Brush   Any geometry created from the Brush Primitive tools on the left side of the UDK Editor, including the red builder brush.

BSP (Binary Space Partitioning)   Sometimes referred to as CSG, this is a data structure that is used to organize objects within a space of the level. While it is not semantically correct to use this term to refer to geometry, it is loosely accepted as referring to the geometry created with the builder brush. In simpler words, BSP is a type of geometry that can be added or subtracted from a level to sculpt the space of the environment.

Build   The act of compiling the level so that it can perform all of the necessary pre-calculations such as lighting, path generation, and resolving geometry.

Builder brush   The red brush that one can use to subtract out or add in BSP volumes to the level. *See also* Brush.

Byte   The next smallest measure of digital data and is composed of eight bits. *See also* bit.

C

Camera   Just as cameras are used in motion pictures to capture the visuals and display the story to your audience, cameras in video games are used to display the game world to the player. You will always have at least one camera in each scene, but you can have more than one. Multiple cameras can give you a two-player split-screen or create advanced custom effects. You can animate cameras or control them with physics. Practically anything you can imagine is possible with cameras.

Casual gamer   A person who plays for the sheer satisfaction of the experience and is less intense about the games he or she plays as opposed to a core gamer. *See also* core gamer.

Coin-op game   A coin-operated game, often enclosed in a box and set in an arcade.

Collision detection   A method in game programming used to make sure that when objects come in contact with one another they behave with a causal response as they would in the real world.

Collision model   Less complicated geometric volumes created along with and stored in a static mesh. The collision model is used to facilitate faster collision calculations than would be possible with just a complex static mesh.

Computer graphics   Anything of a visual nature that artists create using the computer as a tool.

Console (aka command prompt, command line)   A field at the bottom of the UDK Editor that allows one to enter console commands in the editor.

Core/game mechanics   The particular rules by which a player plays a specific video game.

Core gamer   A person who routinely plays lots of games and plays for the thrill of beating games (as opposed to a casual gamer). *See also* Casual gamer.

Crowd sharing   A relatively new practice of fundraising for the development of motion picture or video game production. You basically beg for donations from web users to make your product.

Crunch time   The more intense period of game production as developers get closer to deadline time, resulting in overtime and working obscene hours to get a project finished on time.

CSG (Constructive Solid Geometry)   This is a more semantically accurate term for BSP (Binary Space Partitioning). The term CSG refers to the geometry created with the builder brush.

Cull   To hide from the rendered scene, or in other words, to have the rendered scene not draw something.

Cut-scene   A brief cinematic that progresses the narrative of a video game while removing the player from gameplay temporarily. Cut-scenes are supposed to provide expositional information to help the player make informed decisions in game.

D

Deintersect   An action that will leave the remainder of builder brush selection that is in negative/subtracted space.

Dialogue tree   A set of text dialogue common to RPGs, the dialogue tree has branching outcomes based on the player's choices.

Drag grid   A toggle that allows one to snap certain actors (such as static meshes, movers, and brushes) to a grid in the UDK Editor. The Drag Grid size can be adjusted by powers of 2 going from as low as 1 to as high as 4096.

DXTC (DirectX Texture Compression)   A method of texture compression that is the primary algorithm for texture compression in the UDK Editor.

E

Easter egg   An industry name for a secret reward in a game, something few people but core gamers will find. For instance, game designers will sometimes hide treasure chests in hard-to-reach places in the game environment, knowing casual gamers might not spot them.

Edge   The straight line making up a ray between two vertices and the side of a polygon.

Emitter (particle system)   An actor that can spawn a series of other actors such as static meshes and sprites as particles to achieve various special effects. Emitters can be used in conjunction with each other to create particle systems.

Emotioneering   A cluster of techniques created by David Freeman; these techniques seek to evoke in gamers a breadth and depth of rich emotions to keep them engaged in playing a game.

F

Face   One side of a BSP object. A face is made up of two triangles.

Fetch quest   A common type of quest whereby the player must find and return with a particular item in their possession.

File transfer protocol (FTP)   A set of instructions that allows you to upload and download files to and from a web server.

Flowchart   A schematic representation of an algorithm or other systematic process, showing each step as a box or symbol and connecting them with arrows to show their progression.

Foley sounds   Sounds that are not natural but are custom recorded to emphasize sounds as they should be heard in context.

FPS (frames per second)   A measure of the rate at which pictures are shown for a motion video. Television runs at roughly 30 fps, film usually runs at 24 fps, while games often have variation in their fps rates.

First-person shooter   A style of game that depicts the scene from a first-person perspective and the primary interaction with the world is a gun of some sort.

G

Game   Any activity conducted in a pretend reality that has a core component of play.

Game design document   A written document that tells the team all the details of the game, including which levels and characters will be in the game and how the player controls will work.

Game developer   A person who, frequently with the help of others, designs video games using specialized computer software.

Game loop   A cycle of repetitive steps the player takes to win at any given game challenge.

Game pace (or flow)   The speed at which a player makes interactive actions and is guided through the game.

Gameplay   The way a game is played, especially in the way player interaction, meaningful direction, and an engaging narrative come together to entertain the player.

Game proposal   A written document intended to knock the socks off potential publishers and investors, and which puts a game in its very best light.

Game prototype   A raw unfinished game demo often used for business pitches.

Game school   A place of higher education that offers degree or certificate programs in game development and/or design.

Game testing   Often done iteratively to ensure there are no glaring mistakes; this means that testing is done every step along the way and after a mistake is fixed the game is tested again to make sure the fix didn't break something else.

Game world   A complete background setting for a game.

Garbage collection   Automatic destruction of unreferenced objects (as in Java, C#, or UnrealScript).

Geometry   Anything constructed out of triangles in the level, such as StaticMeshes, BSP, Terrain, etc.

Gimmick   A clear and representational image of an idea; in level design, gimmicks are archetypal level types that are immediately memorable for players because of their familiar themes. For example, a sewer level, mine-cart ride, or lava field are all in-game gimmicks.

Gold master   The final edition of a game with all the bugs removed.

Graphical user interface (GUI)   The look of the shell extension of a game, including the windows, interactive menus, and heads-up display.

Green light   When you hear this, it means that a game development group has completed the preproduction phase, the required tools and finances to begin proper game creation have been acquired, and that the team is now geared up to start development in earnest.

Group (Groups browser)   Actors can be assigned to a group using the Groups Browser. These groups can be used to better visually manage all the different actors that can clutter up a scene.

H

High-concept statement   A two-to-three sentence description of a game, akin to film/TV blurbs.

Huizinga's Magic Circle A concept stating that artificial effects appear to have importance and are bound by a set of made-up rules while inside their circle of use.

Human-machine interfacing (HMI) The way in which a person, or user, interacts with a machine or special device, such as a computer.

I, J, & K

Immersion A key element of a game's popularity that creates addictive gameplay by submerging players in the entertainment form; with immersion, you get so engrossed in a game that you forget it's a game.

Instance a) object of any class; b) sub-object created based on a template, contained within an object instance.

Instantiation One difficult subject in networking games online is ownership of an object. Who controls what object? Network instantiation determines the logic for you.

Internet A global network of networks.

InterpActor A special static mesh that can be assigned keyframes within the editor and then assigned to move along a path determined by these keyframes when triggered by an event such as player collision, weapon fire, or a trigger. InterpActors are called movers in Unreal but InterpActors in UDK.

Invisible A surface property for BSP geometry that will cause surfaces marked as Invisible to not be rendered. Invisible surfaces, however, will still collide as if they were visible.

iOS The operating system developed by Apple for its mobile technology, including the iPad, iPod Touch, and iPhone.

JavaScript A prototype-based C-style scripting language that is dynamic and supports object-oriented programming styles.

Keyframe A pose in an animation or mover path that is used to interpolate the motion of an animation or of the movement of an InterpActor.

L

Level A level defines a set of actors and other complex data that can be loaded and unloaded automatically. The world in UDK may consist of many levels; a typical game may contain several hundred individual levels. These levels may be dynamically loaded and unloaded based on proximity, explicit load/unload triggers, and other criteria.

Light An actor that casts light on the nearby surfaces.

Light-map   A technique used by UDK to encode the light hitting a surface, including an approximation of the direction the light is coming from.

Local area network (LAN)   A local infrastructure system of multiple computers connected over a single network; often used to support multiplayer gaming.

Lock mechanism   A structure that prevents the player's access to some area or reward in a game until the moment when the player beats the challenge and unlocks the next area or recovers the reward.

LOD (level of detail)   A feature that allows the resolution of the geometry to decrease over distance in order to increase the frame rate of a scene (specifically in animated characters).

Log   A window that prints out actions either in game or in the editor that shows every action that takes place.

Ludology   The academic study of games for the features that are distinctly related to play, including rules and simulation.

M

Map   The file that contains all of the placed actor properties and thus the layout of the entire scene you have created.

Masked   A texture property that uses the alpha channel to determine whether a section of the texture is transparent or opaque. Masked textures have no translucency.

Massively multiplayer online game (MMO)   Any game played over a network or the Internet that can be played by many gamers simultaneously.

Massively multiplayer online role-playing game (MMORPG)   A genre role-playing game played over a network or the Internet that can be played by many gamers simultaneously. *See also* Multi-user dungeon (MUD) and Role-playing games (RPGs).

Master server   Similar to a game lobby where servers can advertise their presence to clients; the Master Server is also a solution to enabling communication from behind a firewall or home network. When needed to, it makes it possible to use a technique called NAT punch-through to make sure your players can always connect with each other.

Material   A tool used for creating special effects with textures. Materials show up and can be browsed in the texture browser and they are also saved in texture packages.

Matinee   An in-editor keyframing tool that allows one to move objects and change properties in the game. You can also use it for camera paths and to create in-game cut-scenes.

Mesh emitter   An individual emitter that emits static meshes in a pattern that can be designed within the UDK Editor.

Meshes   A model created in a third-party program that represents some entity; the term Mesh is often used interchangeably with the terms static mesh and skeletal mesh even though they are not the same thing.

Milestone   A step of production that can be accomplished on a game production timeline.

Mod   User-created content that is largely based on another commercial game (such as *Unreal Tournament*) but is modified to create a different, or modified, gameplay experience.

Modifier   A material that can modify a texture or another material in a variety of ways, including (but not limited to) allowing it to pan, waiver, rotate, and scale.

Monomyth   Also known as the "hero's journey," this is a pattern of legendary steps that follow one another in a chain of events common among most myths, fairy tales, and stories.

Motion cycle   A looping animation of a character or other object going frame-by-frame through its motions.

Multi-user dungeon (MUD)   One of the first types of online multiplayer role-playing games, MUDs are often text-based games. Popular examples include *Age of Chaos* and *Dark Prophecy. See also* Massively multiplayer online role-playing game (MMORPG).

Music   Song files that can be added to a level to be played in the background or triggered after an event.

N & O

Non-player characters (NPCs)   Characters not controlled by the player but by the computer's artificial intelligence.

Objective-C   A simple object-oriented programming language used primarily on Apple's Mac OS X and iOS operating systems.

Online communities   Websites designed to foster communication and social networking; they've been compared to bulletin boards, social clubs, and schoolyards.

Orthographic view   A 3D term meaning that you can see only two of three dimensions at one time. *See also* Perspective view.

P

Package   High-level data structure used as a container for UObjects. All UObjects contained within a package have that package as the value for its Outer property.

Package Groups   A subdivision of assets within a package (such as a texture, static mesh, and sound packages) that allows for easier management of the assets within the browser.

Particle   A 2D image rendered in 3D space. These are primarily used for effects such as smoke, fire, water droplets, snow, or falling leaves.

Particle emitter   An individual type of Emitter inside a Particle System (such as a Beam Emitter, Mesh Emitter, Spark Emitter, or Sprite Emitter. *See also* Emitter.

Particle system   *See* Emitter.

Pass   One time that the scene is drawn in the renderer. A scene can require several passes by the renderer before it is drawn to the screen. In other words, if a triangle requires three passes, it is being drawn three times by the renderer.

Path node   A point in a network of lines that determines where a bot can travel. Path nodes appear as apples in the editor.

Pawn   A character or class that can navigate (either on its own or by player control) through a level.

Perspective view   A 3D term meaning that you can see more than two dimensions at the same time. *See also* Orthographic view.

PhysX   The physics engine by Ageia (formerly Novodex) that was integrated into Unreal Engine 3 and, by extent, UDK.

Pick-your-path game book   A book in which the narrative is not linear but branching and the reader must make decisions that carry the story forward to multiple possible endings.

Pixel   A tiny square of color, one of many that make up a bitmap, that has a dot of red, green, and blue information in it that sets the color tone for that square. *See also* Bitmap.

Play   Any grouping of recreational human activities, often centered on having fun.

Player   An actual human user of the map as it is running in real time.

Player interaction   A complex human-computer interface where the player gives her input or feedback to the game engine and the engine responds proportionally;

this interaction can reside on mouse and keyboard or on a handheld game controller, but it comes in the form of key or button combinations and directs the course of action in game.

PlayerStart   A spawn point for a player's pawn or bot in the level.

Play map   Running the level in real time as the end user would be running the map.

Plot   The sequence of events that take place over time, from beginning to end.

Poly (polygon)   A triangle.

Portal (zone portal)   A particular type of special brush usually in the form of a sheet that can divide one zone into two different zones.

Portfolio   A list, often visual in nature, of what a designer has accomplished in his or her career thus far.

Postproduction phase (of game development)   During this development phase, testing, quality assurance, and bug-fixing are initiated, followed by a public relations campaign to get a game noticed by its target audience. *See also* Production phase, Preproduction phase.

Preproduction phase (of game development)   The phase that takes place before designers ever get their tools out and get started. *See also* Postproduction phase, Production phase.

Primitive   One of the standard, unaltered BSP shapes that can be created with the tools on the left side of the editor (i.e., cube, curved stair, cylinder, cone, sheet, etc.).

Production phase (of game development)   During this phase of development, the artists design the assets, characters, and environments on their computers, the writers set out dialogue and scripted events, the programmers code the controls and character behaviors, and the leaders make sure no one walks off the job. *See also* Postproduction phase, Preproduction phase.

Properties   The settings for any actor or texture. To access the Properties of an actor, just press F4 or right-click on the actor.

Protagonist   Another word for the central character or hero of a story. *See also* Antagonist.

Q & R

Quality assurance (QA)   Apart from game testing and beta testing, testing must be done to look at the game as a whole and check it against the initial concept for consistency.

Quest   A special sets of challenges that take place in both stories and games, thus linking narrative and play.

Ragdoll   A realistic physics simulation applied to character models that allows them to act like limp ragdolls.

Ramping   A game gets increasingly harder the longer someone plays it.

Randomization   A method by which a computerized system can change the way in which a game is played.

Rapid iterative prototyping   A production method where designers test ideas daily, see what's working and what's not, and abandon hurdles that are too difficult to get over.

Reactive environments   The game world responds to the player in logical and meaningful ways that help immerse the player in that game world.

Rebuild   *See* Build.

Remote procedure call (RPC)   A method of calling a function on a remote machine. This may be a client calling a function on the server or the server calling a function on all or specific clients.

Renderer   The part of the Unreal engine that actually draws what the player sees on the screen.

Replayability   The "sweet spot" for game designers, where the player doesn't play the game only once through but wants to play the game repeatedly, either motivated by the need to excel or by the sheer excitement that comes from experiencing a compelling narrative.

Rigidbody   Program controls that simulate physical objects they are attached to. You use Rigidbody controls for things the player can push around, such as crates and barrels.

Rogue-like game   Any game in which the world is not persistent but changes every time the game is played.

Role   The part a player plays in a game, especially a role-playing game, often reflected as an avatar.

Role-playing games (RPGs)   Games in which the main goal is for the players to gain enough experience or treasure for completing missions and beating monsters to make their near-infinitely customizable characters stronger.

Rotation gizmo   An interface for rotating and translating actors.

Runtime   The mode when the level is actually running and one can interact as a player within the world.

S

Script *See* Unreal Script.

Scrum A relatively new project management process that helps keep game teams organized and progressing toward product completion in a timely manner. Using this iterative, incremental process, developers check their progress at regular intervals and have a playable work-in-progress early on.

Seamless worlds The seamless world system is aimed at dynamically background-loading and unloading the complex data associated with levels. This works in conjunction with streaming so that, together, all of the data associated with worlds may be dynamically loaded.

Search engine A program that searches the Web for specific keywords and returns a list of documents in which those keywords are found.

Shadow-map A texture or per-vertex mask that stores a pre-computed shadowing term for a specific light to each point on a mesh or BSP surface.

Shadow volume A technique for rendering hard-edged dynamic shadows. Unreal renders the shadows cast by dynamic light using shadow volumes.

Shape Editor (2D Shape Editor) A tool in the UDK Editor that allows one to create unique BSP brushes.

Sheet A 2D brush often used for creating ZonePortals.

Shooters Games in which the characters are equipped with firearms and focus on fast-paced movement, shooting targets, and blowing up nearly everything in sight.

Side-scrolling A visual technique in games where the player's character starts on the left side of the screen (usually) and the player navigates the character to the right side of the screen; the invisible camera that the game is viewed from is locked onto the player character, following its movements.

Skeletal mesh A mesh that can be animated using a skeleton and animations created in a third-party modeling program.

Skeleton The bones set up in a third-party modeling program for an animated character.

Skin The texture(s) applied to a mesh (static mesh, skeletal mesh, etc.).

Sky dome A large hemisphere static-mesh used to create the illusion of a far-off sky.

Snap A feature that aligns geometry to the grid whenever it is moved or rotated.

Socket A named attachment point on a bone of a skeletal mesh.

Sorting Choosing the order or hierarchy of what the renderer will draw first.

Sound effects (SFX)   Short recorded sounds interjected relative to visual effects to enhance the whole experience and give aural clues to what is happening onscreen.

Spawning   Making an object appear in-game at a specific or random location, often referring to the dynamic generation of enemies or pickup items.

Sprint   A short iteration in project development using the scrum method.

Sprite   A 2D rectangular bitmap image that makes up most of the visual elements in a 2D game. *See also* Animated sprite or Static sprite.

Sprite emitter   An individual emitter that emits sprites in a pattern that can be designed within the UDK Editor.

State synchronization   A method of regularly updating a specific set of data across two or more game instances running on a network.

StaticMesh (aka static mesh)   A model created in a third-party program that remains stationary in the level when added to a map.

Static sprite   A single sprite image that consists of a non-animating character, object, or element.

Strategy games   Mental-challenge-based games, where the players build an empire, fortress, realm, world, or other construct, manage the resources therein, and prepare against inevitable problems like decay, hardship, economic depravity, revolution, or foreign invaders.

Sub-object   Object contained within another object (with the exception of UObjects contained within packages).

Subtractive BSP   BSP space that has been subtracted from the solid and/or additive world space. Subtractive BSP is open space in the level that the players can walk around in. *See also* BSP.

Surface properties   The attributes that can be assigned to a BSP surface.

T

Tabletop role-playing game   Any role-playing game played with pencils, paper, and dice with multiple players.

Target market   A specific group of people to sell to.

Teleporter   An actor that can instantly send a player from one point in the map to any other point in the map or even a point in another map.

Texture   An image file that can be assigned to geometry in the world. Materials are also sometimes referred to as textures.

Touchscreen   An electronic visual display that detects the presence and location of a touch within the display area. This generally refers to touching the device's display surface with a finger or hand.

Triangle   The smallest renderable building block of world geometry out of which everything in the scene is constructed.

Trigger   An actor that can activate an event during gameplay.

Triple-A (AAA) title   A game that sells big, in other words has a high cost to make and a higher return-on-investment; refers to an individual title's success or anticipated success if it is still in development.

U

Unreal Developer Network (UDN)   The team that supports the licensees of the Unreal Engine.

Unreal Development Kit (UDK)   The editing tool that allows one to create playable interactive worlds.

UnrealScript   A simple coding language native to Unreal that can be used for creating scripted sequences (a series of actions) for AI as well as game events.

V

Variable   Any observable attribute in a programming language that changes its values when ordered to.

Vertex   A point in Cartesian space made up of three coordinates (X, Y, and Z) and often the point at which the sides of an angle intersect. Plural is vertices.

Viewport   A display window in the UDK Editor that can show a front, side, top, or perspective views.

Voiceovers (VOs)   Sounds done by artists recorded reading dialogue and narration scripts in a recording studio for purposes of providing spoken dialogue and narration in games.

Volume   A 3D space that can affect various gameplay features such as movement, visibility, and player damage.

W

WarpZone   A special zone that contains a WarpZoneInfo that allows players to instantly travel from that WarpZone to another corresponding WarpZone.

Web browser   A software program that is used to locate and display web pages.

Web pages   Specially formatted documents created using languages such as Hypertext Markup Language (HTML) and Extensible Hypertext Markup Language (XHTML).

Web server   A computer that is hooked up to the Internet 24/7 that might have one or more websites stored on it at any given time.

Work breakdown   A project management plan that breaks down the overall project into tasks and sub-tasks, assigns team members to those tasks, and estimates the time it will take to get those tasks done.

World   The construct which forms the entire scene in the game. Worlds in UDK may consist of many smaller constructs known as levels. Worlds are stored in map files. *See also* Level and Map.

World Wide Web (WWW or the Web)   A subset of the Internet that supports web pages.

X, Y, & Z

Xcode   A suite of tools developed by Apple for specifically developing software for Mac OS X and iOS operating systems.

ZBuffer   The section of video memory in a graphics card that keeps track of which onscreen elements can be viewed and which are hidden behind other objects.

Zone   An area in the level that is sectioned off by portals for optimization purposes.

INDEX